Scoring High

Iowa Tests of Basic Skills®

A Test Prep Program for ITBS®

Book 7
Now with Science

Columbus, OH

The **McGraw-Hill** Companies

SRAonline.com

 SRA

Copyright © 2007 by SRA/McGraw-Hill.

Send all inquiries to:
SRA/McGraw-Hill
4400 Easton Commons
Columbus, OH 43219

Printed in the United States of America.

ISBN 0-07-604386-X

2 3 4 5 6 7 8 9 QPD 09 08

The **McGraw-Hill** Companies

On Your Way to Scoring High

On the Iowa Tests of Basic Skills®

Book 7

Family Letter

Greetings!

This year, your child, like many students across the country, will be taking a standardized achievement test called the *Iowa Tests of Basic Skills® (ITBS)*. We will be administering this test for several reasons.

- It gives us a snapshot of what your child has learned (achieved). It is one of many ways we assess the skills and knowledge of students because no one test or assessment tool can give an accurate, ongoing picture of your child's development.

- We use ITBS to help us determine where to strengthen our curriculum to better meet the needs of the students. It also helps us see if we are meeting the learning goals we set previously.

In order to give students the best opportunity to show what they know on this standardized achievement test, we will be using SRA/McGraw-Hill's test preparation program, *Scoring High on the Iowa Tests of Basic Skills.* It is designed specifically for the *Iowa Tests of Basic Skills.* Why will we be spending time preparing for this test?

- What happens to your heartbeat when you hear the word *test*? When students hear that word, their anxiety level can rise. However, when they know what to expect, their confidence soars—they are less nervous.

- Test-taking skills can be learned. When preparing, we focus on such skills as reading and listening carefully to directions; budgeting time; answering the easy questions first so more time can be spent on the harder ones; eliminating answer choices that are obviously wrong, and more. These are life skills that students will take with them and use again and again.

- Preparing for the test assures that students won't be surprised by the format of the test. They won't be worried about the type of questions they will see, or how hard the questions will be. They'll know how to fill in answers appropriately. These, and other skills learned ahead of time, will free students to focus on the content of the test and thus give a much more accurate picture of what they know.

How can you help?

- Talk with your child about the purpose of the test. Be positive about the experience.

- Talk to us here at school if you have any questions. Remember, we are a team with the **same** goals in mind—the improvement of your child's educational experience.

- Assure your child that the results of the test are private and won't be used on his or her report card. Remind your child that the test does not measure how smart he or she is, nor does it predict how successful he or she will be in the future.

- Encourage reading at home, and spend time together talking about what you read.

- Be sure your child has plenty of rest on a regular basis, and eats nourishing foods. That's important every day—not just on the day of the test.

Additional information will be provided about the specific subject areas and dates of the tests. Until then, please feel free to contact me if you have any questions about your child's performance or about standardized testing.

Sincerely,

_____

Your child's teacher

Scoring High on the Iowa Tests of Basic Skills
A program that teaches achievement test behaviors

Scoring High on the Iowa Tests of Basic Skills is designed to prepare students for these tests. The program provides instruction and practice in reading, spelling, language, mathematics, science and study skills. *Scoring High* also familiarizes students with the kinds of test formats and directions that appear on the tests and teaches test-taking strategies that promote success.

Students who are used to a comfortable learning environment are often unaccustomed to the structured setting in which achievement tests are given. Even students who are used to working independently may have difficulty maintaining a silent, sustained effort or following directions that are read to a large group. *Scoring High*, with its emphasis on group instruction, teaches these test-taking skills systematically.

Using *Scoring High* to help prepare students for the *Iowa Tests of Basic Skills* will increase the probability of your students doing their best on the tests. Students' self-confidence will be at a maximum, and their proficiency in the skills tested will be higher as a result of the newly learned test-taking strategies and increased familiarity with test formats.

Scoring High can be used effectively along with your regular reading, language, science and mathematics curriculums. By applying subject-area skills within the context of the test-taking situation, students will not only strengthen their skills, but will accumulate a reserve of test-taking strategies.

Eight Student Books for Grades 1–8

To choose the most appropriate book for each student, match the level of the *Iowa Tests of Basic Skills* that the student will take to the corresponding *Scoring High* book.

Grade Levels	Test Levels
Book 1	Level 7
Book 2	Level 8
Book 3	Level 9
Book 4	Level 10
Book 5	Level 11
Book 6	Level 12
Book 7	Level 13
Book 8	Level 14

Sequential Skill Development

Each student book is organized into units reflecting the subject areas covered in the corresponding levels of the *Iowa Tests of Basic Skills.* This book covers reading, spelling, language, mathematics, science and study skills. Each lesson within a unit focuses on one or two of the subject-area skills and the test-taking strategies that complement the skills. The last lesson in each unit is designed to give students experience in taking an achievement test in that subject area.

The Test Practice section at the end of each book also provides practice in taking achievement tests and will increase students' confidence in their test-taking skills.

Features of the Student Lessons

Each student lesson in subject-area skills contains:

- A Sample(s) section including directions and one or more teacher-directed sample questions
- A Tips section providing test-taking strategies
- A Practice section

Each Test Yourself lesson at the end of a unit is designed like an achievement test in the unit's subject areas.

How the Teacher's Edition Works

Since a program that teaches test-taking skills as well as subject-area skills may be new to your students, the Teacher's Edition makes a special effort to provide detailed lesson plans. Each lesson lists subject-area and test-taking skills. In addition, teaching suggestions are provided for handling each part of the lesson—Sample(s), Tips, and Practice. The text for the subject-area and Test Yourself lessons is designed to help students become familiar with following oral directions and with the terminology used on the tests.

Before you begin Lesson 1, you should use the Orientation Lesson on pages xii–xv to acquaint students with the program organization and the procedure for using the student book.

Scope and Sequence: Test-taking Skills

UNIT

	1	2	3	4	5	6	7	8	9	10	11
Analyzing answer choices		✓		✓	✓					✓	✓
Comparing or evaluating answer choices						✓	✓		✓		✓
Computing carefully							✓	✓			✓
Considering every answer choice	✓										✓
Converting items to a workable format							✓	✓			✓
Eliminating answer choices					✓				✓	✓	✓
Finding the answer without computing						✓	✓				✓
Following printed directions	✓	✓		✓	✓	✓	✓				✓
Identifying and using key words, numbers, and pictures		✓				✓	✓			✓	✓
Indicating that an item has no mistakes			✓	✓	✓						✓
Indicating that the correct answer is not given							✓	✓			✓
Managing time effectively	✓	✓	✓	✓	✓	✓	✓	✓	✓	✓	✓
Noting the lettering of answer choices	✓	✓									✓
Performing the correct operation							✓	✓			✓
Reasoning from facts and evidence		✓									✓
Recalling error types			✓		✓						✓
Recalling special capitalization rules				✓							✓
Recalling word meanings	✓										✓
Referring to a graphic						✓					✓
Referring to a passage to answer questions		✓								✓	✓
Referring to a reference source									✓		✓
Rereading or restating a question						✓			✓		✓
Reworking a problem							✓				✓
Skimming a passage		✓									✓
Skimming a reference source									✓		✓
Skimming questions or answer choices				✓							✓
Skimming text					✓						✓
Skipping difficult items and returning to them later				✓				✓	✓		✓
Substituting answer choices											✓
Subvocalizing answer choices			✓		✓						✓
Taking the best guess when unsure of the answer	✓		✓		✓		✓	✓	✓		✓
Transferring numbers accurately							✓	✓			✓
Understanding unusual item formats				✓	✓						✓
Using charts, diagrams, and graphs							✓				✓
Using context to find an answer					✓						✓
Working methodically	✓	✓	✓	✓	✓	✓	✓	✓	✓	✓	✓

Scope and Sequence: Reading

	UNIT										
	1	2	3	4	5	6	7	8	9	10	11
Identifying synonyms	✓										✓
Analyzing characters		✓									✓
Comparing and contrasting		✓									✓
Deriving word meanings		✓									✓
Drawing conclusions		✓									✓
Making inferences		✓									
Recognizing an author's technique		✓									✓
Recognizing an author's purpose		✓									✓
Recognizing details		✓									
Recognizing genre or text source		✓									✓
Understanding literary devices											✓
Understanding reasons											✓
Understanding the main idea		✓									✓

Scope and Sequence: Language Skills

	UNIT										
	1	2	3	4	5	6	7	8	9	10	11
Identifying spelling errors			✓								✓
Choosing the best paragraph for a given purpose					✓						✓
Choosing the best word to complete a sentence											✓
Identifying capitalization errors				✓							✓
Identifying correctly formed sentences					✓						✓
Identifying mistakes in usage					✓						✓
Identifying punctuation errors				✓							✓
Identifying the best closing sentence for a paragraph					✓						✓
Identifying the best location for a sentence in a paragraph					✓						✓
Identifying the best opening sentence for a paragraph					✓						✓
Identifying the sentence that does not fit in a paragraph					✓						✓

Scope and Sequence: Mathematics Skills

	UNIT										
	1	2	3	4	5	6	7	8	9	10	11
Adding, subtracting, multiplying, and dividing whole numbers, fractions, and decimals									✓		✓
Comparing and ordering whole numbers, decimals, fractions, and integers							✓				✓
Estimating and rounding							✓				✓
Estimating measurement							✓				✓
Identifying parts of a figure							✓				✓
Identifying the best measurement unit							✓				
Interpreting tables, diagrams, and graphs								✓			
Naming numerals							✓				✓
Recognizing alternate forms of a number							✓				
Recognizing equivalent fractions and decimals							✓				✓
Recognizing fractional parts							✓				
Recognizing plane figures							✓				
Sequencing numbers or shapes							✓				✓
Solving measurement problems							✓				
Solving simple equations							✓				✓
Solving word problems								✓			✓
Understanding average (mean)							✓				✓
Understanding characteristics of related numbers							✓				✓
Understanding factors and remainders											✓
Understanding lines and angles							✓				✓
Understanding number sentences							✓				✓
Understanding ordered pairs							✓				✓
Understanding ratio and proportion							✓				
Understanding simple probability											✓
Understanding variability							✓				
Using a coordinate grid							✓				

Scope and Sequence: Study Skills

	UNIT										
	1	2	3	4	5	6	7	8	9	10	11
Differentiating among reference sources									✓		
Understanding a diagram									✓		✓
Understanding a map									✓		✓
Understanding the Dewey Decimal Classification system									✓		
Using a chart									✓		
Using a dictionary									✓		✓
Using a table of contents									✓		
Using an encyclopedia									✓		
Using an index									✓		
Using guide words									✓		
Using key words									✓		✓

Scope and Sequence: Science Skills

	UNIT										
	1	2	3	4	5	6	7	8	9	10	11
Classifying things based on characteristics										✓	✓
Differentiating plants and animals										✓	
Differentiating the source of natural and manufactured products											✓
Recalling characteristics of Earth and bodies in space										✓	✓
Recalling characteristics and functions of the human body										✓	
Recognizing chemical changes										✓	✓
Recognizing forms, sources, and principles of energy										✓	✓
Recognizing importance of environmentally sound practices										✓	✓
Recognizing states, properties, and composition of matter										✓	✓
Understanding characteristics of bodies of water										✓	
Understanding electricity and circuits										✓	
Understanding foods and food groups											✓
Understanding form and function										✓	
Understanding fossilization											✓
Understanding gravity, inertia, and friction										✓	✓
Understanding the history and language of science										✓	✓
Understanding life cycles and reproduction										✓	
Understanding magnetism										✓	
Understanding plant and animal behaviors and characteristics										✓	✓
Understanding properties of light										✓	✓
Understanding scientific instruments, measurement, and processes										✓	✓
Understanding weather, climate, and seasons										✓	✓
Using illustrations, charts, and graphs										✓	✓

Orientation Lesson

Focus
Understanding the purpose and structure of *Scoring High on the Iowa Tests of Basic Skills*

Note: Before you begin Lesson 1, use this introductory lesson to acquaint the students with the program orientation and procedures for using this book.

Say Taking a test is something that you do many times during each school year. What kind of tests have you taken? *(math tests, reading tests, spelling tests, daily quizzes, etc.)* Have you ever taken an achievement test that covers many subjects? An achievement test shows how well you are doing in these subjects compared to other students in your grade. Do you know how achievement tests are different from the regular tests you take in class? *(many students take them on the same day; special pencils, books, and answer sheets are used; etc.)* Some students get nervous when they take achievement tests. Has this ever happened to you?

Encourage the students to discuss their feelings about test taking. Point out that almost everyone feels anxious or worried when facing a test-taking situation.

Display the cover of *Scoring High on the Iowa Tests of Basic Skills*.

Say Here is a new book that you'll be using for the next several weeks. The book is called *Scoring High on the Iowa Tests of Basic Skills*.

Distribute the books to the students.

Say This book will help you improve your reading, language, mathematics, science and study skills. It will also help you gain the confidence and skills you need to do well on achievement

Scoring High

Iowa Tests of Basic Skills®
A Test Prep Program for ITBS®

Book 7
Now with Science

SRA

tests. What does the title say you will be doing when you finish this book? *(scoring high)* Scoring high on achievement tests is what this program is all about. If you learn the skills taught in this book, you will be ready to do your best on the *Iowa Tests of Basic Skills*.

Share this information with the students if you know when they will be taking the *Iowa Tests of Basic Skills*. Then make sure the students understand that the goal of their *Scoring High* books is to improve their test-taking skills.

Tell the students to turn to the table of contents in the front of their books.

Say This page is a progress chart. It shows the contents of the book. How many units are there? *(11)* Let's read the names of the units together.

Read the titles of the units with the students.

Say In these units you will learn reading, spelling, language, mathematics, science study skills, and test-taking skills. The last lesson in each unit is called Test Yourself. It reviews what you have learned in the unit. In Unit 11, the Test Practice section, you will have a chance to use all the skills you have learned on tests that are somewhat like real achievement tests. This page will also help you keep track of the lessons you have completed. Do you see the box beside each lesson number? When you finish a lesson, you will write your score in the box to show your progress.

Make sure the students understand the information presented on this page. Ask questions such as, "On what page does Lesson 9b start?" *(45)* "What is Lesson 2a called?" *(Reading Comprehension)* "What do you think Lesson 10a is about?" *(solving mathematics problems)*

 Book 7

On Your Way to Scoring High
On the Iowa Tests of Basic Skills®

Name _____

Say Now let's look at two of the lessons. Turn to Lesson 1a on page 1. Where is the lesson number and title? *(at the top of the page, beside the unit number)* What is the title of the lesson? *(Vocabulary)*

Familiarize the students with the lesson layout and sequence of instruction. Have them locate the directions and sample items. Explain that you will work through the Samples section together. Then have the students find the STOP sign in the lower right-hand corner of the page. Explain that when they come to the STOP sign at the bottom of a page, they should not continue on to the next page. They may check their work on the present lesson.

Have the students locate the Tips sign below the Samples section.

Say What does the sign point out to you? *(the tips)* Each lesson has tips that suggest new ways to work through the items. Tests can be tricky. The tips will tell you what to watch out for. They will help you find the best answer quickly.

Have the students locate the Practice section below the tips. Explain that they will do the practice items by themselves. Tell the students they will have an opportunity to discuss any problems they had after they complete the Practice section.

Ask the students to turn to the Test Yourself lesson on page 3 of their books. Tell the students the Test Yourself lessons may seem like real tests, but they are not. The Test Yourself lessons are designed to give them opportunities to apply the skills and tips they have learned in timed, trial-run situations. Then have the students find the GO sign in the lower right-hand corner of the page. Explain that when they come to the GO sign at the bottom of a page, they should turn to the next page and continue working until they come to the STOP sign.

Explain that you will go over the answers together after the students complete each lesson. Then they will figure out their scores and record the number of correct answers in the boxes on the progress chart. Be sure to point out that the students' scores are only for them to see how well they are doing.

 Unit 1

Vocabulary
Lesson 1a **Vocabulary**

Directions: Read the phrase and the answer choices. Choose the answer that means the same as the underlined word.

Sample A	Enjoy solitude	Sample B	Inform his friends
	A being with others		J withhold information from
	B crowded place		*K give information to
	C high mountain		L avoid
	*D being alone		M join

- Read each answer choice carefully.
- If you are not sure which answer is correct, take your best guess.

1 Explore a <u>cavern</u>
A forest
*B cave
C desert
D mountain

2 <u>Barter</u> for goods
J argue
*K trade
L wish
M pay

3 <u>Cramped</u> rooms
A rented
B spacious
*C crowded
D hospital

4 <u>Endorse</u> a check
J cash
K lose
L spend
*M sign

5 Make changes <u>gradually</u>
A all at once
*B little by little
C with much help
D all alone

6 An exciting <u>journey</u>
*J trip
K ride
L game
M party

7 A <u>passage</u> through the mountains
A train
B river
C vacation
*D route

8 The <u>region</u> near the lake
J park
*K area
L houses
M dock

STOP

Answer rows A ⒶⒷⒸ● 1 Ⓐ●ⒸⒹ 3 ⒶⒷⒸ● 5 Ⓐ●ⒸⒹ 7 ⒶⒷⒸ●   1
B Ⓙ●ⓁⓂ 2 Ⓙ●ⓁⓂ 4 Ⓙ●ⓁⓂ 6 ●ⓀⓁⓂ 8 Ⓙ●ⓁⓂ

Say Each lesson will teach you new skills and tips. What will you have learned when you finish this book? *(vocabulary, reading, spelling, language arts, mathematics, study skills, and test-taking skills; how to do my best on an achievement test)* When you know you can do your best, how do you think you will feel on test day? You may be a little nervous, but you should also feel confident that you are ready to do your best.

Unit 1

Background

This unit contains three lessons that deal with vocabulary skills. Students are asked to identify words with similar meanings.

• **In Lesson 1a,** students identify words that have the same meaning as target words in phrases. Students are encouraged to follow printed directions. They note the lettering of answer choices, consider every answer choice, and take their best guess when unsure of the answer.

• **In Lesson 1b,** students identify words that have the same meaning as target words in phrases. In addition to reviewing the test-taking skills introduced in Lesson 1a, students learn the importance of recalling word meanings.

• **In the Test Yourself lesson,** the vocabulary skills and test-taking skills introduced and used in Lessons 1a and 1b are reinforced and presented in a format that gives students the experience of taking an achievement test. Techniques for managing time effectively when taking a standardized test are reinforced.

Instructional Objectives

Lesson 1a **Vocabulary** Lesson 1b **Vocabulary**	Given a phrase with a target word, the students identify which of four answer choices means the same as the target word.
Test Yourself	Given questions similar to those in Lessons 1a and 1b, students utilize vocabulary skills and test-taking strategies on achievement test formats.

Focus

Reading Skill
• identifying synonyms

Test-taking Skills
• following printed directions
• noting lettering of answer choices
• considering every answer choice
• taking the best guess when unsure of the answer

Samples A and B

Say Turn to Lesson 1a on page 1. The page number is at the bottom of the page on the right.

Check to see that the students have found the right page.

Say In this lesson you will find words that have the same or nearly the same meaning as another word used in a phrase. Read the directions at the top of the page to yourself while I read them aloud to you.

Read the directions to the students.

Say Let's do Sample A. Listen carefully. Read the phrase with the underlined word. Think about what the word means as it is used in the phrase. Now, look at the four answer choices below the phrase. Which of the four answers means about the same as the underlined word? *(pause)* The answer is D, *being alone*, because *solitude* means *being alone*. Fill in answer D for Sample A in the answer rows at the bottom of the page. Be sure your answer circle is completely filled in with a dark mark and that you have marked the correct answer circle.

Check to see that the students have marked the correct circle.

Say Now do Sample B by yourself. Read the phrase and fill in the circle for the word or phrase that means the same as the underlined word. *(pause)* Which answer choice is correct? *(answer K)* Yes, *inform* means *give information to*. Make sure that circle K for Sample B is

---

Vocabulary
Lesson 1a Vocabulary

Unit 1

Directions: Read the phrase and the answer choices. Choose the answer that means the same as the underlined word.

Sample A	**Enjoy solitude**		**Sample B**	**Inform his friends**
	A being with others			J withhold information from
	B crowded place			*K give information to
	C high mountain			L avoid
	*D being alone			M join

TIPS
• Read each answer choice carefully.
• If you are not sure which answer is correct, take your best guess.

1 **Explore a cavern**
A forest
*B cave
C desert
D mountain

2 **Barter for goods**
J argue
*K trade
L wish
M pay

3 **Cramped rooms**
A rented
B spacious
*C crowded
D hospital

4 **Endorse a check**
J cash
K lose
L spend
*M sign

5 **Make changes gradually**
A all at once
*B little by little
C with much help
D all alone

6 **An exciting journey**
*J trip
K ride
L game
M party

7 **A passage through the mountains**
A train
B river
C vacation
*D route

8 **The region near the lake**
J park
*K area
L houses
M dock

STOP

Answer rows A Ⓐ Ⓑ Ⓒ ●   1 Ⓐ ● Ⓒ Ⓓ   3 Ⓐ Ⓑ ● Ⓓ   5 ● Ⓑ Ⓒ Ⓓ   7 Ⓐ Ⓑ Ⓒ ●
         B ● Ⓚ Ⓛ Ⓜ   2 Ⓙ ● Ⓛ Ⓜ   4 Ⓙ Ⓚ Ⓛ ●   6 ● Ⓚ Ⓛ Ⓜ   8 Ⓙ ● Ⓛ Ⓜ

1

---

completely filled in. Press your pencil firmly so your mark comes out dark.

Check to see that the students have marked the correct circle.

TIPS

Say Now let's look at the tips.

Read the tips aloud to the students.

Say Be sure to read the question and look at each answer choice carefully. Choose the answer that means about the same as the underlined word. If you are not sure which answer is correct, take your best guess. It is better to guess than to leave an answer blank.

Practice

Say We are ready for the Practice items. Remember, the letters for the answer choices change from question to question. For odd-numbered questions, they are A-B-C-D. For even-numbered questions, they are J-K-L-M. You must pay careful attention to the letters for the answer choices and the circles in the answer rows at the bottom of the page. It's a good idea to double-check to be sure that you have filled in the circle for the answer choice you think is correct. Check both the item number and the answer letter. If you make a mistake when you fill in the answer circle, your answer will still be counted wrong, even if you knew what the correct answer was.

Work until you come to the STOP sign at the bottom of the page. Fill in your answer circles with dark marks and completely erase any marks for answers that you change. Do you have any questions? Start working now.

Allow time for the students to do Numbers 1 through 8.

Say It's time to stop. You have finished Lesson 1a.

Review the answers with the students. Ask them if they remembered to look at all the answer choices and take the best guess if they were unsure of the correct answer. Did they have any difficulty marking the circles in the answer rows? If any questions caused particular difficulty, work through each of the answer choices.

Have the students indicate completion of the lesson by entering their score for this activity on the progress chart at the beginning of the book.

Unit 1 Vocabulary
Lesson 1a **Vocabulary**

Directions: Read the phrase and the answer choices. Choose the answer that means the same as the underlined word.

Sample A Enjoy solitude
- A being with others
- B crowded place
- C high mountain
- *D being alone

Sample B Inform his friends
- J withhold information from
- *K give information to
- L avoid
- M join

TIPS
- Read each answer choice carefully.
- If you are not sure which answer is correct, take your best guess.

1 Explore a <u>cavern</u>
- A forest
- *B cave
- C desert
- D mountain

2 <u>Barter</u> for goods
- J argue
- *K trade
- L wish
- M pay

3 <u>Cramped</u> rooms
- A rented
- B spacious
- *C crowded
- D hospital

4 <u>Endorse</u> a check
- J cash
- K lose
- L spend
- *M sign

5 Make changes <u>gradually</u>
- A all at once
- *B little by little
- C with much help
- D all alone

6 An exciting <u>journey</u>
- *J trip
- K ride
- L game
- M party

7 A <u>passage</u> through the mountains
- A train
- B river
- C vacation
- *D route

8 The <u>region</u> near the lake
- J park
- *K area
- L houses
- M dock

STOP

Answer rows   A ⒶⒷⒸ●   1 Ⓐ●ⒸⒹ   3 ⒶⒷ●Ⓓ   5 Ⓐ●ⒸⒹ   7 ⒶⒷⒸ●
              B Ⓙ●ⓁⓂ   2 Ⓙ●ⓁⓂ   4 ⒿⓀⓁ●   6 ●ⓀⓁⓂ   8 Ⓙ●ⓁⓂ

1

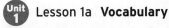

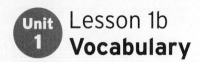

Unit 1 Lesson 1b Vocabulary

Focus

Reading Skill
• identifying synonyms

Test-taking Skills
• working methodically
• following printed directions
• noting lettering of answer choices
• considering every answer choice
• recalling word meanings

Samples A and B

Say Turn to Lesson 1b on page 2. The page number is at the bottom of the page on the left.

Check to see that the students have found the right page.

Say In this lesson you will find more words that have the same or nearly the same meaning as another word used in a phrase. Read the directions at the top of the page to yourself while I read them out loud to you.

Read the directions to the students.

Say Read the phrase with the underlined word for Sample A. Think about what the word means as it is used in the phrase. Now, look at the four answer choices below the phrase. Which of the four answers means about the same as the underlined word? *(pause)* The answer is A, *beginning*. In this phrase, *origin* and *beginning* mean the same thing. Fill in the circle for answer A in the answer rows at the bottom of the page. Be sure your answer circle is completely filled in with a dark mark and that you have marked the correct answer circle.

Check to see that the students have marked the correct circle.

Say Now do Sample B by yourself. Read the phrase and fill in the circle for the word that means the same as the underlined word. *(pause)* Which answer choice is correct? *(answer L)* Yes, *compassion* and *deep sympathy* mean about the same thing. Make sure that circle L for Sample B is completely filled in.

Unit 1 Vocabulary
Lesson 1b **Vocabulary**

Directions: Read the phrase and the answer choices. Choose the answer that means the same as the underlined word.

Sample A Find the origin
* **A** beginning
  B end
  C middle
  D opposite

Sample B Feel compassion
  J great joy
  K much confusion
* **L** deep sympathy
  M nothing at all

 • Think about where you might have read or heard a word before.

1 Have a routine day
  A unusual
  B busy
  C profitable
* **D** typical

2 A willing assistant
  J unhappy to help
* **K** happy to help
  L too busy to help
  M unable to help

3 Tireless workers
  A unusual
  B unfriendly
* **C** untiring
  D uninvited

4 Feel sluggish
  J unhappy
  K unkind
  L unwelcome
* **M** unenergetic

5 The novice sailor
  A experienced
  B skilled
* **C** inexperienced
  D unfriendly

6 A flimsy package
* **J** without strength
  K without a label
  L empty
  M full

7 Attend an elegant party
  A very loud
  B very exciting
* **C** very fine
  D very crowded

8 Delay making a decision
* **J** put off
  K enjoy
  L decide quickly
  M hate to

STOP

2   Answer rows   A ●BCD   1 ABC●   3 AB●D   5 AB●D   7 AB●D
                    B JK●M   2 J●LM   4 JKL●   6 ●KLM   8 ●KLM

Press your pencil firmly so your mark comes out dark.

Check to see that the students have marked the correct circle.

⭐**TIPS**

Say Let's review the tip.

Read the tip aloud to the students.

Say A good strategy to use for vocabulary items is to think about where you might have heard or read a word before. This will give you a clue about its meaning.

Practice

Say We are ready for the Practice items. Remember, the letters for the answer choices change from question to question. For odd-numbered questions, they are A-B-C-D. For even-numbered questions, they are J-K-L-M. You must pay careful attention to the letters for the answer choices and the circles in the answer rows at the bottom of the page. It's a good idea to double-check to be sure that you have filled in the circle for the answer choice you think is correct. Check both the item number and the answer letter. If you make a mistake when you fill in the answer circle, your answer will still be counted wrong, even if you knew what the correct answer was. And remember, if you aren't sure which answer is correct, take your best guess.

Work until you come to the STOP sign at the bottom of the page. Fill in your answer circles with dark marks and completely erase any marks for answers that you change. Do you have any questions? Start working now.

Allow time for the students to do Numbers 1 through 8.

Say It's time to stop. You have finished Lesson 1b.

Review the answers with the students. Ask them if they remembered to look at all the answer choices and take the best guess if they were unsure of the correct answer. If any questions caused particular difficulty, work through each of the answer choices. You may want to discuss with the students where they heard or read a word before.

Have the students indicate completion of the lesson by entering their score for this activity on the progress chart at the beginning of the book.

 **Unit 1** **Vocabulary**
Lesson 1b **Vocabulary**

Directions: Read the phrase and the answer choices. Choose the answer that means the same as the underlined word.

Sample A	Find the **origin**	*Sample* B	Feel **compassion**
	*A beginning		J great joy
	B end		K much confusion
	C middle		*L deep sympathy
	D opposite		M nothing at all

 • **Think about where you might have read or heard a word before.**

1 Have a **routine** day
A unusual
B busy
C profitable
*D typical

2 A **willing** assistant
J unhappy to help
*K happy to help
L too busy to help
M unable to help

3 **Tireless** workers
A unusual
B unfriendly
*C untiring
D uninvited

4 Feel **sluggish**
J unhappy
K unkind
L unwelcome
*M unenergetic

5 The **novice** sailor
A experienced
B skilled
*C inexperienced
D unfriendly

6 A **flimsy** package
*J without strength
K without a label
L empty
M full

7 Attend an **elegant** party
A very loud
B very exciting
*C very fine
D very crowded

8 **Delay** making a decision
*J put off
K enjoy
L decide quickly
M hate to

 STOP

2   **Answer rows**   A ●Ⓑ©Ⓓ   1 ⒶⒷ©●   3 Ⓐ Ⓑ●Ⓓ   5 Ⓐ Ⓑ●Ⓓ   7 ⒶⒷ●Ⓓ
                       B ⒿⓀ●Ⓜ   2 Ⓙ●ⓁⓂ   4 ⒿⓀⓁ●   6 ●ⓀⓁⓂ   8 ●ⓀⓁⓂ

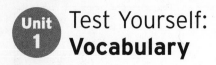

Test Yourself: Vocabulary

Focus

Reading Skill
- identifying synonyms

Test-taking Skills
- managing time effectively
- following printed directions
- noting the lettering of answer choices
- considering every answer choice
- recalling word meanings
- working methodically
- taking the best guess when unsure of the answer

This lesson simulates an actual test-taking experience. Therefore, it is recommended that the directions be read verbatim and the suggested procedures and time allowances be followed.

Directions

Administration Time: approximately 15 minutes

Say Turn to the Test Yourself lesson on page 3.

Check to be sure the students have found the right page. Point out to the students that this Test Yourself lesson is timed like a real test, but that they will score it themselves to see how well they are doing. Explain that it is important to work quickly and to answer as many questions as possible.

Say This lesson will check how well you understand word meanings. Remember to make sure that the circles for your answer choices are completely filled in. Press your pencil firmly so that your marks come out dark. Completely erase any marks for answers that you change. Do not write anything except your answer choices in your books.

Look at Sample A. Read the phrase and fill in the circle for the word that means the same as the underlined word. Mark your answer in the row for Sample A at the bottom of the page.

Test Yourself: Vocabulary

Directions: Read the phrase and the answer choices. Choose the answer that means the same as the underlined word.

Sample A	A beautiful <u>dwelling</u>		Sample B	A <u>hearty</u> meal
	A painting			J expensive
∗ B house				K small
	C park			L late
	D statue			∗ M nourishing

1 A huge <u>freighter</u>
  A passenger train
  B jet plane
∗ C cargo ship
  D pack horse

2 Become <u>inactive</u>
∗ J not moving
  K not present
  L not paid
  M not friendly

3 <u>Mislead</u> the public
  A give correct information to
∗ B give wrong information to
  C govern
  D control

4 To <u>reside</u> in Montana
  J visit
∗ K live
  L arrive
  M hunt

5 Parking is <u>scarce</u> here.
  A easy to find
  B against the law
∗ C hard to find
  D for residents only

6 <u>Tedious</u> work
  J short and exciting
∗ K long and tiring
  L paying well
  M paying poorly

7 A large <u>stall</u>
  A hotel
  B barn
  C car
∗ D booth

8 <u>Pretend</u> to be sad
∗ J make believe
  K act truly
  L try to avoid
  M enjoy

Answer rows
A Ⓐ●ⒸⒹ 1 Ⓐ Ⓑ●Ⓓ 3 Ⓐ●ⒸⒹ 5 Ⓐ Ⓑ●Ⓓ 7 Ⓐ Ⓑ Ⓒ●
B Ⓙ Ⓚ Ⓛ● 2 ●Ⓚ Ⓛ Ⓜ 4 Ⓙ●Ⓛ Ⓜ 6 Ⓙ●Ⓛ Ⓜ 8 ●Ⓚ Ⓛ Ⓜ

GO

3

Allow time for the students to read the item and mark their answers.

Say You should have filled in answer circle B because a *dwelling* is a kind of *house*. If you did not fill in answer B, erase your answer and fill in answer B now.

Check to see that the students have filled in the correct answer circle.

Say Do Sample B now. Read the phrase and fill in the circle for the word that means the same as the underlined word. Mark the circle for the answer you think is correct for Sample B in the answer rows at the bottom of the page.

Allow time for the students to read the item and mark their answers.

Say You should have filled in answer circle M because *hearty* means about the same as *nourishing*. If you did not fill in answer M, erase your answer and fill in answer M now.

Check to see that the students have filled in the correct answer circle.

Say Now you will answer more questions. Fill in the spaces for your answers in the rows at the bottom of the page. When you come to the GO sign at the bottom of the page, turn to the next page and continue working. Work until you come to the STOP sign at the bottom of page 4. When you have finished, you can check over your answers to this test. Then wait for the rest of the group to finish. Any questions?

Answer any questions that the students have.

Say Start working now. You have 10 minutes.

Allow 10 minutes.

Say It's time to stop. You have completed the Test Yourself lesson. Check to see that you have completely filled in your answer circles with dark marks. Make sure that any marks for answers that you changed have been completely erased. Now you may close your books.

Have the students indicate completion of the lesson by entering their score for this activity on the progress chart at the beginning of the book. Collect the students' books if this is the end of the testing session.

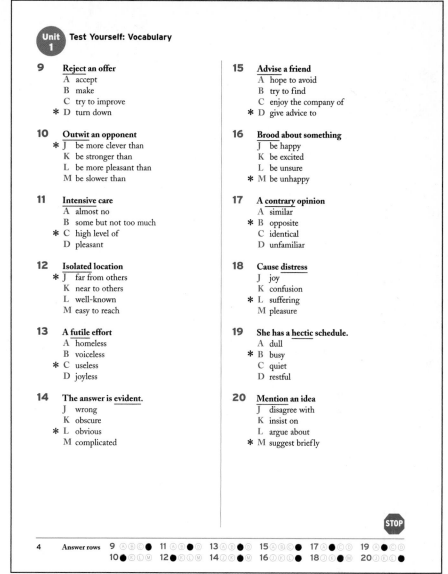

Unit 1 Test Yourself: Vocabulary

9 Reject an offer
A accept
B make
C try to improve
∗ D turn down

10 Outwit an opponent
∗ J be more clever than
K be stronger than
L be more pleasant than
M be slower than

11 Intensive care
A almost no
B some but not too much
∗ C high level of
D pleasant

12 Isolated location
∗ J far from others
K near to others
L well-known
M easy to reach

13 A futile effort
A homeless
B voiceless
∗ C useless
D joyless

14 The answer is evident.
J wrong
K obscure
∗ L obvious
M complicated

15 Advise a friend
A hope to avoid
B try to find
C enjoy the company of
∗ D give advice to

16 Brood about something
J be happy
K be excited
L be unsure
∗ M be unhappy

17 A contrary opinion
A similar
∗ B opposite
C identical
D unfamiliar

18 Cause distress
J joy
K confusion
∗ L suffering
M pleasure

19 She has a hectic schedule.
A dull
∗ B busy
C quiet
D restful

20 Mention an idea
J disagree with
K insist on
L argue about
∗ M suggest briefly

STOP

4   Answer rows   9 Ⓐ Ⓑ Ⓒ ●   11 Ⓐ Ⓑ ● Ⓓ   13 Ⓐ Ⓑ ● Ⓓ   15 Ⓐ Ⓑ Ⓒ ●   17 Ⓐ ● Ⓒ Ⓓ   19 Ⓐ ● Ⓒ Ⓓ
            10 ● Ⓚ Ⓛ Ⓜ   12 ● Ⓚ Ⓛ Ⓜ   14 Ⓙ Ⓚ ● Ⓜ   16 Ⓙ Ⓚ Ⓛ ●   18 Ⓙ Ⓚ ● Ⓜ   20 Ⓙ Ⓚ Ⓛ ●

Unit 2

Background

This unit contains three lessons that deal with reading comprehension skills. Students answer questions about stories they read.

• **In Lesson 2a**, students read a passage and answer questions based on the content of the passage. Students are encouraged to skim a passage and refer to the passage to answer questions. They use key words to find the answer, work methodically, and reason from facts and evidence.

• **In Lesson 2b,** students read a passage and answer questions based on the content of the passage. In addition to reviewing the test-taking skills introduced in Lesson 2a, students learn the importance of analyzing answer choices.

• **In the Test Yourself lesson,** the reading skills and test-taking skills introduced and used in Lessons 2a and 2b are reinforced and presented in a format that gives students the experience of taking an achievement test. Techniques for managing time effectively when taking a standardized test are reinforced.

Instructional Objectives

Lesson 2a **Reading Comprehension** Lesson 2b **Reading Comprehension**	Given a written passage and a literal or inferential question based on the passage, students identify which of four answer choices is correct.
Test Yourself	Given questions similar to those in Lessons 2a and 2b, students utilize reading skills and test-taking strategies on achievement test formats.

Unit 2 Lesson 2a Reading Comprehension

Focus

Reading Skills
- analyzing characters
- recognizing details
- deriving word meanings
- making inferences
- drawing conclusions
- understanding reasons
- comparing and contrasting
- recognizing an author's technique

Test-taking Skills
- skimming a passage
- referring to a passage to answer questions
- using key words to find the answer
- working methodically
- reasoning from facts and evidence

Sample A

Say Turn to Lesson 2a on page 5. In this lesson you will answer questions about passages that you read. Begin by reading the directions at the top of the page to yourself while I read them out loud.

Read the directions to the students.

Say Now we'll do Sample A. Skim the passage to yourself. *(pause)* Now, read the question next to the passage. To find the correct answer, look back at the passage. What is the correct answer? *(answer C)* You can tell from the first sentence that Renee was concentrating. Fill in answer circle C for Sample A in the answer rows at the bottom of the page. Make sure the circle is completely filled in. Press your pencil firmly so that your mark comes out dark.

Check to see that the students have marked the correct answer circle.

 Reading Comprehension
Lesson 2a **Reading Comprehension**

Directions: Read the passage and the answer choices. Choose the best answer.

Sample A As Renee approached the end of the board, she thought of nothing but her dive. Her last step on the board threw her high into the air. Up she went until she felt gravity begin to pull her back to earth. She completed her dive and ripped into the water like a knife.

Which of these describes Renee's state of mind as she began her dive?
A Distracted
B Frightened
* C Concentrating
D Agitated

TIPS
- Don't waste too much time reading the passage. Just skim it to get an idea of what it is about.
- Look for key words in the question and answer choices. Refer back to the passage to find the answer.

When young people listen to music today, they probably don't realize they are enjoying the legacy of "Leadbelly." Born in 1888 in Louisiana, Huddie Ledbetter was a blues guitarist who inspired generations of musicians. He is generally considered to be one of our national treasures.

As a child, Leadbelly learned to play several instruments. His favorite instrument was the twelve-string guitar, which eventually made him famous. Leadbelly's playing had a unique sound that many musicians tried to imitate.

For much of Huddie Ledbetter's adult life, he wandered from place to place, playing anywhere he could. In 1934, he was discovered by John and Alan Lomax, who helped Leadbelly find a larger audience for his music. He was soon playing in colleges, clubs, and music halls around the country. Leadbelly was featured on radio and television shows, gave concerts in New York's Town Hall, and performed in Europe.

Leadbelly died in 1949, but his music lives on. Musicians in every style credit him with laying the foundation for today's popular music.

1 What was the turning point in Leadbelly's life?
A Learning to play music as a young boy
B Being imitated by other musicians
* C Being discovered by the Lomax brothers
D Appearing on television and radio shows

2 How did Leadbelly probably get his nickname?
* J Leadbelly sounds like Ledbetter.
K His guitar had lead strings.
L He led an interesting life.
M He was probably overweight.

3 In the second paragraph, what does the word "unique" mean?
A Similar to everyone else's
B Meant for people from the South
C Meant for large concert halls
* D Different from everyone else's

 GO

Answer rows A ⒶⒷ●Ⓓ 1 ⒶⒷ●Ⓓ 2 ●ⓀⓁⓂ 3 ⒶⒷⒸ●   5

★TIPS

Say Now let's look at the tips. Who will read them?

Have a volunteer read the tips aloud.

Say The best way to answer reading comprehension questions is to skim the passage quickly and then read the questions. Refer back to the passage to answer the questions, but don't reread the story for each question. Key words in the question will tell you where in the passage to look for the correct answer. If you can find the same key words in the passage, you can usually find the correct answer nearby.

Practice

Say Now we are ready for Practice. You will read more passages and answer questions about them in the same way that we did the sample. Work as quickly as you can. Skim the passage and then read the questions. Use the meaning of the passage to find the answers. Use key words in the question to find the part of the passage that contains the answer. Fill in your answers in the circles at the bottom of the page. When you see a GO sign, turn the page and continue working. Work until you come to the STOP sign at the bottom of page 7. Remember to make sure that your answer circles are filled in with dark marks. Completely erase any marks for answers that you change. Do you have any questions? Start working now.

Allow time for the students to read the stories and answer the questions.

Unit 2 Lesson 2a **Reading Comprehension**

It was Maria's worst nightmare. Her mother was going to work in South America for July and August, and she was going to stay with her aunt and uncle in Utah. She loved Aunt Regina, Uncle Louis, and her cousins, Lillian and Zack, but as far as Maria was concerned, Utah was at the end of the earth. She was born and raised in Chicago, and she loved the excitement of the city, especially in the summer. Maria had convinced herself that this would be the worst summer of her life.

The flight from Chicago to Salt Lake City, Maria's first, was uneventful. She spent most of it reading and sleeping and even discovered that airplane food was not as bad as she had expected. Every once in a while she looked out the window, however, and her fears were confirmed. The farther the plane got from Chicago, the fewer signs of civilization she saw. The landscape below was mostly hills, plains, deserts, and mountains. The only cities she saw were tiny, and their number got smaller as the plane got closer to Salt Lake City.

While the plane was circling before landing in Salt Lake City, Maria saw that the city was large, although much smaller than Chicago. A huge lake was nearby, just like Chicago, and incredible mountains were toward the east. "It's pretty neat," she thought to herself, "but it isn't the Windy City."

Uncle Louis and Aunt Regina met Maria as she came out of the jetway. As they walked to the baggage area, Aunt Regina explained that Lillian and Zack were back at the hotel waiting for them. They were all going to spend the night in the city rather than make the long drive back to St. George in the southern part of the state.

By the time they had picked up the luggage and driven to the hotel, it was late in the afternoon. They decided to go out to dinner, and then the kids would go to a concert at the Delta Center. Maria was surprised because the group that was playing was scheduled to perform in Chicago in a few weeks.

The next morning, as they headed south toward St. George, Maria, Lillian, and Zack slept in the backseat of the car. Whenever they woke up, they talked about the great time they had enjoyed the night before. After dinner, they had gone to a mall for an hour before the concert. After the concert, they went to a party with some other kids Lillian and Zack knew. They had been able to get around easily by bus and arrived back at the hotel just before midnight, as they had promised. Maria hated to admit it, but the night was just as much fun as she would have had in Chicago.

The ride to St. George was through beautiful country. Maria was amazed at how far she could see. In Chicago, the tall buildings prevented any great views, although you could always go to the lake and see for miles. Here, however, vistas were in every direction, with mountains and mesas breaking up the desert landscape. Even the colors were unusual, with lots of reds, browns, and tans, but not many greens.

When they were almost to St. George, Zack started giggling and said, "Can we tell her now, Mom? I'm ready to explode."

"Okay," said Aunt Regina. "Maria, we're not going home quite yet. There's a huge lake nearby, Lake Powell, and we've rented a houseboat for a few days. It's a lot of fun, and we're sure you're going to like it." Maria didn't quite know what to say. It sounded wonderful, and she had already had such a good time. Maybe this summer wouldn't be so bad after all. In fact, maybe this would be one of the best summers ever.

GO →

6

Say It's time to stop. You have finished Lesson 2a.

Review the answers with the students. Ask them if they remembered to look back at the passage to find the answers to the questions. If any questions caused particular difficulty, work through the story, questions, and answer choices. Ask the students which key words helped them find the answers and discuss any strategies they used.

Have the students indicate completion of the lesson by entering their score for this activity on the progress chart at the beginning of the book.

4 In the second paragraph, what does the word "uneventful" mean?
∗ J Without any unusual happenings
K Without a meal
L Without enjoyment
M Without anyone knowing her

5 The story implies that
A Maria had often been to Utah before.
B Maria's mother would meet her in Utah.
C the weather is hot in Chicago in the summer.
∗ D this was Maria's first airplane flight.

6 Why did Zack say "I'm ready to explode"?
J He had eaten too much.
K It was hot in the back of the car.
∗ L He was having a hard time keeping a secret.
M He was angry because of the long car ride.

7 Which of these changes occurs in the story?
A Maria comes to dislike Chicago.
∗ B Maria's attitude toward Utah improves.
C Maria decides she wants to live in Utah.
D Maria's cousins learn to appreciate her.

8 It is clear from the story that
J Maria was bored on her first night in Salt Lake City.
∗ K Maria's aunt and uncle have done a lot to make her feel happy.
L Maria's cousins are jealous because of all the attention she is receiving.
M Maria didn't mind leaving Chicago for the summer.

9 In what way are Chicago and Salt Lake City alike?
A Both cities are about the same size.
B Maria has cousins in both cities.
∗ C Both cities are near a large lake.
D Mountains are near both cities.

10 The three children in this story
J had never met before.
K were not very responsible.
L stayed out too late on the first night.
∗ M are about the same age.

11 How does the author set the tone in the first paragraph?
A By making Maria seem like an unhappy person
B By making the job Maria's mother has sound exciting
∗ C By making the reader think Maria will be unhappy in Utah
D By making the reader think Chicago is a great place to be in the summer

Answer rows
4 ●ⓀⓁⓂ 6 ⒿⓀ●Ⓜ 8 Ⓙ●ⓁⓂ 10 ⒿⓀⓁ●
5 ⒶⒷⒸ● 7 Ⓐ●ⒸⒹ 9 ⒶⒷ●Ⓓ 11 ⒶⒷ●Ⓓ

7

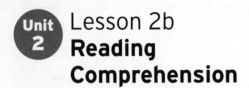

Unit 2 Lesson 2b Reading Comprehension

Focus

Reading Skills
- drawing conclusions
- identifying feelings
- deriving word meanings
- understanding reasons
- recognizing an author's technique
- recognizing an author's purpose
- making inferences

Test-taking Skills
- reasoning from facts and evidence
- working methodically

Sample A

Say Turn to Lesson 2b on page 8. In this lesson you will answer questions about passages that you read. Begin by reading the directions at the top of the page to yourself while I read them out loud.

Read the directions to the students.

Say Now we'll do Sample A. Skim the passage to yourself. *(pause)* Now, read the question next to the passage. To find the correct answer, look back at the passage. What is the correct answer? *(answer D)* You can conclude from the story that it must be a sunny day. Fill in answer circle D for Sample A in the answer rows at the bottom of the page. Make sure the circle is completely filled in. Press your pencil firmly so that your mark comes out dark.

Check to see that the students have marked the correct answer circle.

TIPS

Say Now let's look at the tip. Who will read it?

Have a volunteer read the tip aloud.

Reading Comprehension
Lesson 2b Reading Comprehension

Directions: Read the passage and the answer choices. Choose the best answer.

Sample A Brenda put lots of sunscreen on. She wore a long-sleeve shirt even though she was warm. Her hat had a big brim that would shade her face. She would be outside all day, and she really didn't want to get sunburned.

Which of these can you conclude from this story?
A Brenda is going to a picnic.
B Brenda is playing baseball.
C The weather will get cooler.
∗D It is a sunny day.

 TIPS
• Some questions can be answered with information from the story. For other questions, you have to "read between the lines."

We are beginning to learn that wolves play an important part in the balance of nature and that humans and wolves can live together.

Wolves are near the top of the food chain. They prey on plant-eating animals. When wolves are removed from the environment, the food chain is usually disrupted and plant-eating animals can increase so greatly in number that they overgraze.

At one time, wolves roamed over much of the United States and northern Mexico, as well as most of Canada. As people moved into wilderness areas, wolves were pushed into smaller, more remote areas. They were also hunted for sport and for their pelts and to prevent them from destroying livestock.

In 1995, wolves were reintroduced to the area in and around Yellowstone National Park. Some ranchers disagreed with the return of the wolf, but there was a great deal of popular and scientific support for the idea.

Curiously, while wolves were being destroyed in the wild, they were increasing in popularity as pets. A wolf puppy is a cute ball of fur. When it grows into an adult, however, it is a 150-pound wild animal. What's worse, these wolves can't be returned to the wild because they have never learned to hunt for themselves.

1 Which of these animals is also near the top of the food chain?
A Squirrel
∗B Lion
C Rabbit
D Deer

2 What is the meaning of the word "disrupted" in the second paragraph?
J Improved
K Made longer
∗L Broken apart
M Shortened

3 People who buy wolves for pets
∗A have not given much thought to what happens when their pets grow up.
B are really doing the right thing and should stick it out.
C should just let them go free when they get tired of them.
D have thought about what they are doing and decided it is the right thing.

GO ➡

8   Answer rows   A Ⓐ Ⓑ Ⓒ ●   1 Ⓐ ● Ⓒ Ⓓ   2 Ⓙ Ⓚ ● Ⓜ   3 ● Ⓑ Ⓒ Ⓓ

Say Sometimes you can answer a question from information that is in the story, but other times you have to *read between the lines*. This means you use the information in the story and your experience to find the answer.

Explain the tip further, if necessary. Have the students identify the information in the story that leads to the conclusion that it must be a sunny day.

Practice

Say Now we are ready for Practice. You will read more passages and answer questions about them in the same way that we did the sample. Work as quickly as you can. Skim the passage and then read the questions. Use the meaning of the passage to find the answers. Use key words in the question to find the part of the passage that contains the answer. Fill in your answers in the circles at the bottom of the page. When you see a GO sign, continue working. Work until you come to the STOP sign at the bottom of page 10. Remember to make sure that your answer circles are filled in with dark marks. Completely erase any marks for answers that you change. Do you have any questions? Start working now.

Allow time for the students to read the stories and answer the questions.

 Unit 2 Lesson 2b **Reading Comprehension**

No one believes me, and I can understand why. Here's what happened, and I swear it's the truth.

Aunt Tiki, my sister Lydia, and I were fishing in the Delaware River just north of Easton. On this particular Saturday in May, I had wandered about half a mile up the river to a spot I loved. The river was wide here, and a bend just below me made it impossible for Lydia and Aunt Tiki to see me. This is an important detail, as you will see later.

I tied a lure on my line and cast out about twenty yards. I retrieved the lure slowly, and after a few feet, I hooked a fish. It was a bass, and I returned it to the water after I brought it in. I release almost all of my fish and use barbless hooks so they are not injured.

In the next half hour, I caught three more bass and was having a wonderful time. It's not often that I catch this many fish in such a short period of time, and I was beginning to believe I was becoming a bass master. My confidence rose, and I decided to walk out into the river a little farther.

My next cast was one of the longest I had ever made, and it took my lure into the deepest part of the river, where the current was the strongest. I let it sink for a few seconds, then started bringing it back. When I turned the handle of my reel, however, the lure wouldn't budge. It felt as if I had hooked the bottom.

I was trying to decide if I should walk closer to the lure and see if I could unhook it when something unusual happened. My line moved upriver. I had hooked a fish, and it felt huge!

The fish swam upstream so fast I thought I was going to run out of line. I decided to chase after it and began running. After a few steps, I caught my foot on a rock and went tumbling into the river. I held onto the rod, however, and even though I was soaking wet, I got up and continued the chase.

After about a hundred yards, the fish reached a deep pool and stopped swimming upstream. This gave me a chance to continue the battle, which lasted for about fifteen minutes. Eventually I brought the fish in. I didn't know what kind of fish it was, but it was almost three feet long!

Just then I heard some clapping and turned around. A bunch of people on the bank were shouting, waving, and whistling at me. They must have seen the whole thing. Being a ham, I took a bow, then picked up the fish to show it to them. They clapped even louder, and I felt like a really big deal.

I looked at the fish and saw how beautiful it was. At first, I thought about how good it would look hanging on my wall. The more I thought about it though, the worse I felt. There was only one thing to do. I put the fish in the water, carefully removed the hook, and moved the fish back and forth to make sure water was passing through its gills. After a moment, it swam away slowly, and as if to say it was all right, jumped into the air and landed with a splash. I headed back to shore.

An older gentleman came up to me and asked to shake my hand. He said the fish was a salmon, which was very rare in the Delaware, and the one I had returned was a female loaded with eggs. If she could find a male, there was a chance she would lay her eggs and young salmon would someday return to the river.

I ran back to Lydia and Aunt Tiki and told them the story. They didn't believe me. When I got back to school, I told all my friends, but none of them believed me. Someday when we go back to the river, that kind, older gentleman will show up, and Lydia and Aunt Tiki will believe me.

9

Say It's time to stop. You have finished Lesson 2b.

Review the answers with the students. Ask them if they remembered to look back at the passage to find the answers to the questions. If any questions caused particular difficulty, work through the story, questions, and answer choices.

Have the students indicate completion of the lesson by entering their score for this activity on the progress chart at the beginning of the book.

 Unit 2 Lesson 2b **Reading Comprehension**

6 When the author returned to Aunt Tiki and Lydia, he was probably
J sad.
K unpleasant.
∗ L wet.
M confused.

7 In the fourth paragraph, what is a "bass master"?
A Someone who enjoys eating bass
B Someone who returns bass to the river
∗ C Someone who is good at catching bass
D Someone who fishes for bass alone

8 What is the author's purpose in writing this passage?
J To explain how to catch large fish in unexpected places
K To show that Aunt Tiki and Lydia were wrong
L To help the reader understand the author's love of fishing
∗ M To please the reader by sharing an unusual story

9 Why did the older gentleman want to shake the author's hand?
∗ A The author did the right thing by returning the fish to the river.
B The author caught a large and unusual fish.
C No one would believe the author later when he told the story.
D The author put on a good show.

10 What does it mean to be a "ham"?
J To clap for people
K To catch large fish in unexpected places
L To enjoy a picnic more than fishing
∗ M To put on a show in front of a crowd

11 What made the author sad?
A Knowing no one would believe him
∗ B Thinking of killing the fish
C Tumbling into the river
D Knowing Aunt Tiki and Lydia hadn't seen his fish

12 Why does the author start out by insisting the story is true?
J The story is about fish.
K He doesn't know the reader.
L It is a fiction story.
∗ M Nobody else believes him.

13 Why is it important to know that a bend in the river prevented Aunt Tiki and Lydia from seeing the author?
∗ A Had they seen him, they would have believed him.
B The best fishing was around the bend in the river.
C The bend in the river brought the author closer to the deep part.
D The current was strongest above the bend in the river.

 STOP

---

10   Answer rows    6 Ⓙ Ⓚ ● Ⓜ   8 Ⓙ Ⓚ Ⓛ ●   10 Ⓙ Ⓚ Ⓛ ●   12 Ⓙ Ⓚ Ⓛ ●
7 Ⓐ ● Ⓒ Ⓓ   9 ● Ⓑ Ⓒ Ⓓ   11 Ⓐ ● Ⓒ Ⓓ   13 ● Ⓑ Ⓒ Ⓓ

Test Yourself: Reading Comprehension

Focus

Reading Skills
- drawing conclusions
- making inferences
- understanding reasons
- analyzing characters
- deriving word meanings
- understanding literary devices
- identifying feelings
- recognizing an author's technique
- recognizing details
- understanding sequence
- comparing and contrasting

Test-taking Skills
- managing time effectively
- following printed directions
- noting the lettering of answer choices
- skimming a passage
- referring to a passage to answer questions
- using key words to find the answer
- working methodically
- reasoning from facts and evidence
- analyzing answer choices

Test Yourself: Reading Comprehension

Directions: Read the passage and the answer choices. Choose the best answer.

Sample A

In many parts of the United States, deer are becoming a problem. There are simply too many of them. When new housing developments are built on farmlands or near forests, the environment is improved for deer. They just love the lawns, plants, and flowers homeowners put in, which make for the perfect deer fast-food restaurant.

Which of these is a problem for many suburban gardeners?

A Observing deer in their yards
B Finding plants that deer enjoy
* C Keeping deer out of gardens
D Deer coming into houses

1 "Shel Silverstein is an expert at finding humor and truth in childhood experiences…"
2 Tony listened as the first contestant began her introduction. Wringing his hands, Tony tried to concentrate on the reader. His mind kept spinning around all the advice his coach had given him before the first round: be sure to make eye contact with the audience; pause between the introduction and the poem; don't go too fast. Swimming in his nervous anticipation and the fear of messing up, he finally closed his eyes and took a deep breath.
3 The audience of contestants and coaches laughed suddenly, then clapped. Tony looked up to see the expression on the reader's face. Her eyes were bulging with expression as she froze, hanging on to the last word of the poem with her mouth.
4 Tony looked down at the crumpled piece of paper that he drew when he entered the room. Number five. What was he doing here? Though he loved poetry and had received compliments for his ability to interpret it well, standing in front of strangers and a judge was an altogether different feeling. He knew that everyone in the room had spent at least as many hours as he had in front of mirrors, parents, and coaches, trying to gain an edge in their ability to communicate their poem's meaning.
5 Number four began his introduction, and Tony once again breathed deeply.
6 "I can do this. I can do this," he repeated in his mind. The clapping came after what seemed like a few seconds. The judge called, "Number five."
7 Tony made his way to the front of the room. As he faced the audience with his black book at his side, something changed. He smiled, nodded at the timekeeper to begin, and easily, as if having a conversation, began his introduction.
8 When he finished the last word and closed his book, he felt like his whole world was a different color. The audience clapped, his coach gave him a thumbs-up, and the timer flashed the six-minute card. He had entered the room feeling like an alien. He left knowing he had found a new talent.

Answer rows   A Ⓐ Ⓑ ● Ⓓ

11

This lesson simulates an actual test-taking experience. Therefore, it is recommended that the directions be read verbatim and the suggested procedures and time allowances be followed.

Directions

Administration Time: approximately 30 minutes

Say Turn to the Test Yourself lesson on page 11.

Check to be sure the students have found the right page. Point out to the students that this Test Yourself lesson is timed like a real test, but that they will score it themselves to see how well they are doing. Explain that it is important to work quickly and to answer as many questions as possible.

Say This lesson will check how well you understand what you read. Remember to make sure that the circles for your answer choices are completely filled in. Press your pencil firmly so that your marks come out dark. Completely erase any marks for answers that you change. Do not write anything except your answer choices in your books.

Look at Sample A. Read the passage and answer the question about it. The answer rows are at the bottom of the page.

Allow time for the students to fill in their answers.

Say The correct answer is C. The story suggests that *keeping deer out of a garden* is a problem. If you chose another answer, erase yours and fill in answer C now.

Check to see that the students have correctly filled in their answer circles with a dark mark.

Say Now you will do more items like Sample A. There are different passages for this part of the lesson. When you come to the GO sign at the bottom of a page, turn the page and continue working. Work until you come to the STOP sign at the bottom of page 15. Fill in your answers in the rows at the bottom of the page. Make sure you fill in the circles completely with dark marks. Completely erase any marks for answers you change. You will have 25 minutes. You may begin.

Allow 25 minutes.

 Unit 2 Test Yourself: Reading Comprehension

1 Why did the audience clap and laugh at the first contestant?
  A She made a joke at the end of the poem.
  B She wore a funny costume.
  C Her reading was not very good.
  *D She finished reading a funny poem.

2 In paragraph 3, what does "hanging on to the last word" mean?
  *J The reader stood still after she said her last word.
  K The reader forgot the last line of her poem.
  L The audience helped her finish by saying the last word.
  M Tony mouthed the last word of the poem with the reader.

3 What made Tony think differently about the competition?
  A He left his black book at the chair where he was sitting.
  *B His attitude changed when he came to the front of the room.
  C He realized that he knew the timekeeper and the judge.
  D His coach was the first person he saw in the audience.

4 How did Tony feel about the competition after he read?
  *J Comfortable
  K Silly
  L Nervous
  M Adventurous

5 Whose thoughts does the narrator express in paragraph 4?
  A The judge's
  B The other contestants'
  *C Tony's
  D The coach's

6 In paragraph 8, what is the effect of the description of Tony "feeling like an alien"?
  J It describes Tony's confidence at the start of the contest.
  K It explains that Tony was from another country.
  L It emphasizes the fact that Tony's poem was about immigrants from Russia.
  *M It suggests that Tony considered himself an outsider when he entered the contest.

7 The use of a series of imperative statements in paragraph 2 helps the reader understand that
  A his coach was demanding and expected too much of Tony.
  B the audience was allowed to give the readers advice.
  *C Tony had to keep in mind many technical details when he read.
  D the judge helped coach the readers during the contest.

8 What made Tony feel nervous at first?
  J The first contestant read his poem.
  K His coach sat too close to him.
  *L This was his first poetry reading contest.
  M The other readers were better than he was.

 GO

12 Answer rows 1 (A)(B)(C)● 3 (A)●(C)(D) 5 (A)(B)●(D) 7 (A)(B)●(D)
                2 ●(K)(L)(M) 4 ●(K)(L)(M) 6 (J)(K)(L)● 8 (J)(K)●(M)

After the Revolutionary War, the citizens of the newly formed United States thought their problems were over. They had defeated the most powerful nation in the world and now occupied a rich land.

However, the governing body of the United States, the Continental Congress, was facing bankruptcy because it had no guaranteed source of revenue. In addition, armed mobs in Massachusetts were revolting against the state government, which had imposed heavy taxes and created harsh laws to punish those who owed money. The individual states were not working together well, which weakened the international trading position of the United States and affected its ability to defend itself.

A convention was called by the Continental Congress and several of the states in 1787. Taking place in Philadelphia, the Constitutional Convention was meant to create amendments to the existing Articles of Confederation, which were considered at the time to be America's constitution. The Articles of Confederation were thought to be so weak, however, that those attending the convention decided to create a whole new constitution.

More than fifty delegates from twelve of the thirteen states attended. They included lawyers, farmers, merchants, and heroes of the Revolutionary War. George Washington presided over the meeting, which many historians believe created a brilliant document that has withstood the test of time.

At the beginning of the convention, the delegates agreed on a three-part government that included the legislative, executive, and judicial branches. They disagreed, however, on how the states would be represented in the legislature. The large population states wanted representation by population, while the small states wanted each state to be represented by the same number of legislators. A compromise was reached in which the legislature would have two houses, a Senate and a House of Representatives. Each state would have two senators, but the number of representatives would be determined by the population of the state. This compromise is reflected in the makeup of Congress today.

Disputes also arose between delegates from manufacturing and agricultural states who wanted the Constitution to favor their particular industry. Another disagreement was how the president, the chief of the executive branch of government, would be elected.

In spite of the disputes, a draft of the Constitution was signed on September 17, 1887. The matter now went to the individual states, which debated the Constitution and eventually agreed to it. The last state to ratify the Constitution was Rhode Island, which agreed to it on May 29, 1790.

The Constitution is "the supreme law of the land." The first eight articles established the responsibilities of the branches of government, how the president is elected, the relationship among the states, and how the Constitution can be amended. To these articles were quickly added ten amendments, which we know as the Bill of Rights. The Bill of Rights defines the most important rights of individuals and also delegates to the states any powers not held by the federal government. Since 1791, when the Bill of Rights was created, seventeen more amendments have been added to the Constitution.

The Constitution and the Bill of Rights are as important today as they were two hundred years ago. The first amendment, for example, guarantees citizens freedom to practice the religion of their choice, freedom of speech and the press, the right to gather together peaceably, and the opportunity to criticize the government without fear of retaliation. These guarantees were necessary in the 1700s because people were concerned that the new government of the United States would be as oppressive as the British government they had just defeated. Today these same rights are exercised by Americans every day.

13

9 The phrase "withstood the test of time" means the Constitution

A was created long ago.

B was written on durable paper.

C was signed by many people who were old and knowledgeable.

✳ D has proven useful over many years.

10 How many amendments to the Constitution are there?

✳ J 27

K 17

L 10

M 8

11 If there is a conflict between the laws of a state and the Constitution,

A the state law is considered to be the higher law.

✳ B the Constitution is considered to be the higher law.

C they are considered to be equal.

D both laws are considered to be invalid.

12 Why did the large states want representation by population?

J The greater a state's population, the fewer votes it would have.

✳ K The greater a state's population, the more votes it would have.

L They wanted to give equal power to all the states.

M They wanted people to move to low population states.

13 In the last paragraph, what does the word "retaliation" mean?

✳ A Punishment

B Payment

C Privacy

D Performance

14 If a person is accused of a crime, that person is guaranteed a trial by a jury. This guarantee would probably be found in

J the first eight articles of the Constitution.

K the Constitutional Convention.

✳ L the Bill of Rights.

M the last amendment.

15 The current Constitution is our

A first.

✳ B second.

C third.

D fourth.

16 What was necessary before the Constitution could be enacted?

J England had to agree to it.

K The states had to fight with one another.

L There had to be three branches of government.

✳ M The states had to agree to it.

GO

14　Answer rows　**9** Ⓐ Ⓑ Ⓒ ●　**11** Ⓐ ● Ⓒ Ⓓ　**13** ● Ⓑ Ⓒ Ⓓ　**15** Ⓐ ● Ⓒ Ⓓ

10 ● Ⓚ Ⓛ Ⓜ　**12** Ⓙ ● Ⓛ Ⓜ　**14** Ⓙ Ⓚ ● Ⓜ　**16** Ⓙ Ⓚ Ⓛ ●

Say It's time to stop. You have completed the Test Yourself lesson.

Check to see that the students have correctly filled in their answer circles. At this point, go over the answers with the students. Did they have enough time to complete the lesson? Did they remember to skim the passage and to look for key words in the questions? Did they take the best guess when they were unsure of the answer?

Work through any questions that caused difficulty. It may be helpful to discuss the strategies students used to answer the comprehension items. You may also want to have the students identify the specific part of a passage that helped them find the right answer.

Have the students indicate completion of the lesson by entering their score for this activity on the progress chart at the beginning of the book.

 Unit 2 Test Yourself: Reading Comprehension

As the sun drops low in the west
And begins its journey that makes the night,
Its final rays turn the eastern mountains pink,
The color of an open watermelon in July.
I pull the reins and slow the horse to a steady trot,
Then turn and face the mountain rich with color.
It fades to purple, then to darkness,
And the evening breeze cools the air.
I think about the wanderers of long ago
Who reached this spot so far from home.
"There is no better place," they must have said
And felt my joy at the desert sunset.

17 An "open watermelon in July" is
  A one that is almost ripe.
  B one that is delicious.
  C an unusual one that has pink skin.
✳ D one that has been cut open.

18 The narrator and the horse
  J had been riding slower.
✳ K had been riding faster.
  L had been herding cows.
  M had been exploring the mountain.

19 The area in which the narrator is riding
  A is near a river.
  B is on the eastern side of a mountain.
  C is close to a large city.
✳ D had been settled long ago.

20 The "journey that makes the night" is
✳ J the time when the sun is below the horizon.
  K the long trip the poet has yet to take.
  L the trip made by wanderers of long ago.
  M the time when the sun rises behind the mountain.

Answer rows **17** Ⓐ Ⓑ Ⓒ ● **18** Ⓙ ● Ⓛ Ⓜ **19** Ⓐ Ⓑ Ⓒ ● **20** ● Ⓚ Ⓛ Ⓜ   15

Unit 3

Background

This unit contains three lessons that deal with spelling skills. Students are asked to identify a misspelled word in isolation.

• **In Lesson 3a,** students identify an incorrectly spelled word. Students work methodically, take the best guess when unsure of the answer, and indicate that an item has no mistakes.

• **In Lesson 3b,** students identify an incorrectly spelled word. In addition to reviewing the test-taking skills introduced in Lesson 3a, students learn about recalling error types.

• **In the Test Yourself lesson,** the spelling skills and test-taking skills introduced and used in Lessons 3a and 3b are reinforced and presented in a format that gives students the experience of taking an achievement test. Techniques for managing time effectively when taking a standardized test are reinforced.

Instructional Objectives

Lesson 3a Spelling **Lesson 3b Spelling**	Given four words, students identify which of the four is misspelled or indicate that there are no mistakes.
Test Yourself	Given questions similar to those in Lessons 3a and 3b, students utilize spelling skills and test-taking strategies on achievement test formats.

Lesson 3a
Spelling

Focus

Spelling Skill
• identifying spelling errors

Test-taking Skills
• working methodically
• subvocalizing answer choices
• taking the best guess when unsure of the answer
• indicating that an item has no mistakes

Samples A and B

Say Turn to Lesson 3a on page 16. In this lesson you will find misspelled words. Read the directions at the top of the page to yourself while I read them out loud.

Read the directions out loud to the students.

Say Let's look at Sample A. Look at the answer choices. Find the word that has a spelling mistake. If none of the words has a mistake, choose the last answer, No mistakes. Which answer did you choose? *(answer C, c-h-a-n-g-a-b-l-e)* Mark circle C for Sample A in the answer rows at the bottom of the page. Make sure the circle is completely filled in. Press your pencil firmly so that your mark comes out dark.

Check to see that the students have filled in the correct answer circle. Review the correct spelling of the word *changeable*.

Say Do Sample B yourself. Find the word that has a spelling mistake. If none of the words has a mistake, choose the last answer. *(pause)* Which answer should you choose? *(answer J)* You should have marked answer J because *e-x-s-t-r-a* is an incorrect spelling. What should you do now? *(mark the circle for answer J in the answer rows)* Make sure the circle is completely filled in with a dark mark.

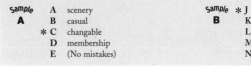

Spelling
Lesson 3a Spelling

Directions: Fill in the space for any word that has a spelling mistake. If there is no mistake, fill in the last answer space.

Sample A			Sample B		
	A	scenery		* J	exstra
	B	casual		K	station
	* C	changable		L	awaken
	D	membership		M	pillow
	E	(No mistakes)		N	(No mistakes)

• Say the words to yourself while you look at them. This can help you find the word with a spelling mistake.

• If you are not sure which answer to choose, take your best guess.

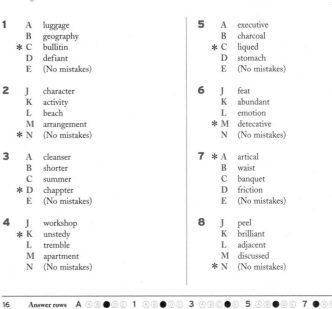

1	A	luggage		5	A	executive
	B	geography			B	charcoal
	* C	bullitin			* C	liqued
	D	defiant			D	stomach
	E	(No mistakes)			E	(No mistakes)
2	J	character		6	J	feat
	K	activity			K	abundant
	L	beach			L	emotion
	M	arrangement			* M	detecative
	* N	(No mistakes)			N	(No mistakes)
3	A	cleanser		7	* A	artical
	B	shorter			B	waist
	C	summer			C	banquet
	* D	chappter			D	friction
	E	(No mistakes)			E	(No mistakes)
4	J	workshop		8	J	peel
	* K	unstedy			K	brilliant
	L	tremble			L	adjacent
	M	apartment			M	discussed
	N	(No mistakes)			* N	(No mistakes)

STOP

16   Answer rows   A ⒶⒷ●ⒹⒺ   1 ⒶⒷ●ⒹⒺ   3 ⒶⒷⒸ●Ⓔ   5 ⒶⒷ●ⒹⒺ   7 ●ⒷⒸⒹⒺ
               B ●⒦ⓁⓂⓃ   2 ⒿⓀⓁⓂ●   4 Ⓙ●ⓁⓂⓃ   6 ⒿⓀⓁ●Ⓝ   8 ⒿⓀⓁⓂ●

Check to see that the students have filled in the correct answer circle. Review the correct spelling of the word *extra*.

⭐ **TIPS**

Say Now let's look at the tips.

Have a volunteer read the tips aloud.

Say Don't forget, you are looking for the word that is spelled wrong. You might find it helpful to say the words to yourself while you look at them letter by letter. Sometimes you may not be able to figure out which word has a mistake. When this happens, take your best guess.

Practice

Say Now we are ready for Practice. Do Numbers 1 through 8 in the same way that we did the samples. Work as quickly as you can, and if you aren't sure which word has a mistake, take your best guess. Don't forget, if all the words are spelled correctly, choose the last answer, No mistakes. Work until you come to the STOP sign at the bottom of the page. Remember to make sure that your answer circles are completely filled in with dark marks. Completely erase any marks for answers that you change. Any questions? Start working now.

Allow time for the students to mark their answers.

Say It's time to stop. You have finished Lesson 3a.

Review the answers with the students. If any items caused particular difficulty, work through each of the answer choices.

Have the students indicate completion of the lesson by entering their score for this activity on the progress chart at the beginning of the book.

Spelling
Lesson 3a Spelling

Directions: Fill in the space for any word that has a spelling mistake. If there is no mistake, fill in the last answer space.

Sample A			Sample B		
	A	scenery		*J	exstra
	B	casual		K	station
	*C	changable		L	awaken
	D	membership		M	pillow
	E	(No mistakes)		N	(No mistakes)

- Say the words to yourself while you look at them. This can help you find the word with a spelling mistake.
- If you are not sure which answer to choose, take your best guess.

1
A luggage
B geography
*C bullitin
D defiant
E (No mistakes)

2
J character
K activity
L beach
M arrangement
*N (No mistakes)

3
A cleanser
B shorter
C summer
*D chappter
E (No mistakes)

4
J workshop
*K unstedy
L tremble
M apartment
N (No mistakes)

5
A executive
B charcoal
*C liqued
D stomach
E (No mistakes)

6
J feat
K abundant
L emotion
*M detecative
N (No mistakes)

7
*A artical
B waist
C banquet
D friction
E (No mistakes)

8
J peel
K brilliant
L adjacent
M discussed
*N (No mistakes)

16 **Answer rows** A Ⓐ Ⓑ ● Ⓓ Ⓔ   1 Ⓐ Ⓑ ● Ⓓ Ⓔ   3 Ⓐ Ⓑ Ⓒ ● Ⓔ   5 Ⓐ Ⓑ ● Ⓓ Ⓔ   7 ● Ⓑ Ⓒ Ⓓ Ⓔ
B ● Ⓙ Ⓚ Ⓛ Ⓜ Ⓝ   2 Ⓙ Ⓚ Ⓛ Ⓜ ●   4 Ⓙ ● Ⓛ Ⓜ Ⓝ   6 Ⓙ Ⓚ Ⓛ ● Ⓝ   8 Ⓙ Ⓚ Ⓛ Ⓜ ●

Unit 3 Lesson 3b
Spelling

Focus

Spelling Skill
• identifying spelling errors

Test-taking Skills
• recalling error types
• working methodically
• indicating that an item has no mistakes

Samples A and B

Say Turn to Lesson 3b on page 17. In this lesson you will find misspelled words. Read the directions at the top of the page to yourself while I read them out loud.

Read the directions out loud to the students.

Say Find Sample A at the top of the page. Look at the answer choices. Find the word that has a spelling mistake. If none of the words has a mistake, choose the last answer. Which answer did you choose? (answer B, m-e-a-n-w-i-l-e) Mark circle B for Sample A in the answer rows at the bottom of the page. Make sure the circle is completely filled in. Press your pencil firmly so that your mark comes out dark.

Check to see that the students have filled in the correct answer circle. Review the correct spelling of the word *meanwhile*.

Say Do Sample B yourself. Find the word that has a spelling mistake. If none of the words has a mistake, choose the last answer. (pause) Which answer should you choose? (answer L, t-h-i-r-d-i-e-t-h) What should you do now? (mark circle L) Yes, mark circle L for Sample B in the answer rows at the bottom of the page. Make sure the circle is completely filled in. Press your pencil firmly so that your mark comes out dark.

Check to see that the students have filled in the correct answer circle.

Spelling
Unit 3 Lesson 3b Spelling

Directions: Fill in the space for any word that has a spelling mistake. If there is no mistake, fill in the last answer space.

Sample A			Sample B		
	A	reject		J	flounder
	*B	meanwile		K	heed
	C	empire		*L	thirdieth
	D	dictionary		M	conserve
	E	(No mistakes)		N	(No mistakes)

• **Look for different kinds of spelling mistakes: missing letters, extra letters, and wrong letters.**

1
A health
B opportunity
C dropping
*D acident
E (No mistakes)

2
J historic
*K inormous
L orbiting
M icicle
N (No mistakes)

3
A foretell
B ourselves
C underwater
D flagpole
*E (No mistakes)

4 *J propertie
K wonderful
L crumble
M numerous
N (No mistakes)

5
A ore
B particle
*C surjeon
D shoulder
E (No mistakes)

6
J repeated
K security
L privacy
*M charidy
N (No mistakes)

7
A idle
B proposing
*C dependant
D admission
E (No mistakes)

8
J emotion
K umbrella
L cancel
M situation
*N (No mistakes)

STOP

Answer rows A Ⓐ●ⒸⒹⒺ 1 ⒶⒷⒸ●Ⓔ 3 ⒶⒷⒸⒹ● 5 Ⓐ●ⒸⒹⒺ 7 ⒶⒷ●ⒹⒺ   17
            B ⒿⓀ●ⓂⓃ 2 Ⓙ●ⓁⓂⓃ 4 ●ⓀⓁⓂⓃ 6 ⒿⓀⓁ●Ⓝ 8 ⒿⓀⓁⓂ●

★**TIPS**

Say Now let's look at the tip.

Have a volunteer read the tip aloud.

Say There are many different kinds of spelling mistakes. They include missing letters, extra letters, and wrong letters. When you look at the answer choices, look for all of these mistakes.

Demonstrate various misspellings of the words in the sample items, errors such as *regect* or *hede*. Point out that the error in sample A is a missing letter and in Sample B it is a wrong letter.

Practice

Say Now we are ready for Practice. Do Numbers 1 through 8 in the same way that we did the samples. Work as quickly as you can and remember that there are different kinds of spelling errors. Work until you come to the STOP sign at the bottom of the page. Remember to make sure that your answer circles are completely filled in with dark marks. Completely erase any marks for answers that you change. Any questions? Start working now.

Allow time for the students to mark their answers.

Say It's time to stop. You have finished Lesson 3b.

Review the answers with the students. If any items caused particular difficulty, work through each of the answer choices. Do an informal item analysis to determine which items were most difficult. Discuss with the students the words that gave them the most difficulty, including the misspelled words and the distractors that are spelled correctly and that the students identify as wrong.

Have the students indicate completion of the lesson by entering their score for this activity on the progress chart at the beginning of the book.

Unit 3

Spelling
Lesson 3b **Spelling**

Directions: Fill in the space for any word that has a spelling mistake. If there is no mistake, fill in the last answer space.

Sample A			Sample B		
	A	reject		J	flounder
*	B	meanwile		K	heed
	C	empire	*	L	thirdieth
	D	dictionary		M	conserve
	E	(No mistakes)		N	(No mistakes)

- Look for different kinds of spelling mistakes: missing letters, extra letters, and wrong letters.

1
A health
B opportunity
C dropping
* D acident
E (No mistakes)

2
J historic
* K inormous
L orbiting
M icicle
N (No mistakes)

3
A foretell
B ourselves
C underwater
D flagpole
* E (No mistakes)

4
* J propertie
K wonderful
L crumble
M numerous
N (No mistakes)

5
A ore
B particle
* C surjeon
D shoulder
E (No mistakes)

6
J repeated
K security
L privacy
* M charidy
N (No mistakes)

7
A idle
B proposing
* C dependant
D admission
E (No mistakes)

8
J emotion
K umbrella
L cancel
M situation
* N (No mistakes)

STOP

Answer rows A Ⓐ●ⒸⒹⒺ 1 ⒶⒷⒸ●Ⓔ 3 ⒶⒷⒸⒹ● 5 ⒶⒷ●ⒹⒺ 7 ⒶⒷ●ⒹⒺ
B Ⓙ●ⓀⓁⓂ 2 Ⓙ●ⓁⓂⓃ 4 ●ⓀⓁⓂⓃ 6 ⒿⓀⓁ●Ⓝ 8 ⒿⓀⓁⓂ●

17

Unit 3 Test Yourself: Spelling

Focus

Spelling Skill
• identifying spelling errors

Test-taking Skills
• managing time effectively
• working methodically
• subvocalizing answer choices
• taking the best guess when unsure of the answer
• indicating that an item has no mistakes
• recalling error types

This lesson simulates an actual test-taking experience. Therefore it is recommended that the directions be read verbatim and that the suggested procedures and time allowances be followed.

Directions

Administration Time: approximately 20 minutes

Say Turn to the Test Yourself lesson on page 18.

Point out to the students that this Test Yourself lesson is timed like a real test, but that they will score it themselves to see how well they are doing. Remind the students to work quickly and to mark the answer as soon as they are sure which word is misspelled.

Say This lesson will check how well you can find words with spelling errors. Remember to make sure that the circles for your answer choices are completely filled in. Press your pencil firmly so that your marks come out dark. Completely erase any answers that you change. Do not write anything except your answer choices in your books.

Look at the answer choices for Sample A. Find the answer choice that has a spelling error. If there is no error, choose the last answer choice. Mark the circle for your answer.

Allow time for the students to mark their answers.

Unit 3 Test Yourself: Spelling

Directions: Fill in the space for any word that has a spelling mistake. If there is no mistake, fill in the last answer space.

Sample A			Sample B		
	A	usable		J	quotation
	B	horse		K	elaborate
	C	rotate		L	miner
*	D	freaze		M	inscription
	E	(No mistakes)	*	N	(No mistakes)

1	A	thunder	6	*J	interier
	B	vanilla		K	compare
	C	tease		L	jogging
*D		harvist		M	frightened
	E	(No mistakes)		N	(No mistakes)

2	J	wrote	7	A	congratulate
	K	successful		B	veil
	L	award		C	resource
	M	decorate		*D	trackked
*N		(No mistakes)		E	(No mistakes)

3	A	revenue	8	J	dormitory
	B	permitted		K	misprint
	C	basis		L	spacious
*D		symble		*M	publicatun
	E	(No mistakes)		N	(No mistakes)

4	J	orchard	9	A	obey
	K	scribble		B	receipt
	L	measure		C	napkin
	M	album		D	impulse
*N		(No mistakes)		*E	(No mistakes)

5	A	fascination	10	*J	estabalish
	B	cafeteria		K	vitamin
	C	scientific		L	scent
*D		interferance		M	moisture
	E	(No mistakes)		N	(No mistakes)

GO

18 Answer rows

Say The circle for answer D should have been marked because it is the incorrect spelling of *f-r-e-e-z-e*. If you chose another answer, erase yours and fill in circle D now.

Check to see that the students have correctly marked their answer circles for Sample A.

Say Do Sample B yourself. Mark the circle for the answer choice that has a spelling mistake. If there is no error, choose the last answer choice. Mark the circle for your answer.

Allow time for the students to fill in their answers.

Say You should have filled in the circle for answer N because none of the words has a spelling error. If you chose another answer, erase yours and fill in circle N now.

Check to see that the students have correctly marked their answer circles for Sample B.

Say Now you will do Numbers 1 through 22 in the same way that we did the samples. When you come to the GO sign at the bottom of the page, continue working. Work until you come to the STOP sign at the bottom of page 19. When you have finished, you can check over your answers to this lesson. Then wait for the rest of the group to finish. Any questions? You will have 15 minutes. Begin working now.

Allow 15 minutes.

Say It's time to stop. You have completed the Test Yourself lesson. Check to see that you have completely filled in your answer circles with dark marks. Make sure that any marks for answers that you changed have been completely erased.

Go over the lesson with the students. Ask them if they had enough time to finish the lesson. Ask for volunteers to identify the spelling errors in each item.

Work through any questions that caused difficulty. Discuss any rules the students used to determine whether or not a word is spelled correctly. If necessary, provide additional practice questions similar to the ones in this unit.

Have the students indicate completion of the lesson by entering their score for this activity on the progress chart at the beginning of the book.

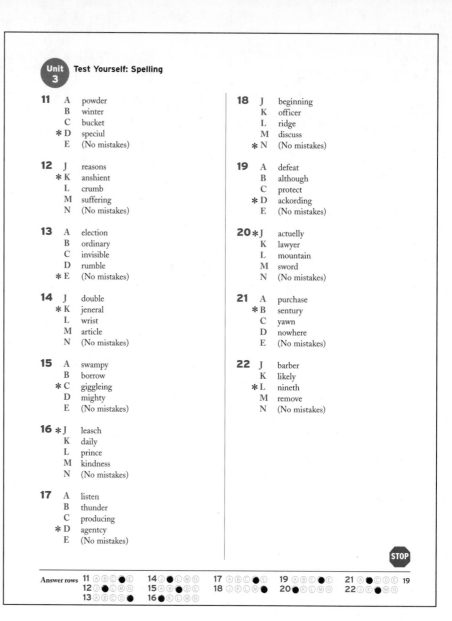

Unit 3 Test Yourself: Spelling

11
A powder
B winter
C bucket
*D speciul
E (No mistakes)

12
J reasons
*K anshient
L crumb
M suffering
N (No mistakes)

13
A election
B ordinary
C invisible
D rumble
*E (No mistakes)

14
J double
*K jeneral
L wrist
M article
N (No mistakes)

15
A swampy
B borrow
*C giggleing
D mighty
E (No mistakes)

16
*J leasch
K daily
L prince
M kindness
N (No mistakes)

17
A listen
B thunder
C producing
*D agentcy
E (No mistakes)

18
J beginning
K officer
L ridge
M discuss
*N (No mistakes)

19
A defeat
B although
C protect
*D ackording
E (No mistakes)

20
*J actually
K lawyer
L mountain
M sword
N (No mistakes)

21
A purchase
*B sentury
C yawn
D nowhere
E (No mistakes)

22
J barber
K likely
*L nineth
M remove
N (No mistakes)

STOP

Answer rows
11 Ⓐ Ⓑ Ⓒ ● Ⓔ
12 Ⓙ ● Ⓛ Ⓜ Ⓝ
13 Ⓐ Ⓑ Ⓒ Ⓓ ●
14 Ⓙ ● Ⓛ Ⓜ Ⓝ
15 Ⓐ Ⓑ ● Ⓓ Ⓔ
16 ● Ⓚ Ⓛ Ⓜ Ⓝ
17 Ⓐ Ⓑ Ⓒ ● Ⓔ
18 Ⓙ Ⓚ Ⓛ Ⓜ ●
19 Ⓐ Ⓑ Ⓒ ● Ⓔ
20 ● Ⓚ Ⓛ Ⓜ Ⓝ
21 Ⓐ ● Ⓒ Ⓓ Ⓔ
22 Ⓙ Ⓚ ● Ⓜ Ⓝ
19

Background

This unit contains five lessons that deal with capitalization and punctuation skills.

• **In Lessons 4a and 4b,** students identify mistakes in capitalization in written text. Students work methodically and practice understanding unusual item formats. They also analyze answer choices, indicate that an item has no mistakes, and recall special capitalization rules.

• **In Lessons 5a and 5b,** students identify mistakes in punctuation in written text. In addition to reviewing the test-taking skills introduced in the two previous lessons, students learn the importance of skimming answer choices, analyzing answer choices, and skipping difficult items and returning to them later.

• **In the Test Yourself lesson,** the capitalization and punctuation skills and test-taking skills introduced in Lessons 4a through 5b are reinforced and presented in a format that gives students the experience of taking an achievement test. Techniques for managing time effectively when taking a standardized test are reinforced.

Instructional Objectives

Lesson 4a **Capitalization** Lesson 4b **Capitalization**	Given text divided into three parts, students identify which part has a capitalization mistake or indicate that there is no mistake.
Lesson 5a **Punctuation** Lesson 5b **Punctuation**	Given text divided into three parts, students identify which part has a punctuation mistake or indicate that there is no mistake.
Test Yourself	Given questions similar to those in Lessons 4a through 5b, students utilize capitalization, punctuation, and test-taking strategies on achievement test formats.

Unit 4
Lesson 4a
Capitalization

Focus

Language Skill
- identifying capitalization errors

Test-taking Skills
- working methodically
- understanding unusual item formats
- analyzing answer choices
- indicating that an item has no mistakes

Samples A and B

Say Turn to Lesson 4a on page 20. In this lesson you will look for capitalization in sentences. Read the directions at the top of the page to yourself while I read them out loud.

Read the directions out loud to the students.

Say Let's begin with Sample A. It is a sentence divided into three parts. You are to find the part that has a mistake in capitalization. If there is no mistake, choose the last answer, No mistakes. Read the answer choices to yourself. Does one of them have a mistake in capitalization? *(yes, answer A)* Answer A has a mistake because *Aunt* should begin with a capital letter. Fill in circle A for Sample A in the answer rows at the bottom of the page. Check to make sure your answer circle is completely filled in with a dark mark.

Check to see that the students have filled in the correct answer circle.

Say Do Sample B yourself. Mark the circle for the answer choice that has a capitalization mistake. If there is no error, choose the last answer choice. Mark the circle for your answer.

Allow time for the students to fill in their answers.

Say You should have filled in the circle for answer M, *No mistakes*. If you chose another answer, erase yours and fill in circle M now.

Unit 4
Capitalization and Punctuation

Lesson 4a Capitalization

Directions: Fill in the space for the answer that has a mistake in capitalization. Fill in the last answer space if there is no mistake.

Sample A	*A	I called aunt Farani to ask
	B	if she would sponsor me in
	C	the race on Saturday.
	D	(No mistakes)

Sample B	J	Before he went to school,
	K	Chuck got his equipment
	L	ready for the hockey game.
	*M	(No mistakes)

TIPS
- Take your time. Read each answer choice word by word.
- The first word of a sentence and proper nouns should be capitalized.

1
A "The CD you want is out of stock
*B right now," Answered the clerk. "We
C expect it in soon," she added.
D (No mistakes)

2
J My cousin was an exchange student
K last year. She spent six months living
*L with a family in austria.
M (No mistakes)

3
A This movie is based on a book called
*B *maybe next time.* I was surprised to
C find that I enjoyed the movie more.
D (No mistakes)

4
J The wagon train arrived in Oregon
K in October. The families had time to
L build shelters before winter came.
*M (No mistakes)

5
A For years, families would do
*B their shopping at bunting's. The
C store will close for good this week.
D (No mistakes)

6
J My mother visited New York
K last summer. She loved all
*L the shops on Fifth avenue.
M (No mistakes)

7
A When asked about the movie,
*B Willard answered, "it was good,
C but I thought it was too long."
D (No mistakes)

8
J Engineers say that each drop
K of water in the Colorado River is
L used at least three times.
*M (No mistakes)

STOP

20 Answer rows A ●ⒷⒸⒹ 1 Ⓐ●ⒸⒹ 3 Ⓐ●ⒸⒹ 5 Ⓐ●ⒸⒹ 7 Ⓐ●ⒸⒹ
B ⒿⓀⓁ● 2 ⒿⓀ●Ⓜ 4 ⒿⓀⓁ● 6 ⒿⓀ●Ⓜ 8 ⒿⓀⓁ●

Check to see that the students have filled in the correct answer circle.

★TIPS

Say Now let's look at the tips.

Have a volunteer read the tips aloud.

Say Look at the answer choices word by word. Be sure the first word in a sentence and important words in a sentence are capitalized. And don't forget, sometimes the mistake will be a word that begins with a capital letter when it should not.

Discuss with the students the different kinds of words that should begin with a capital letter.

Practice

Say Now you will do the Practice items. Remember to look carefully at all of the answer choices for a capitalization mistake. Make sure you fill in the circles in the answer rows with dark marks. Do not write anything except your answer choices in your books. Completely erase any marks for answers that you change. Work until you come to the STOP sign at the bottom of the page. Any questions? Start working now.

Allow time for the students to fill in their answers.

Say It's time to stop. You have finished Lesson 4a.

Review the answers with the students. It will be helpful to discuss the errors in the items and the capitalization rules with which the errors are associated. If any questions caused particular difficulty, work through each of the answer choices.

Have the students indicate completion of the lesson by entering their score for this activity on the progress chart at the beginning of the book.

Capitalization and Punctuation

Lesson 4a **Capitalization**

Directions: Fill in the space for the answer that has a mistake in capitalization. Fill in the last answer space if there is no mistake.

Sample A	* A	I called aunt Farani to ask
	B	if she would sponsor me in
	C	the race on Saturday.
	D	(No mistakes)

Sample B	J	Before he went to school,
	K	Chuck got his equipment
	L	ready for the hockey game.
	* M	(No mistakes)

- Take your time. Read each answer choice word by word.
- The first word of a sentence and proper nouns should be capitalized.

1 A "The CD you want is out of stock
* B right now," Answered the clerk. "We
C expect it in soon," she added.
D (No mistakes)

2 J My cousin was an exchange student
K last year. She spent six months living
* L with a family in austria.
M (No mistakes)

3 A This movie is based on a book called
* B *maybe next time*. I was surprised to
C find that I enjoyed the movie more.
D (No mistakes)

4 J The wagon train arrived in Oregon
K in October. The families had time to
L build shelters before winter came.
* M (No mistakes)

5 A For years, families would do
* B their shopping at bunting's. The
C store will close for good this week.
D (No mistakes)

6 J My mother visited New York
K last summer. She loved all
* L the shops on Fifth avenue.
M (No mistakes)

7 A When asked about the movie,
* B Willard answered, "it was good,
C but I thought it was too long."
D (No mistakes)

8 J Engineers say that each drop
K of water in the Colorado River is
L used at least three times.
* M (No mistakes)

20 **Answer rows** A ●ⒷⒸⒹ 1 Ⓐ●ⒸⒹ 3 Ⓐ●ⒸⒹ 5 Ⓐ●ⒸⒹ 7 Ⓐ●ⒸⒹ
B ⒿⓀⓁ● 2 ⒿⓀ●Ⓜ 4 ⒿⓀⓁ● 6 ⒿⓀ●Ⓜ 8 ⒿⓀⓁ●

Unit 4 Lesson 4b Capitalization

Focus

Language Skill
• identifying capitalization errors

Test-taking Skills
• working methodically
• understanding unusual item formats
• recalling special capitalization rules
• indicating that an item has no mistakes

Samples A and B

Say Turn to Lesson 4b on page 21. This is another lesson about capitalization. Read the directions at the top of the page to yourself while I read them out loud.

Read the directions out loud to the students.

Say Let's do Sample A. It is one sentence divided into three parts. You are to find the part that has a mistake in capitalization. If there is no mistake, choose the last answer, No mistakes. Does one of the answer choices have a mistake in capitalization? *(yes, answer C)* Answer C has a mistake. The word *because* should not begin with a capital letter. Fill in circle C for Sample A in the answer rows at the bottom of the page. Check to make sure your answer circle is completely filled in with a dark mark.

Check to see that the students have filled in the correct answer circle.

Say Do Sample B yourself. Mark the circle for the answer choice that has a capitalization mistake. If there is no error, choose the last answer choice. Mark the circle for your answer.

Allow time for the students to fill in their answers.

Say You should have filled in the circle for answer M. None of the answer choices has a mistake in capitalization. If you chose another answer, erase yours and fill in circle M now.

Unit 4 Capitalization and Punctuation

Lesson 4b Capitalization

Directions: Fill in the space for the answer that has a mistake in capitalization. Fill in the last answer space if there is no mistake.

Sample A	A	Not many people use
	B	this trail any more
	*C	Because it is steep.
	D	(No mistakes)

Sample B	J	The book you are looking
	K	for is on loan. It will be
	L	back next week.
	*M	(No mistakes)

• Remember, letters need special capitalization.

1
A   16 Hale Avenue
*B   seeley, CA 92273
C   March 4, 2001
D   (No mistakes)

2
*J   Western boot Co.
K   Lima, OH 45805
L   Dear Ms. Harrison:
M   (No mistakes)

3
A   Thank you for responding to my
B   letter. I received a new pair of
C   boots a week after writing.
*D   (No mistakes)

4
J   I returned my old boots on the
*K   following Day. You should have
L   received them by now.
M   (No mistakes)

5
A   Again, thank you for your help.
B   Gratefully,
*C   Asa ferdig
D   (No mistakes)

6
J   The library and headquarters of
*K   the Association of American railroads
L   is located in Washington, D.C.
M   (No mistakes)

7
*A   After Richard the lion-hearted
B   became king, he joined with France
C   in a crusade to the Holy Land.
D   (No mistakes)

8
J   Before Julia Child was a famous
K   chef, she worked for a secret agency
*L   called the Office of strategic services.
M   (No mistakes)

STOP

Answer rows
A Ⓐ Ⓑ ● Ⓓ   1 Ⓐ ● Ⓒ Ⓓ   3 Ⓐ Ⓑ Ⓒ ●   5 Ⓐ Ⓑ ● Ⓓ   7 ● Ⓑ Ⓒ Ⓓ
B Ⓙ Ⓚ Ⓛ ●   2 ● Ⓚ Ⓛ Ⓜ   4 Ⓙ ● Ⓛ Ⓜ   6 Ⓙ ● Ⓛ Ⓜ   8 Ⓙ Ⓚ ● Ⓜ

21

Check to see that the students have filled in the correct answer circle.

 TIPS

Say Now let's look at the tip.

Have a volunteer read the tip aloud.

Say Some of the items in this lesson are parts of a letter. Keep in mind that the parts of a letter need special capitalization. You should look at these items very carefully and think about how they should be capitalized.

Remind the students that street names, city names, state abbreviations, dates, and the greeting and closing of a letter have special capitalization.

Practice

Say Now you will do the Practice items. Remember to look carefully at all of the answer choices for a capitalization mistake, especially the items that involve parts of a letter. Make sure you fill in the circles in the answer rows with dark marks. Do not write anything except your answer choices in your books. Completely erase any marks for answers that you change. Work until you come to the STOP sign at the bottom of the page. Any questions? Start working now.

Allow time for the students to fill in their answers.

Say It's time to stop. You have finished Lesson 4b.

Review the answers with the students. It will be helpful to discuss the errors in the items and the rules for capitalization. If any questions caused particular difficulty, work through each of the answer choices.

Have the students indicate completion of the lesson by entering their score for this activity on the progress chart at the beginning of the book.

Unit 4 Capitalization and Punctuation

Lesson 4b **Capitalization**

Directions: Fill in the space for the answer that has a mistake in capitalization. Fill in the last answer space if there is no mistake.

Sample A	A	Not many people use
	B	this trail any more
	*C	Because it is steep.
	D	(No mistakes)

Sample B	J	The book you are looking
	K	for is on loan. It will be
	L	back next week.
	*M	(No mistakes)

- Remember, letters need special capitalization.

1
A   16 Hale Avenue
*B   seeley, CA 92273
C   March 4, 2001
D   (No mistakes)

2
*J   Western boot Co.
K   Lima, OH 45805
L   Dear Ms. Harrison:
M   (No mistakes)

3
A   Thank you for responding to my
B   letter. I received a new pair of
C   boots a week after writing.
*D   (No mistakes)

4
J   I returned my old boots on the
*K   following Day. You should have
L   received them by now.
M   (No mistakes)

5
A   Again, thank you for your help.
B   Gratefully,
*C   Asa ferdig
D   (No mistakes)

6
J   The library and headquarters of
*K   the Association of American railroads
L   is located in Washington, D.C.
M   (No mistakes)

7
*A   After Richard the lion-hearted
B   became king, he joined with France
C   in a crusade to the Holy Land.
D   (No mistakes)

8
J   Before Julia Child was a famous
K   chef, she worked for a secret agency
*L   called the Office of strategic services.
M   (No mistakes)

Answer rows   A ⒶⒷ●Ⓓ   1 Ⓐ●ⒸⒹ   3 ⒶⒷⒸ●   5 ⒶⒷ●Ⓓ   7 ●ⒷⒸⒹ
              B ⒿⓀⓁ●   2 ●ⓀⓁⓂ   4 Ⓙ●ⓁⓂ   6 Ⓙ●ⓁⓂ   8 ⒿⓀ●Ⓜ

21

Lesson 5a
Punctuation

Focus

Language Skill
• identifying punctuation errors

Test-taking Skills
• working methodically
• understanding unusual item formats
• skimming answer choices
• analyzing answer choices
• indicating that an item has no mistakes

Samples A and B

Say Turn to Lesson 5a on page 22. In this lesson you will look for punctuation mistakes in sentences. Read the directions at the top of the page to yourself while I read them out loud.

Read the directions out loud to the students.

Say Let's begin with Sample A. It is two sentences divided into three parts. You are to find the part that has a mistake in punctuation. If there is no mistake, choose the last answer. Read the answer choices to yourself. Does one of them have a mistake in punctuation? *(yes, the first one)* The first answer has a mistake because there should be a *comma* after said. Fill in circle A for Sample A in the answer rows at the bottom of the page. Check to make sure your answer circle is completely filled in with a dark mark.

Check to see that the students have filled in the correct answer circle.

Say Now do Sample B yourself. Read the answer choices and look for a mistake in punctuation. Choose the last answer if the punctuation is correct. *(pause)* Which answer did you choose? *(the last one, M)* Yes, the punctuation in this item is correct. Fill in circle M for Sample B in the answer rows at the bottom of the page. Check to make sure that answer circle M is completely filled in with a dark mark.

Capitalization and Punctuation

Lesson 5a **Punctuation**

Directions: Fill in the space for the answer that has a mistake in punctuation. Fill in the last answer space if there is no mistake.

Sample A	*A	Carl said "Next week is
	B	Joan's birthday. We should
	C	have a party for her."
	D	(No mistakes)

Sample B	J	Our neighbor, Barb Cain,
	K	has an interesting job. She
	L	is an air traffic controller.
	*M	(No mistakes)

• First, skim the answers. Check for punctuation at the end of each sentence.

• Next, read each answer more carefully. Look for a missing comma, apostrophe, quotation mark, or other punctuation in the answers.

1
A Hiking this trail is hard work,
B but you will enjoy it. Just be sure
C to bring lots of water and a sweater.
*D (No mistakes)

2
J Chesapeake Bay has thousands
K of tiny coves. If a storm comes up,
*L sailor's can find safety in them.
M (No mistakes)

3
A "This isn't the road we should
*B be on" sighed Jamal. He looked at
C the map and knew they were lost.
D (No mistakes)

4
*J Covered with mud the puppy
K looked like he had enjoyed his
L visit to the lake with his master.
M (No mistakes)

5
A "How did you ever find us?"
B laughed Chet. "We were sure
*C you would never look there?"
D (No mistakes)

6
J The drive to the bay will take
K about two hours. We can stop
L for breakfast on the way.
*M (No mistakes)

7
*A Sharon was excited Tomas was
B nervous, and I was confused. The
C city was a new experience for us.
D (No mistakes)

8
J Talasha helped her father paint
*K her bedroom: when they finished,
L it looked absolutely wonderful.
M (No mistakes)

22   Answer rows   A ●ⒷⒸⒹ   1 ⒶⒷⒸ●   3 Ⓐ●ⒸⒹ   5 ⒶⒷ●Ⓓ   7 ●ⒷⒸⒹ
                   B ⒿⓀⓁ●   2 ⒿⓀ●Ⓜ   4 ●ⓀⓁⓂ   6 ⒿⓀⓁ●   8 Ⓙ●ⓁⓂ

Check to see that the students have filled in the correct answer circle.

★TIPS

Say Now let's look at the tips.

Have a volunteer read the tips aloud.

Say Always begin by skimming the answers and looking for missing or wrong end punctuation. Then read the answers again and look for missing or wrong punctuation inside the sentence. Be sure to work carefully. It is easy to miss a punctuation mistake.

Discuss with the students the error types for which they should look. The punctuation marks they should look for are end punctuation, comma, apostrophe, and quotation mark.

Practice

Say Now you will do some Practice items. Remember to look carefully at all of the answer choices. Look for errors in end punctuation and punctuation inside a sentence. Make sure you fill in the circles in the answer rows with dark marks. Do not write anything except your answer choices in your books. Completely erase any marks for answers that you change. Work until you come to the STOP sign at the bottom of the page. Any questions? Start working now.

Allow time for the students to fill in their answers.

Say It's time to stop. You have finished Lesson 5a.

Review the answers with the students. It will be helpful to discuss the punctuation errors in the items. If any questions caused particular difficulty, work through each of the answer choices.

Have the students indicate completion of the lesson by entering their score for this activity on the progress chart at the beginning of the book.

Capitalization and Punctuation

Lesson 5a Punctuation

Directions: Fill in the space for the answer that has a mistake in punctuation. Fill in the last answer space if there is no mistake.

Sample A
*A Carl said "Next week is
B Joan's birthday. We should
C have a party for her."
D (No mistakes)

Sample B
J Our neighbor, Barb Cain,
K has an interesting job. She
L is an air traffic controller.
*M (No mistakes)

- First, skim the answers. Check for punctuation at the end of each sentence.
- Next, read each answer more carefully. Look for a missing comma, apostrophe, quotation mark, or other punctuation in the answers.

1
A Hiking this trail is hard work,
B but you will enjoy it. Just be sure
C to bring lots of water and a sweater.
*D (No mistakes)

2
J Chesapeake Bay has thousands
K of tiny coves. If a storm comes up,
*L sailor's can find safety in them.
M (No mistakes)

3
A "This isn't the road we should
*B be on" sighed Jamal. He looked at
C the map and knew they were lost.
D (No mistakes)

4
*J Covered with mud the puppy
K looked like he had enjoyed his
L visit to the lake with his master.
M (No mistakes)

5
A "How did you ever find us?"
B laughed Chet. "We were sure
*C you would never look there?"
D (No mistakes)

6
J The drive to the bay will take
K about two hours. We can stop
L for breakfast on the way.
*M (No mistakes)

7
*A Sharon was excited Tomas was
B nervous, and I was confused. The
C city was a new experience for us.
D (No mistakes)

8
J Talasha helped her father paint
*K her bedroom: when they finished,
L it looked absolutely wonderful.
M (No mistakes)

 STOP

22 Answer rows
A ⒜Ⓑ©Ⓓ 1 ⒶⒷⒸ● 3 Ⓐ●©Ⓓ 5 ⒶⒷ●Ⓓ 7 ●Ⓑ©Ⓓ
B ⒿⓀⓁ● 2 ⒿⓀ●Ⓜ 4 ●ⓀⓁⓂ 6 ⒿⓀⓁ● 8 Ⓙ●ⓁⓂ

Unit 4 Lesson 5b
Punctuation

Focus

Language Skill
• identifying punctuation errors

Test-taking Skills
• working methodically
• analyzing answer choices
• understanding unusual item formats
• indicating that an item has no mistakes
• skipping difficult items and returning to them later

Samples A and B

Say Turn to Lesson 5b on page 23. In this lesson you will look for punctuation mistakes in sentences. Read the directions at the top of the page to yourself while I read them out loud.

Read the directions out loud to the students.

Say Find Sample A at the top of the page. Read the answer choices and look for a mistake in punctuation. Choose the last answer if the punctuation is correct. *(pause)* Which answer did you choose? *(the second one, B)* There should be a *comma* after *dollars*. Fill in circle B for Sample A in the answer rows at the bottom of the page. Check to make sure that answer circle B is completely filled in with a dark mark.

Check to see that the students have filled in the correct answer circle.

Say Now do Sample B yourself. Fill in the space for the answer that has a mistake in punctuation. Choose the last answer if the punctuation is correct. *(pause)* The last answer is correct because none of the answer choices has a punctuation mistake. Fill in circle M for Sample B in the answer rows at the bottom of the page. Check to make sure your answer circle is completely filled in with a dark mark.

Unit 4 — Capitalization and Punctuation

Lesson 5b **Punctuation**

Directions: Fill in the space for the answer that has a mistake in punctuation. Fill in the last answer space if there is no mistake.

Sample A	A	Our first computer cost
	✱ B	more than five thousand dollars
	C	A new one is less than a thousand.
	D	(No mistakes)

Sample B	J	All of us were tired. We had
	K	played ball in the morning
	L	and then had gone swimming.
	✱ M	(No mistakes)

• Take your time when you look at the answer choices. Think about all the places punctuation might be needed.

1
A The highest temperature in the
✱B nation today was in Yuma Arizona.
C It was over one hundred degrees.
D (No mistakes)

2
J The principal smiled and asked,
✱K Are you sure you want the day off?"
L She was joking with us, of course.
M (No mistakes)

3
✱A The Peach Boy is a folktale
B about an elderly couple that
C finds a child inside a peach.
D (No mistakes)

4
J She'd spent all summer training for
K the race. In the end, she was able to
✱L reach her coachs goals and her own.
M (No mistakes)

5
✱A Jo Biggs the girl next door
B took first place in the Rose
C Festival's writing contest.
D (No mistakes)

6
✱J "Is anybody home" hollered
K Alan. This caused Dad, who was
L taking a nap, to awaken suddenly.
M (No mistakes)

7
A Janet King, a math teacher with
B a flair for art, began making quilts at
C the age of 60. She's a talented lady.
✱D (No mistakes)

8
✱J When uncle George was a
K boy, he loved swimming. He won
L many trophies and medals.
M (No mistakes)

STOP

Answer rows
A A ● C D 1 A ● C D 3 ● B C D 5 ● B C D 7 A B C ●
B J K ● M 2 J ● L M 4 J K ● M 6 ● K L M 8 ● K L M

23

Check to see that the students have filled in the correct answer circle.

 TIPS

Say Now let's look at the tip.

Have a volunteer read the tip aloud.

Say When you look at the answer choices, think about places that need punctuation. You should also look for wrong punctuation or a punctuation mark where none is needed.

Discuss some possible error types with the students, such as a question mark being placed where a period should be or a period where a comma should be.

Practice

Say Now you will do some Practice items. Remember to look carefully at all of the answer choices. Think about where a punctuation mark might be needed in an answer. And remember, if an item seems difficult, skip it and come back to it later. Make sure you fill in the circles in the answer rows with dark marks. Do not write anything except your answer choices in your books. Completely erase any marks for answers that you change. Work until you come to the STOP sign at the bottom of the page. Any questions? Start working now.

Allow time for the students to fill in their answers.

Say It's time to stop. You have finished Lesson 5b.

Review the answers with the students. It will be helpful to discuss the punctuation errors in the items. If any questions caused particular difficulty, work through each of the answer choices.

Have the students indicate completion of the lesson by entering their score for this activity on the progress chart at the beginning of the book.

 Unit 4

Capitalization and Punctuation

Lesson 5b **Punctuation**

Directions: Fill in the space for the answer that has a mistake in punctuation. Fill in the last answer space if there is no mistake.

Sample A	A	Our first computer cost
	*B	more than five thousand dollars
	C	A new one is less than a thousand.
	D	(No mistakes)

Sample B	J	All of us were tired. We had
	K	played ball in the morning
	L	and then had gone swimming.
	*M	(No mistakes)

 TIPS

• Take your time when you look at the answer choices. Think about all the places punctuation might be needed.

1
A   The highest temperature in the
*B   nation today was in Yuma Arizona.
C   It was over one hundred degrees.
D   (No mistakes)

2
J   The principal smiled and asked,
*K   Are you sure you want the day off?"
L   She was joking with us, of course.
M   (No mistakes)

3
*A   The Peach Boy is a folktale
B   about an elderly couple that
C   finds a child inside a peach.
D   (No mistakes)

4
J   She'd spent all summer training for
K   the race. In the end, she was able to
*L   reach her coachs goals and her own.
M   (No mistakes)

5
*A   Jo Biggs the girl next door
B   took first place in the Rose
C   Festival's writing contest.
D   (No mistakes)

6
*J   "Is anybody home" hollered
K   Alan. This caused Dad, who was
L   taking a nap, to awaken suddenly.
M   (No mistakes)

7
A   Janet King, a math teacher with
B   a flair for art, began making quilts at
C   the age of 60. She's a talented lady.
*D   (No mistakes)

8
*J   When uncle George was a
K   boy, he loved swimming. He won
L   many trophies and medals.
M   (No mistakes)

STOP

Answer rows   A ⒶⒷ●ⒸⒹ   1 Ⓐ●ⒸⒹ   3 ●ⒷⒸⒹ   5 ●ⒷⒸⒹ   7 ⒶⒷⒸ●
B ⒿⓀⓁ●   2 Ⓙ●ⓁⓂ   4 ⒿⓀ●Ⓜ   6 ●ⓀⓁⓂ   8 ●ⓀⓁⓂ

23

Focus

Language Skills
- identifying capitalization errors
- identifying punctuation errors

Test-taking Skills
- managing time effectively
- following printed directions
- working methodically
- understanding unusual item formats
- analyzing answer choices
- indicating that an item has no mistakes
- recalling special capitalization rules
- skimming answer choices
- analyzing answer choices
- skipping difficult items and returning to them later

This lesson simulates an actual test-taking experience. Therefore, it is recommended that the directions be read verbatim and the suggested procedures and time allowances be followed.

Directions

Administration Time: approximately 20 minutes

Say Turn to the Test Yourself lesson on page 24.

Point out to the students that this Test Yourself lesson is timed like a real test, but that they will score it themselves to see how well they are doing. Remind the students to pace themselves and to check the clock after they have finished the capitalization items to see how much time is left. This is about the halfway point in the lesson. Encourage the students to avoid spending too much time on any one item and to take the best guess if they are unsure of the answer.

Say There are two types of items in the Test Yourself lesson, so you will have to read the directions for each section and pay close

---

Test Yourself: Unit 4 Capitalization and Punctuation

Directions: Fill in the space for the answer that has a mistake in capitalization or punctuation. Fill in the last answer space if there is no mistake.

Sample A	A	We arrived in Seattle on
	B	Thursday afternoon. As usual,
	C	it was rainy and chilly.
	*D	(No mistakes)

Sample B	J	The tennis courts were open,
	*K	but there weren't any nets, we
	L	decided to go home.
	M	(No mistakes)

Directions: For questions 1–12, fill in the space for the answer that has a mistake in capitalization. Fill in the last answer space if there is no mistake.

1
- A The book I just finished is called
- *B *Flowers on the wall.* The title doesn't
- C fit the story very well.
- D (No mistakes)

2
- *J In late august, my family
- K goes to Lincoln City's annual
- L Sand-Castle Building Contest.
- M (No mistakes)

3
- A When experts talk about the
- B geographical areas around Japan,
- *C they often refer to it as the far east.
- D (No mistakes)

4
- *J The Lincoln memorial is spectacular.
- K Most people who visit it come away
- L with a feeling of awe and wonder.
- M (No mistakes)

5
- A Many people disagree with her
- B ideas, but no one complains that
- *C senator Lobianco doesn't work hard.
- D (No mistakes)

6
- J Our school plants a tree in
- *K the park on arbor day. This
- L tradition began in 1950.
- M (No mistakes)

7
- A My cousin and her friends went
- B on a trip to South America. They
- *C hiked the andes mountains.
- D (No mistakes)

8
- J Every Sunday morning my family
- *K walks to the midtown Bakery. We
- L have breakfast and then walk home.
- M (No mistakes)

GO ▶

24   Answer rows

---

attention to what you are doing. Remember to make sure that the circles in the answer rows are completely filled in. Press your pencil firmly so that your marks come out dark. Completely erase any marks for answers that you change. Do not write anything except your answer choices in your books.

Look at Sample A and listen carefully. Read the answer choices to yourself. Mark the circle for the answer that has a mistake in capitalization. Choose the last answer, No mistakes, if none of the answer choices has a mistake. Mark the circle for your answer.

Allow time for the students to fill in their answers.

Say The circle for answer D should be filled in because all of the answer choices are correct. If you chose another answer, erase yours and fill in the circle for answer D now.

Check to see that the students have filled in the correct answer circle.

Say Now do Sample B. Read the answer choices to yourself. Mark the circle for the answer that has a mistake in punctuation. Choose the last answer, No mistakes, if none of the answer choices has a mistake in punctuation. Mark the circle for your answer.

Allow time for the students to fill in their answers.

Say The circle for answer K should be filled in. The *comma* after *nets* should be a *period*. If you chose another answer, erase yours and fill in the circle for answer K now.

Check to see that the students have filled in the correct answer circle.

Say Now you will do more items. Read the directions for each section. When you come to the GO sign at the bottom of the page, continue working. Work until you come to the STOP sign on page 26. If you are not sure of an answer, fill in the circle for the answer you think might be right. Do you have any questions?

Answer any questions the students have.

Say You may begin working. You will have 15 minutes.

Allow 15 minutes.

 Unit 4 Test Yourself: Capitalization and Punctuation

9 *A The Colorado river starts as
B a relatively small stream in the
C mountains and quickly grows larger.
D (No mistakes)

10 J Many people are surprised to see
*K how far North the country of England
L is. Its weather is fairly mild.
M (No mistakes)

11 A Africa is an unusual continent.
*B it has many countries, a variety of land
C forms, and exotic plants and animals.
D (No mistakes)

12 J Our neighbors are from New York
K City. They have never lived in the
*L Country and find it a little strange.
M (No mistakes)

Directions: For questions 13–26, fill in the space for the answer that has a mistake in punctuation. Fill in the last answer space if there is no mistake.

13 A This basketball needs some air.
B Let's walk over to Ted's house and
*C borrow his brother Toms' hand pump.
D (No mistakes)

14 *J Dr. Hennessy who lives up the
K street, comes to our school once
L a week to talk to us about college.
M (No mistakes)

15 A Cherise just joined the soccer
*B team Vera takes tennis lessons,
C and I have taken up volleyball.
D (No mistakes)

16 J The kitchen in our house is small.
K My mother and father want to take
*L out a wall and make it bigger?
M (No mistakes)

 GO

Say It's time to stop. You have finished the Test Yourself lesson. Check to see that you have completely filled in your answer circles with dark marks. Make sure that any marks for answers that you changed have been completely erased.

Go over the lesson with the students. Ask the students if they read the directions for each section. Did they have enough time to finish all the items? Which items were most difficult? Work through any questions that caused difficulty.

Have the students indicate completion of the lesson by entering their score for this activity on the progress chart at the beginning of the book.

17
A   This forest is very healthy.
B   It has a mix of oak, maple,
∗C   and, cherry trees.
D   (No mistakes)

18
J   Almost no one expected
K   that the new mall would cause
L   so many traffic problems.
∗M   (No mistakes)

19
A   The table was made by my
∗B   uncle the chairs are from my
C   grandmother's attic.
D   (No mistakes)

20
J   The store closed at eight
K   o'clock. We got there too late
L   to buy what we needed.
∗M   (No mistakes)

21
A   "This is the longest bike ride
B   I've ever taken. I'm going to be
∗C   tired tomorrow" said Allan.
D   (No mistakes)

22
J   These mountains were formed
∗K   long ago. You can see, one layer
L   of rock was the bottom of a lake.
M   (No mistakes)

23
A   We see our neighbor walk
∗B   her dog's every morning just
C   after the sun comes up.
D   (No mistakes)

24
∗J   Why were you late. You knew
K   it was important for all of the
L   players to be here on time.
M   (No mistakes)

25
A   All of these candles were made
B   by a small company that has a
∗C   factory in Dubuque Iowa.
D   (No mistakes)

26
J   This building was owned
∗K   by CJ Pierce. He was a famous
L   artist in our town.
M   (No mistakes)

 STOP

26   **Answer rows**   17 Ⓐ Ⓑ ● Ⓓ   19 Ⓐ ● Ⓒ Ⓓ   21 Ⓐ Ⓑ ● Ⓓ   23 Ⓐ ● Ⓒ Ⓓ   25 Ⓐ Ⓑ ● Ⓓ
   18 Ⓙ Ⓚ Ⓛ ●   20 Ⓙ Ⓚ Ⓛ ●   22 Ⓙ ● Ⓛ Ⓜ   24 ● Ⓚ Ⓛ Ⓜ   26 Ⓙ ● Ⓛ Ⓜ

Unit 5

Background

This unit contains five lessons that deal with usage and expression skills.

• **In Lessons 6a and 6b,** students identify usage mistakes in written text. Students use context to find an answer, indicate that an item has no mistakes, and skim text. They work methodically, recall usage errors, and take the best guess when unsure of the answer.

• **In Lesson 7a,** students identify the correct word to fit in a sentence and answer questions about a paragraph. In addition to reviewing the test-taking skills learned in previous lessons, they learn the importance of following printed directions and understanding unusual item formats. They eliminate answer choices, take the best guess when unsure of the answer, and work methodically.

• **In Lesson 7b,** students identify correctly formed sentences, identify which paragraph best suits a stated purpose, and answer questions about a paragraph. In addition to reviewing the test-taking skills learned in previous lessons, they practice analyzing answer choices.

• **In the Test Yourself lesson,** the usage and expression skills and test-taking skills introduced in Lessons 6a through 7b are reinforced and presented in a format that gives students the experience of taking an achievement test. Techniques for managing time effectively when taking a standardized test are reinforced.

Instructional Objectives

Lesson 6a Usage **Lesson 6b Usage**	Given text divided into three parts, students identify which part has a usage mistake or indicate that there is no mistake.
Lesson 7a Expression **Lesson 7b Expression**	Given a sentence with an underlined word or words, students identify which of three answer choices should replace the word or words or indicate that there should be no change. Given four paragraphs, students identify which paragraph best suits a stated purpose. Given a paragraph and questions about it, students identify which of four answer choices is correct. Given four sentences, students identify the best way to express the underlying idea.
Test Yourself	Given questions similar to those in Lessons 6a through 7b, students utilize usage and expression skills and test-taking strategies on achievement test formats.

Lesson 6a
Usage

Focus

Language Skill
• identifying mistakes in usage

Test-taking Skills
• using context to find an answer
• indicating that an item has no mistakes
• subvocalizing answer choices

Samples A and B

Say Turn to Lesson 6a on page 27. In this lesson you will look for mistakes in the correct use of English. Read the directions at the top of the page to yourself while I read them out loud.

Read the directions out loud to the students.

Say Let's begin with Sample A. It is a sentence divided into three parts. You are to find the part that has a mistake in English. If there is no mistake, choose the last answer, No mistakes. Read the answer choices to yourself. Does one of them have a mistake? *(yes, the second one)* The second answer choice has a mistake. The word *hisself* should be *himself*. Fill in circle B for Sample A in the answer rows at the bottom of the page. Check to make sure your answer circle is completely filled in with a dark mark.

Check to see that the students have filled in the correct answer circle.

Say Now do Sample B. Read the answer choices and look for a mistake in English. Choose the last answer if there is no mistake. *(pause)* Which answer did you choose? *(answer L)* The third answer choice has a mistake. The word *singed* should be *sang*. Fill in circle L for Sample B in the answer rows at the bottom of the page. Check to make sure the answer circle is completely filled in with a dark mark.

Check to see that the students have filled in the correct answer circle.

Unit 5

Usage and Expression
Lesson 6a **Usage**

Directions: Fill in the space for the answer that has a mistake in usage. Fill in the last answer space if there is no mistake.

Sample A			
	A		Last year Tashani taught
	*B		hisself how to use a computer
	C		and word processing software.
	D		(No mistakes)

Sample B			
	J		The students had fun at
	K		the zoo. On the way home,
	*L		they singed funny songs.
	M		(No mistakes)

TIPS
• Say the answer choices to yourself carefully word by word.
• If one of the answers sounds wrong, it probably is wrong.

1
 A   The phone rang five times. Jilisa
 B   ran as fast as she could, but by the
 C   time she got there, it had stopped.
*D   (No mistakes)

2
*J   Can you borrow me your pen?
 K   Mine is out of ink, and I have to
 L   take notes in science lab today.
 M   (No mistakes)

3
 A   Roberto knew it was going to
 B   be a bad day. It started when he
*C   couldn't find no milk for his cereal.
 D   (No mistakes)

4
 J   The football coach asked Rollie
*K   and I if we were interested in
 L   playing for the school team this year.
 M   (No mistakes)

5
*A   The smaller of the six students
 B   was asked to crawl under the desk
 C   to try to find the missing hamster.
 D   (No mistakes)

6
 J   A box full of used paperback books
*K   were on sale for a dollar. My older
 L   sister said she was going to buy them.
 M   (No mistakes)

7
 A   Jill and I wanted to stay at the
 B   mall, but since it was getting
*C   kinda late, we went home.
 D   (No mistakes)

8
*J   Eric and his sister was surprised
 K   to learn that their parents were
 L   thinking about buying a new house.
 M   (No mistakes)

GO

Answer rows   A Ⓐ●©Ⓓ   1 ⒶⒷ©●   3 Ⓐ●©Ⓓ   5 ●Ⓑ©Ⓓ   7 ⒶⒷ●Ⓓ
               B ⒿⓀ●Ⓜ   2 ●ⓀⓁⓂ   4 Ⓙ●ⓁⓂ   6 Ⓙ●ⓁⓂ   8 ●ⓀⓁⓂ   27

★ TIPS

Say Now let's look at the tips.

Have a volunteer read the tips aloud.

Say You might find it helpful to say the answer choices to yourself carefully. Choose the one that has a part that sounds incorrect. Think about the meaning of the answer choices as you say them to yourself. Their meaning will help you choose the correct answer.

Practice

Say Let's do the Practice items now. Say the answer choices to yourself and listen for the one that sounds incorrect. Make sure you fill in the circles in the answer rows with dark marks. Do not write anything except your answer choices in your books. Completely erase any marks for answers that you change. When you come to the GO sign at the bottom of the page, turn the page and continue working. Work until you come to the STOP sign at the bottom of page 28. Any questions? Start working now.

Allow time for the students to fill in their answers.

Say It's time to stop. You have finished Lesson 6a.

Review the answers with the students. It will be helpful to discuss the error types that appear in the lesson and have the students read aloud the correct form of the sentences. If any questions caused particular difficulty, work through each of the answer choices.

Have the students indicate completion of the lesson by entering their score for this activity on the progress chart at the beginning of the book.

 Lesson 6a **Usage**

9 A   I enjoy reading science fiction,
    B   but I am usually embarrassed
    C   to tell my friends about it.
  * D   (No mistakes)

10 J   It rained all weekend. Celine
    K   and her friends were bored because
  * L   they couldn't find nothing to do.
    M   (No mistakes)

11 A   The game was fun, but I
  * B   maked too many mistakes. Next
    C   time I'll try to do better.
    D   (No mistakes)

12 J   Cats can swim, but they don't
    K   usually like to. My cat is strange
    L   because she loves the water.
  * M   (No mistakes)

13 * A   Last week was awful windy.
    B   The dust was terrible, and
    C   our trash cans blew away.
    D   (No mistakes)

14 J   Lisa and Bill saved their money
  * K   and bought theirselves a telescope.
    L   Astronomy is their favorite hobby.
    M   (No mistakes)

15 A   To get ready for our annual
    B   family reunion, we set up lots of
  * C   benchs and tables under the trees.
    D   (No mistakes)

16 * J   The bread might of been better
    K   if we had let it rise more. Even so,
    L   it tasted great right from the oven.
    M   (No mistakes)

17 A   The door to Jeremy's apartment
    B   was locked, so he spent the afternoon
    C   at Fannie's house doing homework.
  * D   (No mistakes)

18 J   The single-use camera we
  * K   bought took wonderfuller pictures,
    L   almost as good as a standard camera.
    M   (No mistakes)

28   Answer rows   9 Ⓐ Ⓑ Ⓒ ●   11 Ⓐ ● Ⓒ Ⓓ   13 ● Ⓑ Ⓒ Ⓓ   15 Ⓐ Ⓑ ● Ⓓ   17 Ⓐ Ⓑ Ⓒ ●
                  10 Ⓙ Ⓚ ● Ⓜ   12 Ⓙ Ⓚ Ⓛ ●   14 Ⓙ ● Ⓛ Ⓜ   16 ● Ⓚ Ⓛ Ⓜ   18 Ⓙ ● Ⓛ Ⓜ

Focus

Language Skill
• identifying mistakes in usage

Test-taking Skills
• working methodically
• recalling usage errors
• indicating that an item has no mistakes
• taking the best guess when unsure of the answer

Samples A and B

Say Turn to Lesson 6b on page 29. This is another lesson in which you will look for mistakes in the correct use of English. Read the directions at the top of the page to yourself while I read them out loud.

Read the directions out loud to the students.

Say Sample A is two sentences divided into three parts. You are to find the part that has a mistake in English. If there is no mistake, choose the last answer, No mistakes. *(pause)* Answer B has a mistake. The word *had* is not needed in the sentence. Fill in answer circle B for Sample A in the answer rows at the bottom of the page. Check to make sure that the answer circle is completely filled in with a dark mark.

Check to see that the students have filled in the correct answer circle.

Say Now do Sample B. Read the answer choices and look for a mistake in English usage. Choose the last answer if there is no mistake. *(pause)* Which answer did you choose? *(answer J)* The word *weather* should be spelled *whether*. Fill in circle J for Sample B in the answer rows at the bottom of the page. Make sure the circle is completely filled in with a dark mark.

Check to see that the students have filled in the correct answer circle.

 Usage and Expression
Lesson 6b **Usage**

Directions: Fill in the space for the answer that has a mistake in usage. Fill in the last answer space if there is no mistake.

Sample A			
	A		On our trip, the pilot
	∗B		had flew over the storm,
	C		so we had a good flight.
	D		(No mistakes)

Sample B			
	∗J		Juanita didn't know weather
	K		to buy a gift for her father or
	L		to take him to a ball game.
	M		(No mistakes)

 • **Look for incorrect verbs and words that are spelled right but used wrong.**

1
A Last fall our house was hit
B by lightning. It didn't do any
C damage to the house.
∗D (No mistakes)

2
∗J The fish swimmed up the
K river until they reached a large
L dam that stopped them.
M (No mistakes)

3
A The tourists rode on a raft
∗B made of logs. My friend and me
C decided that we wanted to do it.
D (No mistakes)

4
J Mr. Scott has a wonderful
K garden. All of the plants he grows
∗L is healthy and pretty.
M (No mistakes)

5
A The holiday parade will be held
B next week. The band members
∗C had met at the high school.
D (No mistakes)

6
∗J There isn't no way that our
K team will lose this game. We
L will all do our best.
M (No mistakes)

7
A Many people prepare for a
B vacation by reading books about
∗C the places they to plan to go.
D (No mistakes)

8
J The store that just opened on
K Market Street had to close because
L the roof was leaking.
∗M (No mistakes)

 STOP

Answer rows A Ⓐ●ⒸⒹ 1 ⒶⒷⒸ● 3 Ⓐ●ⒸⒹ 5 Ⓐ●●Ⓓ 7 ⒶⒷ●Ⓓ
B ●ⓀⓁⓂ 2 ●ⓀⓁⓂ 4 ⒿⓀ●Ⓜ 6 ●ⓀⓁⓂ 8 ⒿⓀⓁ●

29

★TIPS

Say Now let's look at the tip.

Have a volunteer read the tip aloud.

Say When you read the answers, pay extra attention to verb forms and words that are spelled correctly but used in the wrong way. These kinds of mistakes often appear on tests.

Practice

Say Let's do the Practice items now. Look for the answer that has a mistake in English usage, and remember the different kinds of mistakes we talked about. If you aren't sure which answer is correct, take your best guess. Mark your answers in the rows at the bottom of the page. Make sure you fill in the circles in the answer rows with dark marks. Do not write anything except your answer choices in your books. Completely erase any marks for answers that you change. Work until you come to the STOP sign at the bottom of the page. Any questions? Start working now.

Allow time for the students to fill in their answers.

Say It's time to stop. You have finished Lesson 6b.

Review the answers with the students. It will be helpful to discuss the error types that appear in the lesson and have the students read aloud the correct form of the sentences. If any questions caused particular difficulty, work through each of the answer choices.

Have the students indicate completion of the lesson by entering their score for this activity on the progress chart at the beginning of the book.

 Unit 5

Usage and Expression
Lesson 6b Usage

Directions: Fill in the space for the answer that has a mistake in usage. Fill in the last answer space if there is no mistake.

Sample A	A On our trip, the pilot ∗ B had flew over the storm, C so we had a good flight. D (No mistakes)	**Sample B** ∗ J Juanita didn't know weather K to buy a gift for her father or L to take him to a ball game. M (No mistakes)

 TIPS
- Look for incorrect verbs and words that are spelled right but used wrong.

1   A   Last fall our house was hit
     B   by lightning. It didn't do any
     C   damage to the house.
∗ D   (No mistakes)

2 ∗ J   The fish swimmed up the
     K   river until they reached a large
     L   dam that stopped them.
     M   (No mistakes)

3   A   The tourists rode on a raft
∗ B   made of logs. My friend and me
     C   decided that we wanted to do it.
     D   (No mistakes)

4   J   Mr. Scott has a wonderful
     K   garden. All of the plants he grows
∗ L   is healthy and pretty.
     M   (No mistakes)

5   A   The holiday parade will be held
     B   next week. The band members
∗ C   had met at the high school.
     D   (No mistakes)

6 ∗ J   There isn't no way that our
     K   team will lose this game. We
     L   will all do our best.
     M   (No mistakes)

7   A   Many people prepare for a
     B   vacation by reading books about
∗ C   the places they to plan to go.
     D   (No mistakes)

8   J   The store that just opened on
     K   Market Street had to close because
     L   the roof was leaking.
∗ M   (No mistakes)

 STOP

Answer rows   A ⒶⒷ●ⒸⒹ   1 ⒶⒷⒸ●   3 Ⓐ●ⒸⒹ   5 ⒶⒷ●Ⓓ   7 ⒶⒷ●Ⓓ
            B ●ⓀⓁⓂ   2 ●ⓀⓁⓂ   4 ⒿⓀ●Ⓜ   6 ●ⓀⓁⓂ   8 ⒿⓀⓁ●

29

Unit 5
Lesson 7a
Expression

Focus

Language Skills
- choosing the best word to complete a sentence
- choosing the best paragraph for a given purpose
- identifying the best opening sentence for a paragraph
- identifying the sentence that does not fit in a paragraph

Test-taking Skills
- following printed directions
- understanding unusual item formats
- eliminating answer choices
- taking the best guess when unsure of the answer
- working methodically

Sample A

Say Turn to Lesson 7a on page 30. In this lesson you will work with sentences and paragraphs. There are directions for each section of this lesson, so read them carefully before you answer questions.

Look at Sample A. Read the sentence with the underlined word. Then read each of the answer choices. Find the answer choice that is the best way to write the underlined part of the sentence. If the underlined part is already correct, choose answer D, No change. *(pause)* Which answer choice is correct? *(D, No change)* The underlined part is correct as it is. Mark answer circle D for Sample A in the answer rows at the bottom of the page. Make sure the circle is completely filled in with a dark mark.

Check to see that the students have filled in the correct answer circle. Explain why answer D is better than the other answers.

 TIPS

Say Who will read the tips for us?

 Unit 5
Usage and Expression
Lesson 7a **Expression**

Directions: Fill in the space for the answer that is the best way to write the underlined part of the sentence.

Sample A	The whole family gets together for dinner **whenever** my Uncle George comes for a visit.
	A although B in addition to C however *D (No change)

- Remember, for this lesson, you are choosing the answer that is better than the others.
- Eliminate answer choices you know are wrong. If necessary, take your best guess from the remaining choices.

Directions: For questions 1–4, choose the best way to write the underlined part of the sentence.

1 Everyone who was invited showed up **although** Channi, who had a terrible cold.
   *A except   B yet   C because   D (No change)

2 **To move quietly,** Ursula got within ten feet of the owl and then took a picture.
   J Will have moved   *K Moving quietly   L Moving more quiet   M (No change)

3 The problem of paying for the vacation, **although,** remains to be solved.
   A and   B in spite of   *C however   D (No change)

4 **Feeling angry,** Rico decided to take a walk until he calmed down.
   J To be angry   K Although angrily   L By being angry   *M (No change)

5 Which of these would be most appropriate at the beginning of a story about the U.S. presidency?

A	Many American presidents have been called "great." This title is usually given to those who have led the country during times of war.	*C	The office of president of the United States was established under Article 2 of the Constitution. It is considered to be the highest office in the land.
B	The president is not actually elected by the people. Instead, the electoral college, a group chosen by state legislators, makes the decision.	D	In the beginning, people thought the president should serve an indefinite term. Later this was changed to a limit of two four-year terms.

 GO

30	Answer rows	A ⒶⒷⒸ●	2 Ⓙ●ⓁⓂ	4 ⒿⓀⓁ●
		1 ●ⒷⒸⒹ	3 ⒶⒷ●Ⓓ	5 ⒶⒷ●Ⓓ

Have a volunteer read the tips aloud.

Say In this lesson, you are looking for the answer that is better than the others, not one that has a mistake. Read the directions for each section of the lesson carefully. There are different kinds of items, and if you don't pay attention to the directions, you may make a mistake. You may be able to eliminate some answer choices because you know they are wrong. If you do this and still don't know which answer is correct, take your best guess from the remaining answers. Eliminating and guessing increase your chances of finding the right answer when you are not sure.

Discuss eliminating and guessing until you are confident the students understand these strategies.

Practice

Say Now we are ready for Practice. There are two types of items in this lesson, so be sure to read the directions for each section carefully. Choose the answer you think is correct for each item. Work until you come to the STOP sign at the bottom of page 31. Make sure your answer circles are completely filled in with dark marks. Do not write anything except your answer choices in your books. Completely erase any marks for answers that you change. Any questions? Start working now.

Allow time for the students to fill in their answers. Walk around the room to be sure the students know how to answer the different item types in the lesson.

Say It's time to stop. You have finished Lesson 7a.

Review the answers with the students. If any questions caused particular difficulty, work through each of the answer choices.

Have the students indicate completion of the lesson by entering their score for this activity on the progress chart at the beginning of the book.

 Lesson 7a **Expression**

Directions: Use this paragraph to answer questions 6–9.

> [1] It is caused by an electrical imbalance between clouds and the ground. [2] When the imbalance gets large enough, <u>nature tries to</u> even things out. [3] The result is a lightning flash between cloud and ground. [4] The noise created by the process is the thunder we hear. [5] Another source of natural sound is strong wind. [6] Because sound <u>travels more slower</u> than light, we usually hear thunder after we see the lightning.

6 Choose the best opening sentence to add to this paragraph.
*J Lightning is frightening yet wonderful.
K Benjamin Franklin studied lightning more than 200 years ago.
L Ancient people did not understand lightning.
M Florida has many lightning strikes.

7 What is the best way to write the underlined part of sentence 2?
A nature trying to
B nature to tries
C nature try to
*D (No change)

8 Which sentence should be left out of this paragraph?
J Sentence 2
K Sentence 3
L Sentence 4
*M Sentence 5

9 What is the best way to write the underlined part of sentence 6?
A traveling more slowly
*B travels more slowly
C travel more slower
D (No change)

Answer rows 6 ●ⓀⓁⓂ 7 ⒶⒷⒸ● 8 ⒿⓀⓁ● 9 Ⓐ●ⒸⒹ   31

Focus

Language Skills
- identifying correctly formed sentences
- choosing the best paragraph for a given purpose
- choosing the best word to complete a sentence
- identifying the best opening sentence for a paragraph
- identifying the sentence that does not fit in a paragraph
- identifying the best location for a sentence in a paragraph
- identifying the best closing sentence for a paragraph

Test-taking Skills
- following printed directions
- understanding unusual item formats
- analyzing answer choices

Sample A

Say Turn to Lesson 7b on page 32. In this lesson you will work with sentences and paragraphs. There are directions for each section of this lesson, so read them carefully before you answer questions.

Let's look at Sample A. Read each of the answer choices. Find the one that expresses the meaning of the sentence better than the others. *(pause)* Which answer choice is correct? *(answer D)* Mark answer circle D for Sample A in the answer rows at the bottom of the page. Make sure the circle is completely filled in with a dark mark.

Check to see that the students have filled in the correct answer circle. If necessary, explain why the correct answer is better than the others.

Say Who will read the tip for us?

Have a volunteer read the tip aloud.

Unit 5 Usage and Expression
Lesson 7b **Expression**

Directions: Choose the best way to express the idea.

| Sample A | A The bridge to close for repairs. | C For repairs the bridge is closed. |
| | B The bridge which is closed for repairs. | ＊D The bridge is closed for repairs. |

TIPS
- The sentence that expresses the idea simply and clearly is usually right.

Directions: For questions 1–3, choose the best way to express the idea.

1
- A Recently retiring from his job, Mr. Tanaka as manager of the supermarket.
- B As manager of the supermarket, Mr. Tanaka recently retired from his job.
- ＊C Mr. Tanaka recently retired from his job as manager of the supermarket.
- D Retired from his job recently, Mr. Tanaka, the supermarket manager.

2
- ＊J We will meet you at the airport near the baggage claim.
- K We will meet you near the airport at the baggage claim.
- L Near the baggage claim, we will meet you at the airport.
- M Near the airport, we will meet you at the baggage claim.

3
- A Venice, Italy, is unusual, the city, because of its canals.
- ＊B The city of Venice, Italy, is unusual because of its canals.
- C Because of its canals, the city unusual is Venice, Italy.
- D Unusual because of its canals, Venice, Italy, is a city.

4 Which of these would be most appropriate in the beginning of a report on stars?

- J Stars and planets have different paths through the sky. Because of the spin of the earth, stars seem to have a circular path. Planets, because they rotate around the sun, have erratic paths.
- ＊K We see them every night, but they are billions of miles away. The stars in the night sky are all suns like our own. Some are older and some are younger and some even have planets.
- L Throughout history, people have given names to groups of stars. One of the most familiar groups of stars is the Big Dipper. The Latin name for this group is Ursa Major.
- M New telescopes are giving astronomers an opportunity to study stars more closely than ever before. They have discovered some incredibly old stars as well as those being born even now.

 GO

32   **Answer rows**   A Ⓐ Ⓑ Ⓒ ●   1 Ⓐ Ⓑ ● Ⓓ   2 ● Ⓚ Ⓛ Ⓜ   3 Ⓐ ● Ⓒ Ⓓ   4 Ⓙ ● Ⓛ Ⓜ

Say In this lesson, you are looking for the answer choice that is correct, not a mistake. For some of the items, the correct answer will be easier to understand than the others. There are different kinds of items, however, so be sure to read the directions for each section.

Practice

Say Now we are ready for Practice. There are different types of items in this lesson. Read the directions for each section of the lesson. Choose the answer you think is correct for each item. Work until you come to the STOP sign at the bottom of page 33. Make sure your answer circles are completely filled in with dark marks. Do not write anything except your answer choices in your books. Completely erase any marks for answers that you change. Any questions? Start working now.

Allow time for the students to fill in their answers. Walk around the room to be sure the students know how to answer the different item types in the lesson.

Say It's time to stop. You have finished Lesson 7b.

Review the answers with the students. If any questions caused particular difficulty, work through each of the answer choices.

Have the students indicate completion of the lesson by entering their score for this activity on the progress chart at the beginning of the book.

 Unit 5 Lesson 7b **Expression**

Directions: Use this paragraph to answer questions 5–10.

> [1] Many of them start businesses after they retire from sports. [2] By starting new businesses, they keep themselves busy and earn more money. [3] Some of them simply live off their earnings, so many invest their money and start new businesses. [4] But what is <u>more important</u>, they create jobs for other people and improve the economy. [5] In a healthy economy, there are enough jobs for everyone who wants one.

5 Choose the best opening sentence to add to this paragraph.
 * A Successful athletes often have more than one career.
   B Successful athletes earn a lot of money.
   C Some successful athletes don't have to work after they retire.
   D Only a few people get to become professional athletes.

6 Which sentence should be left out of this paragraph?
   J Sentence 1
   K Sentence 3
   L Sentence 4
 * M Sentence 5

7 What is the best way to write the underlined part of sentence 4?
   A more importanter
   B importanter
   C importantly
 * D (No change)

8 Where is the best place for sentence 3?
   J Where it is now
 * K Between sentences 1 and 2
   L Between sentences 4 and 5
   M After sentence 5

9 What is the best way to write the underlined part of sentence 3?
 * A but
   B too
   C like
   D (No change)

10 Choose the best concluding sentence to add to this paragraph.
   J In a slowing economy, finding a job can be difficult.
   K Successful athletes often become sports announcers.
 * L Not surprisingly, many of these athletes are also successful in business.
   M Finding a job is easier for successful athletes because they are well known.

 STOP

Answer rows 5 ●BCD 7 ABC● 9 ●BCD
             6 JKL● 8 J●LM 10 J K●M

33

Test Yourself: Usage and Expression

Unit 5

Focus

Language Skills
- identifying mistakes in usage
- choosing the best word to complete a sentence
- choosing the best paragraph for a given purpose
- identifying the best opening sentence for a paragraph
- identifying the sentence that does not fit in a paragraph
- identifying the best location for a sentence in a paragraph
- identifying the best closing sentence for a paragraph
- identifying correctly formed sentences

Test-taking Skills
- managing time effectively
- following printed directions
- using context to find an answer
- indicating that an item has no mistakes
- subvocalizing answer choices
- working methodically
- taking the best guess when unsure of the answer
- understanding unusual item formats
- eliminating answer choices
- analyzing answer choices

This lesson simulates an actual test-taking experience. Therefore, it is recommended that the directions be read verbatim and the suggested procedures and time allowances be followed.

Directions

Administration Time: approximately 25 minutes

Say Turn to the Test Yourself lesson on page 34.

Point out to the students that this Test Yourself lesson is timed like a real test, but that they will score it themselves to see how well they are doing. Remind the students to pace themselves and to check the clock after they have finished Number 12

Unit 5 — Test Yourself: Usage and Expression

Directions: Use this paragraph to answer the question.

> [1] Today most telephone calls pass through wires. [2] New technology, however, makes it possible to offer wireless telephone services. [3] With a wireless phone, you will be able to call anywhere at any time. [4] Many people dislike the idea of being so tied to a phone.

Sample A   Where is the best place for sentence 3?
* A   Where it is now
  B   Before sentence 1
  C   Between sentences 1 and 2
  D   After sentence 4

Directions: For questions 1–8, fill in the space for the answer that has a mistake in usage. Fill in the last answer space if there is no mistake.

1   A   The other day a parakeet made
    * B   its way into the art studio. It had flew
      C   away from the pet store downtown.
      D   (No mistakes)

2   J   Dallas had spent the whole day
      K   at the fair, so he wasn't interested
    * L   in going that night with Val and I.
      M   (No mistakes)

3   A   Masks made out of cardboard
    * B   and plaster hangs from floor to ceiling
      C   in Mr. Sakamano's classroom.
      D   (No mistakes)

4   J   I find it very difficult to predict the
      K   weather while visiting that city. The
    * L   temperature changed without warning.
      M   (No mistakes)

5   * A   One of the sails on our boat torn,
      B   so we decided to go back to shore
      C   and get it repaired before it got worse.
      D   (No mistakes)

6   J   When Casey stuck out his chin
    * K   stubborn, it was a signal to Phil that
      L   he had lost his chance of going.
      M   (No mistakes)

7   A   Before the race began, Zack
      B   stood on his toes, looking around
      C   for the familiar faces of his parents.
    * D   (No mistakes)

8   * J   I hadn't barely begun working
      K   when I was rudely interrupted by a
      L   loud and agitated knock at the door.
      M   (No mistakes)

34   Answer rows   A ●ⒷⒸⒹ   2 ⒿⓀⓁ●   4 ⒿⓀ●Ⓜ   6 Ⓙ●ⓁⓂ   8 ●ⓀⓁⓂ
                1 Ⓐ●ⒸⒹ   3 Ⓐ●ⒸⒹ   5 ●ⒷⒸⒹ   7 ⒶⒷⒸ●

---

to see how much time is left. This is about the halfway point in the lesson. Encourage the students to avoid spending too much time on any one item and to take the best guess if they are unsure of the answer.

Say There are different types of items in the Test Yourself lesson, so you will have to read the directions for each section and pay close attention to what you are doing. Remember to make sure that the circles in the answer rows are completely filled in. Press your pencil firmly so that your marks come out dark. Completely erase any marks for answers that you change. Do not write anything except your answer choices in your books.

Say Look at Sample A and listen carefully. Read the paragraph and the question. Decide which answer you think is best. Mark the circle for your answer.

Allow time for the students to fill in their answers.

Say The circle for answer A should be filled in. If you chose another answer, erase yours and fill in the circle for answer A now.

Check to see that the students have filled in the correct answer circle.

Say Now you will do more items. Read the directions for each section. When you come to the GO sign at the bottom of a page, continue working. Work until you come to the STOP sign on page 37. If you are not sure of an answer, fill in the circle for the answer you think might be right. Do you have any questions?

Answer any questions the students have.

Say You may begin working. You will have 20 minutes.

Allow 20 minutes.

 Unit 5 Test Yourself: Usage and Expression

Directions: For questions 9–13, choose the best way to write the underlined part of the sentence.

9 By next week, we **finished** most of the science project.
    A   had finished   ∗ B   will have finished   C would be finishing   D (No change)

10 **About** two weeks, the flu had spread through every grade in the school.
    ∗ J   Within   K   Around   L Beyond   M (No change)

11 It's only a few blocks to school, so Lucy **prefers** walking to taking the bus.
    A   preferring   B   has preferred   C prefer   ∗ D (No change)

12 Mr. Norris **living** in our town since he was born here in 1920.
    J   to live   ∗ K   has lived   L lives   M (No change)

13 **Although** knowing the area, Stan and I were quickly lost.
    A   Because   B   Unless   ∗ C Without   D (No change)

14 Which of these would be most appropriate for the closing of a history report?

  J | President Jefferson decided to explore the new territory. He chose Lewis and Clark to lead the expedition. |

  K | Getting ready for the expedition took a long time. Lewis and Clark didn't want to forget anything. |

  L | So many "firsts" were accomplished by Lewis and Clark that you couldn't begin to name them. It was as if they had landed on a strange planet where everything was new. |

  ∗ M | The journey of Lewis and Clark was a remarkable adventure. Even today, after two centuries have passed, people still find the journey amazing. |

GO

Directions: Use this paragraph to answer questions 15–20.

> [1] A river wanders through the center of the city. [2] San Antonio is an old mission town. [3] The walkway beside the river is <u>lined</u> with trees, shrubs, and flowering plants. [4] In addition, small boats make their way up and down the river. [5] Tourists and residents alike enjoy <u>stroll</u> along the river or riding in one of the boats, which often offers meals and entertainment.

15 Choose the best opening sentence to add to this paragraph.
   A   There is more than just the "wild west" in Texas.
   B   A city is more than concrete and steel.
＊C   San Antonio, Texas, has a unique feature.
   D   Like San Antonio, many cities have been built near rivers.

16 What is the best way to write the underlined part of sentence 3?
   J   will be lined
   K   to be lined
   L   having been lined
＊M   (No change)

17 Which sentence should be left out of this paragraph?
   A   Sentence 1
＊B   Sentence 2
   C   Sentence 4
   D   Sentence 5

18 What is the best place for sentence 3?
＊J   Where it is now
   K   Before sentence 1
   L   Between sentences 4 and 5
   M   After sentence 5

19 What is the best way to write the underlined part of sentence 5?
   A   will stroll
   B   to stroll
＊C   strolling
   D   (No change)

20 Choose the best concluding sentence to add to this paragraph.
   J   Other towns have built walkways beside their rivers.
＊K   The riverwalk is something that people like best about San Antonio.
   L   Many other attractions draw tourists to San Antonio.
   M   When people visit San Antonio, they have more than enough to do.

Say It's time to stop. You have finished the Test Yourself lesson. Check to see that you have completely filled in your answer circles with dark marks. Make sure that any marks for answers that you changed have been completely erased.

Go over the lesson with the students. Ask the students if they read the directions for each section. Did they have enough time to finish all the items? Which items were most difficult? Work through any questions that caused difficulty.

Have the students indicate completion of the lesson by entering their score for this activity on the progress chart at the beginning of the book.

Unit 5 Test Yourself: Usage and Expression

Directions: For questions 21–24, choose the best way to express the idea.

21
A When Michelle left the game, the team captain gave the crowd a standing ovation.
*B When Michelle, the team captain, left the game, the crowd gave her a standing ovation.
C The crowd gave the team captain a standing ovation when Michelle left the game.
D The team captain received a standing ovation from the crowd for Michelle leaving the game.

22
J To the public, the computer lab is open after school from four to nine o'clock.
K After school to the public, the computer lab is open from four to nine o'clock.
*L The computer lab is open to the public after school from four to nine o'clock.
M From four to nine o'clock, the computer lab to the public is open after school.

23
A The leaky hose from the washing machine was fixed by the plumber, being here before.
*B The plumber, who had been here before, fixed the leaky hose from the washing machine.
C Having been here before, the leaky hose from the washing machine was fixed by the plumber.
D The plumber fixed the leaky hose from the washing machine, having been here before.

24
J Always it seems to rain, and on weekends.
K Weekend rains always seem to be.
L Always on the weekends it seems to rain.
*M It always seems to rain on the weekends.

25 Which of these would be most appropriate at the end of a written report about a movie?

A The movie is set in Egypt in the 1800s. The opening scene shows two people entering a tomb. The music suggests that something frightening is going to happen, but it doesn't.

B The lead character is an archaeologist who thinks the ancient Egyptians found a way to travel through time. She and her assistant are looking for clues in different places in Egypt.

*C All in all, I'd give the movie a rating of C+. The characters are strong and the scenery is wonderful but there isn't much action. I'd prefer spending my money on an action film.

D The part I liked best was when the last tomb was opened. Everyone in the theater knew what would happen and it did. It was so predictable that we all laughed and booed.

Answer rows   21 Ⓐ ● Ⓒ Ⓓ   22 Ⓙ Ⓚ ● Ⓜ   23 Ⓐ ● Ⓒ Ⓓ   24 Ⓙ Ⓚ Ⓛ ●   25 Ⓐ Ⓑ ● Ⓓ

37

Background

This unit contains five lessons that deal with math concepts and estimation skills.

• **In Lessons 8a and 8b,** students solve problems involving math concepts. Students identify and use key words, numbers, and pictures. They refer to a graphic, find the answer without computing, work methodically, evaluate answer choices, and reread questions.

• **In Lessons 9a and 9b,** students solve problems involving estimation. They review the test-taking skills introduced in the two previous lessons.

• **In the Test Yourself lesson,** the math concepts and estimation skills and test-taking skills introduced in Lessons 8a through 9b are reinforced and presented in a format that gives students the experience of taking an achievement test. Techniques for managing time effectively when taking a standardized test are reinforced.

Instructional Objectives

Lesson 8a **Math Concepts** Lesson 8b **Math Concepts**	Given a problem involving math concepts, students identify which of four answer choices is correct.
Lesson 9a **Math Estimation** Lesson 9b **Math Estimation**	Given a problem involving estimation, students identify which of four answer choices is correct.
Test Yourself	Given questions similar to those in Lessons 8a through 9b, students utilize math concepts, estimation, and test-taking strategies on achievement test formats.

Focus

Mathematics Skills
- comparing and ordering whole numbers, decimals, fractions, and integers
- estimating measurement
- understanding ordered pairs
- using a coordinate grid
- recognizing plane figures
- solving simple equations
- understanding congruence
- understanding lines and angles
- recognizing equivalent fractions and decimals
- understanding number sentences
- recognizing fractional parts
- estimating and rounding
- understanding variability
- finding area
- understanding ratio and proportion
- solving measurement problems
- recognizing alternate forms of a number

Test-taking Skills
- identifying and using key words, numbers, and pictures
- referring to a graphic
- finding the answer without computing
- working methodically
- evaluating answer choices

Samples A and B

Distribute scratch paper to the students.

Say Turn to Lesson 8a on page 38. In this lesson you will work on math problems. Read the directions at the top of the page to yourself.

Allow time for the students to read the directions.

Say Find Sample A. Read the question to yourselves. *(pause)* Which answer choice is correct? *(answer B, –3)* Yes, answer B is correct. Mark answer B for Sample A in the answer rows. Make sure the circle is completely filled in with a dark mark.

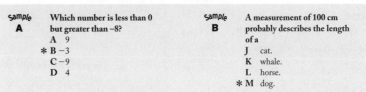

Math Concepts and Estimation

Lesson 8a **Math Concepts**

Directions: Read each mathematics problem. Choose the best answer.

Sample A	Which number is less than 0 but greater than −8?
	A 9
	* B −3
	C −9
	D 4

Sample B	A measurement of 100 cm probably describes the length of a
	J cat.
	K whale.
	L horse.
	* M dog.

TIPS
- Be sure to read the question and answer choices carefully. Look closely at fractions, decimals, numbers, and any picture that is part of the problem.
- It is easy to make a mistake by misreading a problem.
- Before you mark your answer, be sure your choice makes sense.

1 The numbers in the figures below are related by the same rule. What number is missing in the second figure?

| Figure 1 | 0 | 1 | 2 | 3 | 4 | 5 | 6 |
| Figure 2 | 0 | 3 | 6 | 9 | ? | 15 | 18 |

A 10   * C 12
B 11   D 14

2 What are the two coordinates of point *D* in the figure below?

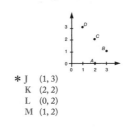

* J (1, 3)
K (2, 2)
L (0, 2)
M (1, 2)

3 Which figure is not a polygon?

A   B

C   * D

4 Which is the value of *a* if $5a = 10$?

* J 2   L 10
K 5   M 20

5 The figures below are congruent. Which pair of parts is identical?

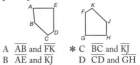

A $\overline{AB}$ and $\overline{FK}$ * C $\overline{BC}$ and $\overline{KJ}$
B $\overline{AE}$ and $\overline{KJ}$ D $\overline{CD}$ and $\overline{GH}$

GO

38   Answer rows   A Ⓐ●ⒸⒹ   1 Ⓐ●●Ⓓ   3 ⒶⒷⒸ●   5 Ⓐ●ⒸⒹ
                     B Ⓙ(Ⓚ)Ⓛ●   2 ●ⒿⓀⓁⓂ   4 ●ⓀⓁⓂ

Check to see that the students have filled in the correct answer circle.

Say Now we'll do Sample B. Read the question to yourself. *(pause)* Think about the important words and numbers in the question that will help you find the answer. Which answer is correct? *(answer M)* Fill in answer M for Sample B in the answer rows at the bottom of the page. Be sure you fill in the circle with a dark mark.

Check to see that the students have filled in the correct answer circle. If necessary, elaborate on the solutions to the sample items.

★**TIPS**

Say Now let's look at the tips.

Have a volunteer read the tips aloud to the group.

Say You should look for key words, numbers, and pictures in a problem. They will help you find the answer. Read the question carefully so you don't make a mistake. And before you mark your answer, be sure it makes sense. Compare it with the question and any graphic that is part of the question.

Practice

Say We are ready for Practice. You are going to do more problems in the same way that we did the samples. Do not write anything except your answer choices in your book. If you think it will help, you may do your work on the scratch paper I gave you. Remember to look for key words, numbers, and pictures in the problems. You should also remember that you don't have to compute to find some of the answers in this lesson. When you have finished working a problem, fill in the circle for your answer in the answer rows at the bottom of the page. Make sure that the circles for your answer choices are completely filled in with dark marks. Completely erase any marks for answers that you change. When you come to the GO sign at the bottom of a page, turn the page and continue working. Work until you come to the STOP sign at the bottom of page 40. Do you have any questions? Start working now.

Allow time for the students to fill in their answers.

6 Which number line shows $x \le 5$?

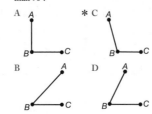

7 In which figure is angle *ABC* greater than 90°?

A

* C

B

D

8 Which is greater in value than 0.287?
J 0.2   L 0.278
* K 0.289   M 0.03

9 Which numeral has the same value as $\frac{11}{4}$?
* A $2\frac{3}{4}$ C $3\frac{3}{4}$
B $3\frac{1}{4}$ D $4\frac{1}{4}$

10 Which should replace the *n* in the number sentence below?

$8 + (2 \times n) = 32$

J 2
K 4
* L 12
M 20

11 The square below is divided into 8 triangles of equal size. If two of the triangles are removed, how much of the original area will be left?

A 25%
B 50%
C 70%
* D 75%

12 If the number 15.18 is rounded to the nearest tenth, it should be written as
J 15.01   L 15.0
* K 15.2   M 10.0

13 Which set of numbers show the least variability?
A {6, 9, 12}
B {2, 12, 24}
* C {8, 9, 10, 11}
D {2, 4, 6, 8}

14 The area of a square porch is 64 square feet. What are the length and width of the porch?
J 2 ft by 32 ft
K 4 ft by 16 ft
* L 8 ft by 8 ft
M 14 ft by 50 ft

Answer rows 6 ⓙ●ⓛⓜ   8 ⓙ●ⓛⓜ   10 ⓙⓀ●ⓜ   12 ⓙ●ⓛⓜ   14 ⓙ●ⓛⓜ   39
7 ⒶⒷ●Ⓓ   9 ●ⒷⒸⒹ   11 ⒶⒷⒸ●   13 ⒶⒷ●Ⓓ

Say You may stop working now. You have finished Lesson 8a.

Review the answers with the students. If any problems caused particular difficulty, work through each of the answer choices. It may be helpful to have the students identify the key words and numbers in each problem. It is also a good idea to have volunteers solve each problem at the chalkboard and discuss the strategy they used.

Have the students indicate completion of the lesson by entering their score for this activity on the progress chart at the beginning of the book.

15 What is the ratio of the number of shaded squares to unshaded squares?

- A 1 to 1
- B 1 to 5
- C 4 to 1
- ∗D 1 to 4

16 Mr. Duncan wants to buy 4 bags of carrots at the store. One bag weighs 2 pounds 5 ounces. How much would 4 bags of carrots weigh?
- J 8 pounds 5 ounces
- ∗K 9 pounds 4 ounces
- L 9 pounds 6 ounces
- M 9 pounds 8 ounces

17 What should replace the ☐ in the number sentence $\frac{2}{3} \div \frac{1}{3} = \frac{\square}{(3 \times 1)}$?
- A 1×1
- B 2×1
- C $2 + 3$
- ∗D 2×3

18 What number is expressed by $(6 \times 10^4) + (7 + 10^3) + (3 \times 10^2) + (5 \times 10) + (2 \times 1)$?
- J 6,735.2
- ∗K 67,352
- L 1,067,352
- M 6,735,200

19 Which of the following figures does not show intersecting line segments?

A   C

∗B   D

20 Which of the following statements about $-\frac{1}{4}$ is true?
- ∗J It is greater than $-\frac{3}{4}$.
- K It is greater than $+\frac{1}{2}$.
- L 2 times $-\frac{1}{4}$ is greater than $-\frac{1}{4}$.
- M $-\frac{1}{3}$ times $-\frac{1}{4}$ is less than $-\frac{1}{4}$.

21 Which is the value of c if $\frac{24}{c+6} = 3$?
- ∗A 2
- B 4
- C 8
- D 28

40   Answer rows   15 Ⓐ Ⓑ Ⓒ ●   17 Ⓐ Ⓑ Ⓒ ●   19 Ⓐ ● Ⓒ Ⓓ   21 ● Ⓑ Ⓒ Ⓓ
16 Ⓙ ● Ⓛ Ⓜ   18 Ⓙ ● Ⓛ Ⓜ   20 ● Ⓚ Ⓛ Ⓜ

Focus

Mathematics Skills
- estimating and rounding
- identifying parts of a figure
- understanding average (mean)
- understanding number sentences
- understanding lines and angles
- recognizing equivalent fractions and decimals
- finding area
- understanding variability
- understanding ratio and proportion
- solving measurement problems
- recognizing alternate forms of a number
- comparing and ordering whole numbers, decimals, fractions, and integers
- naming numerals
- estimating measurement
- identifying the best measurement unit
- understanding characteristics of related numbers
- recognizing equivalent fractions and decimals
- solving simple equations

Test-taking Skills
- rereading a question
- referring to a graphic
- finding the answer without computing
- working methodically

Samples A and B

Distribute scratch paper to the students.

Say Turn to Lesson 8b on page 41. In this lesson you will work on more mathematics problems. Read the directions at the top of the page to yourself.

Allow time for the students to read the directions.

Say Find Sample A. Read the question to yourself. *(pause)* Which answer choice is correct? *(answer B)* Yes, answer B is correct because 2.08 rounded to the nearest tenth is *2.1*. Mark

---

Unit 6

Math Concepts and Estimation

Lesson 8b **Math Concepts**

Directions: Read each mathematics problem. Choose the best answer.

Sample A If the number 2.08 is rounded to the nearest tenth, it should be written as
- A 2.01.
- *B 2.1.
- C 2.8.
- D 10.

Sample B If you divide a square in half diagonally, what figures do you have?
- J Four squares
- K Four rectangles
- L Two squares
- *M Two triangles

- Don't be confused by the numbers in a problem. Read the problem carefully and decide what you should do. Then look at the numbers and solve the problem on scratch paper.

1 On a bike trip, Luke rode 32, 43, 38, and 44 miles over 4 days. The *average* (mean) number of miles of these 4 days is about
- A 30.
- *B 40.
- C 45.
- D 160.

2 In what order should you place the numbers 2, 3, 4, and 5 into the boxes below so that the largest possible answer will be formed?

□ – □ + □ – □ = ?

- J 5, 4, 3, 2
- *K 5, 2, 4, 3
- L 3, 2, 5, 4
- M 3, 2, 4, 5

3 Which is an obtuse angle?

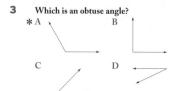

4 Which of the following is <u>not</u> the same as $\frac{6}{30}$?
- J $\frac{1}{5}$
- *K $6\frac{1}{30}$
- L $\frac{3}{15}$
- M $\frac{2}{10}$

GO

Answer rows
A (A)●(C)(D) 1 (A)●(C)(D) 3 ●(B)(C)(D)
B (J)(K)(L)● 2 (J)●(L)(M) 4 (J)●(L)(M)

41

---

answer B for Sample A in the answer rows. Make sure the circle is completely filled in with a dark mark.

Check to see that the students have filled in the correct answer circle.

Say Now we'll do Sample B. Read the question to yourself. *(pause)* Which answer is correct? *(answer M)* Fill in answer M for Sample B in the answer rows at the bottom of the page. Be sure you fill in the circle with a dark mark.

Check to see that the students have filled in the correct answer circle. If necessary elaborate on the solutions to the sample items.

★TIPS

Say Now let's look at the tip.

Have a volunteer read the tip aloud to the group.

Say Math problems can sometimes be confusing. In order to simplify the problem, you should read it first and think about how to solve it. Then look at the problem again and think about the numbers. If necessary, you can solve the problem on scratch paper.

Practice

Say We are ready for Practice. You are going to do more problems in the same way that we did the samples. Do not write anything except your answer choices in your book. If you think it will help, you may do your work on scratch paper. When you have finished working a problem, fill in the circle for your answer in the answer rows at the bottom of the page. Make sure that the circles for your answer choices are completely filled in with dark marks. Completely erase any marks for answers that you change. When you come to the GO sign at the bottom of a page, turn the page and continue working. Work until you come to the STOP sign at the bottom of page 43. Do you have any questions? Start working now.

Allow time for the students to fill in their answers.

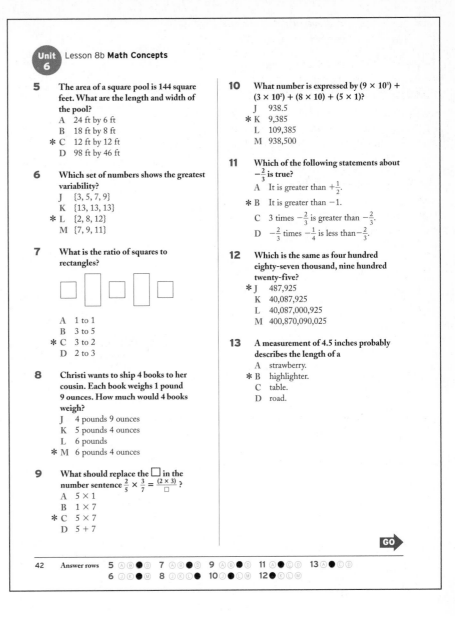

Say You may stop working now.
You have finished Lesson 8b.

Review the answers with the students. If any problems caused particular difficulty, work through each of the answer choices. It may be helpful to have volunteers solve each problem at the chalkboard and discuss the strategy they used.

Have the students indicate completion of the lesson by entering their score for this activity on the progress chart at the beginning of the book.

 Unit 6 Lesson 8b **Math Concepts**

14 The best unit for measuring the cost of a toaster is
* J   tens of dollars.
  K   hundreds of dollars.
  L   thousands of dollars.
  M   millions of dollars.

15 What should replace the ☐ to make the number sentence true?

$(9 - 4) \times \square > 28$
  A   5
  B   4
* C   6
  D   3

16 Which of the following statements is true?
  J $\frac{1}{4} > \frac{1}{3}$
  K $\frac{1}{4} < \frac{1}{5}$
* L $\frac{1}{3} > \frac{1}{5}$
  M $\frac{1}{2} < \frac{1}{4}$

17 How should the numeral 349.247 be written if it is rounded to the nearest tenth?
  A   350
  B   349
* C   349.2
  D   349.25

18 The set of numbers {1, 2, 4, 5, 8, 10, 20, 40} can be described as a set of
  J   prime numbers.
  K   even numbers.
  L   squares of numbers.
* M   factors of 40.

19 Which fraction is <u>not</u> equal to 0.25?
  A $\frac{1}{4}$
  B $\frac{3}{12}$
* C $\frac{4}{20}$
  D $\frac{4}{16}$

20 Which is the correct solution to $0.8 \times \square = 0.32$?
  J   0.04
* K   0.4
  L   4
  M   40

21 When $l = 5$ and $m = 2$, which of these is the value of $4l + 2m$?
  A   18
  B   20
* C   24
  D   26

Answer rows   14 ●ⓀⓁⓂ   16 ⒿⓀ●Ⓜ   18 ⒿⓀⓁ●   20 Ⓙ●ⓁⓂ
           15 ⒶⒷ●Ⓓ   17 ⒶⒷ●Ⓓ   19 ⒶⒷ●Ⓓ   21 ⒶⒷ●Ⓓ

43

Unit 6

Lesson 9a
Math Estimation

Focus

Mathematics Skill
• estimating and rounding

Test-taking Skills
• working methodically
• finding the answer without computing

Sample A

Distribute scratch paper to the students.

Say Turn to Lesson 9a on page 44. In this lesson you will solve mathematics problems involving estimation. Read the directions at the top of the page to yourself.

Allow time for the students to read the directions.

Say Find Sample A. Read the question to yourselves. *(pause)* Think about how to solve the problem. Which answer choice is correct? *(answer D)* Yes, answer A is correct. The closest estimate of the problem is *more than $30*. Mark answer A for Sample D in the answer rows. Make sure the circle is completely filled in with a dark mark.

Check to see that the students have filled in the correct answer circle. If necessary elaborate on the solution to the sample item.

⭐**TIPS**

Say Now let's look at the tip.

Have a volunteer read the tip aloud to the group.

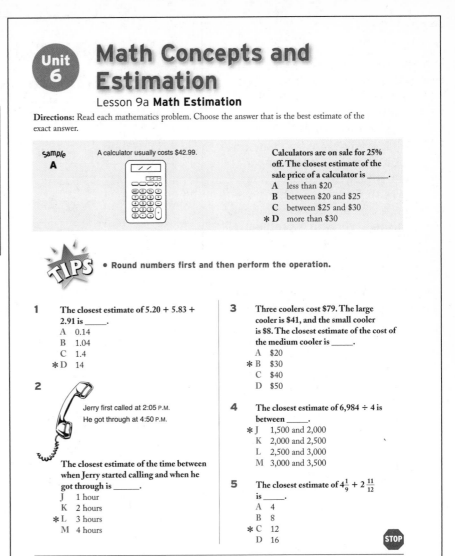

Say Estimation problems are different from other math problems because you do not have to find an exact answer. It is usually a good idea to solve the problems using two steps. First, round the numbers in the problem. Then, perform the operation. You can solve some problems in your head, but you might want to use scratch paper for other problems.

Review the rules for rounding with the students.

Practice

Say We are ready for Practice. You are going to do more problems in the same way that we did the samples. Do not write anything except your answer choices in your book. If you think it will help, you may do your work on scratch paper. Remember that you do not have to find an exact answer to the problems. When you have finished working a problem, fill in the circle for your answer in the answer rows at the bottom of the page. Make sure that the circles for your answer choices are completely filled in with dark marks. Completely erase any marks for answers that you change. Work until you come to the STOP sign at the bottom of the page. Do you have any questions? Start working now.

Allow time for the students to fill in their answers.

Say You may stop working now. You have finished Lesson 9a.

Review the answers with the students. If any problems caused particular difficulty, work through each of the answer choices. It may be helpful to have volunteers solve each problem at the chalkboard and discuss the rounding and estimation strategies they used.

Have the students indicate completion of the lesson by entering their score for this activity on the progress chart at the beginning of the book.

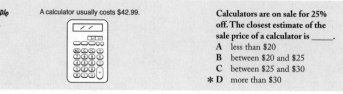

Unit 6 Math Concepts and Estimation

Lesson 9a **Math Estimation**

Directions: Read each mathematics problem. Choose the answer that is the best estimate of the exact answer.

Sample A

A calculator usually costs $42.99.

Calculators are on sale for 25% off. The closest estimate of the sale price of a calculator is _____.
A   less than $20
B   between $20 and $25
C   between $25 and $30
✱D   more than $30

TIPS • Round numbers first and then perform the operation.

1 The closest estimate of 5.20 + 5.83 + 2.91 is _____.
A   0.14
B   1.04
C   1.4
✱D   14

2

Jerry first called at 2:05 P.M.
He got through at 4:50 P.M.

The closest estimate of the time between when Jerry started calling and when he got through is _____.
J   1 hour
K   2 hours
✱L   3 hours
M   4 hours

3 Three coolers cost $79. The large cooler is $41, and the small cooler is $8. The closest estimate of the cost of the medium cooler is _____.
A $20
✱B $30
C $40
D $50

4 The closest estimate of 6,984 ÷ 4 is between _____.
✱J   1,500 and 2,000
K   2,000 and 2,500
L   2,500 and 3,000
M   3,000 and 3,500

5 The closest estimate of $4\frac{1}{9} + 2\frac{11}{12}$ is _____.
A   4
B   8
✱C   12
D   16

 STOP

44   **Answer rows**   A ⒶⒷⒸ●   2 ⓙⓀ●ⓜ   4 ●ⓚⓛⓜ
                          1 ⒶⒷⒸ●   3 Ⓐ●ⒸⒹ   5 ⒶⒷ●Ⓓ

Lesson 9b
Math Estimation

Focus

Mathematics Skill
• estimating and rounding

Test-taking Skills
• finding the answer without computing
• working methodically

Samples A and B

Distribute scratch paper to the students.

Say Turn to Lesson 9b on page 45. In this lesson you will solve more problems involving estimation. Read the directions at the top of the page to yourself.

Allow time for the students to read the directions.

Say Find Sample A. Read the question to yourselves. *(pause)* Think about how to solve the problem. Which answer choice is correct? *(answer A)* Yes, answer A is correct. The closest estimate of the exact answer is 4. Mark answer A for Sample A in the answer rows. Make sure the circle is completely filled in with a dark mark.

Check to see that the students have filled in the correct answer circle.

Say Now we'll do Sample B. Read the question to yourself. Remember to round before you solve the problem. *(pause)* Which answer is correct? *(answer L)* Fill in answer L for Sample B in the answer rows at the bottom of the page. Be sure you fill in the circle with a dark mark.

Check to see that the students have filled in the correct answer circle. If necessary elaborate on the solutions to the sample items.

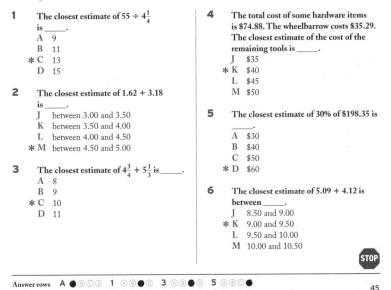

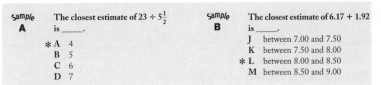

Math Concepts and Estimation
Lesson 9b Math Estimation

Directions: Read each mathematics problem. Choose the answer that is the best estimate of the exact answer.

Sample A The closest estimate of $23 \div 5\frac{1}{2}$ is _____.
* ✱A 4
  B 5
  C 6
  D 7

Sample B The closest estimate of $6.17 + 1.92$ is _____.
  J between 7.00 and 7.50
  K between 7.50 and 8.00
✱ L between 8.00 and 8.50
  M between 8.50 and 9.00

TIPS • Decide whether you should round numbers up or down.

1 The closest estimate of $55 \div 4\frac{1}{4}$ is _____.
  A 9
  B 11
✱C 13
  D 15

2 The closest estimate of $1.62 + 3.18$ is _____.
  J between 3.00 and 3.50
  K between 3.50 and 4.00
  L between 4.00 and 4.50
✱M between 4.50 and 5.00

3 The closest estimate of $4\frac{3}{4} + 5\frac{1}{3}$ is _____.
  A 8
  B 9
✱C 10
  D 11

4 The total cost of some hardware items is $74.88. The wheelbarrow costs $35.29. The closest estimate of the cost of the remaining tools is _____.
  J $35
✱K $40
  L $45
  M $50

5 The closest estimate of 30% of $198.35 is _____.
  A $30
  B $40
  C $50
✱D $60

6 The closest estimate of $5.09 + 4.12$ is between _____.
  J 8.50 and 9.00
✱K 9.00 and 9.50
  L 9.50 and 10.00
  M 10.00 and 10.50

STOP

Answer rows   A ●ⒷⒸⒹ   1 ⒶⒷ●Ⓓ   3 ⒶⒷ●Ⓓ   5 ⒶⒷⒸ●
              B ⒥Ⓚ●Ⓜ   2 ⒥ⓀⓁ●   4 ⒥●ⓁⓂ   6 ⒥●ⓁⓂ

45

★**TIPS**

Say Now let's look at the tip.

Have a volunteer read the tip aloud to the group.

Say The most important thing to remember when you solve estimation problems is to round numbers first. Once you round numbers correctly, it is easy to find the answer. Think about the rules for rounding so you know when to round up or down.

Review rounding rules with the students, emphasizing when to round up and when to round down. Include a discussion of fractions and decimals as well as whole numbers.

Practice

Say We are ready for Practice. You are going to do more problems in the same way that we did the samples. Do not write anything except your answer choices in your book. If you think it will help, you may do your work on scratch paper. Remember that you do not have to find an exact answer to the problems. When you have finished working a problem, fill in the circle for your answer in the answer rows at the bottom of the page. Make sure that the circles for your answer choices are completely filled in with dark marks. Completely erase any marks for answers that you change. Work until you come to the STOP sign at the bottom of the page. Do you have any questions? Start working now.

Allow time for the students to fill in their answers.

Say You may stop working now. You have finished Lesson 9b.

Review the answers with the students. If any problems caused particular difficulty, work through each of the answer choices. It may be helpful to have volunteers solve each problem at the chalkboard and discuss the strategy they used.

Have the students indicate completion of the lesson by entering their score for this activity on the progress chart at the beginning of the book.

Unit 6 — Math Concepts and Estimation

Lesson 9b **Math Estimation**

Directions: Read each mathematics problem. Choose the answer that is the best estimate of the exact answer.

Sample A	The closest estimate of $23 \div 5\frac{1}{2}$ is _____.
	∗A 4
	B 5
	C 6
	D 7

Sample B	The closest estimate of $6.17 + 1.92$ is _____.
	J between 7.00 and 7.50
	K between 7.50 and 8.00
	∗L between 8.00 and 8.50
	M between 8.50 and 9.00

 TIPS • Decide whether you should round numbers up or down.

1 The closest estimate of $55 \div 4\frac{1}{4}$ is _____.
A 9
B 11
∗C 13
D 15

2 The closest estimate of $1.62 + 3.18$ is _____.
J between 3.00 and 3.50
K between 3.50 and 4.00
L between 4.00 and 4.50
∗M between 4.50 and 5.00

3 The closest estimate of $4\frac{3}{4} + 5\frac{1}{3}$ is _____.
A 8
B 9
∗C 10
D 11

4 The total cost of some hardware items is $74.88. The wheelbarrow costs $35.29. The closest estimate of the cost of the remaining tools is _____.
J $35
∗K $40
L $45
M $50

5 The closest estimate of 30% of $198.35 is _____.
A $30
B $40
C $50
∗D $60

6 The closest estimate of $5.09 + 4.12$ is between _____.
J 8.50 and 9.00
∗K 9.00 and 9.50
L 9.50 and 10.00
M 10.00 and 10.50

 STOP

Answer rows A ●ⒷⒸⒹ 1 ⒶⒷ●Ⓓ 3 ⒶⒷ●Ⓓ 5 ⒶⒷⒸ●
B ⒿⓀ●Ⓜ 2 ⒿⓀⓁ● 4 Ⓙ●ⓁⓂ 6 Ⓙ●ⓁⓂ

45

Focus

Mathematics Skills

- naming numerals
- estimating and rounding
- understanding number sentences
- understanding ordered pairs
- solving simple equations
- comparing and ordering whole numbers, decimals, fractions, and integers
- estimating measurement
- understanding characteristics of related numbers
- recognizing equivalent fractions and decimals
- recognizing fractional parts
- finding area
- understanding variability

Test-taking Skills

- managing time effectively
- following printed directions
- identifying and using key words, numbers, and pictures
- referring to a graphic
- finding the answer without computing
- working methodically
- evaluating answer choices
- rereading a question

 Test Yourself: Math Concepts and Estimation

Directions: Read each mathematics problem. Choose the best answer.

Sample A
Which of the following is the name for five hundred ninety and seventeen hundredths?
A 500.9017
B 590.017
* C 590.17
D 590,170

Sample B
The closest estimate of 4.25 ÷ 0.42 is _____.
J 0.1
K 1.0
* L 10.0
M 100.0

1 Which is the same as five hundred sixteen thousand, four hundred twenty-two?
A 51,642
* B 516,422
C 5,016,422
D 500, 160,422

2 If c is a positive number, what should replace the □ to make the equation true?

$$c \times \square = 0$$

* J 0
K 1
L c
M d

3 The numbers in the table below are related to each other by the same rule. What number is missing in the second row?

Row 1	2	7	12	17	22
Row 2	4	□	14	19	24

* A 9
B 10
C 12
D 18

4 If $56 \div z = 8$, what is the value of $8 \times z$?
J z
K 7
L 8
* M 56

5 Which of the following statements is true?
A $\frac{1}{6} < \frac{1}{8}$
* B $\frac{1}{7} > \frac{1}{9}$
C $\frac{1}{5} > \frac{1}{4}$
D $\frac{1}{3} < \frac{1}{7}$

6 How should the numeral 218.772 be written if it is rounded to the nearest tenth?
J 210
K 218
* L 218.8
M 219.10

GO

46   Answer rows   A Ⓐ Ⓑ ● Ⓓ   1 Ⓐ ● Ⓒ Ⓓ   3 ● Ⓑ Ⓒ Ⓓ   5 Ⓐ ● Ⓒ Ⓓ
                      B Ⓙ Ⓚ Ⓛ ●   2 ● Ⓚ Ⓛ Ⓜ   4 Ⓙ Ⓚ Ⓛ ●   6 Ⓙ Ⓚ ● Ⓜ

This lesson simulates an actual test-taking experience. Therefore, it is recommended that the directions be read verbatim and that the suggested procedures and time allowances be followed.

Directions

Administration Time: approximately 30 minutes

Distribute scratch paper to the students.

Say Turn to the Test Yourself lesson on page 46.

Point out to the students that this Test Yourself lesson is timed like a real test, but that they will score it themselves to see how well they are doing. Encourage them to read each question carefully, to think about what they are supposed to do, and to work carefully on scratch paper when necessary.

They should skip difficult problems and return to them later and take the best guess when they are unsure of the answer.

Say This lesson will check how well you can solve mathematics problems. Remember to make sure that the circles for your answer choices are completely filled in. Press your pencil firmly so that your marks come out dark. Completely erase any marks for answers that you change. Do not write anything except your answer choices in your books.

Look at Sample A. Read the question and the answer choices. Mark the circle for the answer you think is correct.

Allow time for the students to fill in their answers.

Say The circle for answer C should be filled in. If you chose another answer, erase yours and fill in circle C now.

Check to see that the students have filled in the correct answer circle.

Say Now read Sample B and the answer choices. Fill in the circle for the answer you think is correct.

Allow time for the students to fill in their answers.

Say The circle for answer L should be filled in because the right answer is *10.0*. If you chose another answer, erase yours and fill in circle L now.

Check to see that the students have filled in the correct answer circle.

Say Now you will do more mathematics problems. You may use the scratch paper I gave you. When you come to a GO sign at the bottom of a page, continue working. Work until you come to the STOP sign at the bottom of page 50. Make sure that the circles for your answers are completely filled in with dark marks. Be sure to fill in the circle in the answer row for the problem you are working on. Completely erase any marks for answers that you change. You will have 25 minutes to solve the problems. You may begin.

Allow 25 minutes.

 Unit 6 — **Test Yourself: Math Concepts and Estimation**

7 A measurement of 1.5 meters probably describes the length of a
  A shoe.
  B classroom.
  C car.
  ✳D kitchen table.

8 What should replace the ☐ to make the number sentence true?

$(9 - 4) \times \square < 45$

  ✳J 8
  K 9
  L 10
  M 11

9 The set of numbers {11, 13, 23, 31, 43} can be described as a set of
  A multiples of 3.
  B even numbers.
  ✳C prime numbers.
  D factors of 111.

10 Which fraction is **not** equal to 0.8?
  J $\frac{8}{10}$
  ✳K $\frac{1}{8}$
  L $\frac{4}{5}$
  M $\frac{80}{100}$

11 About what fraction of the figure is shaded?
  ✳A Less than $\frac{1}{4}$
  B Between $\frac{1}{4}$ and $\frac{1}{2}$
  C Between $\frac{1}{2}$ and $\frac{3}{4}$
  D More than $\frac{3}{4}$

12 Which is the correct solution to $0.2 \times \square = 0.5$?
  J 0.0025
  K 0.025
  L 0.25
  ✳M 2.5

13 The area of a carpet is 81 square feet. What are the length and width of the carpet?
  A 8 ft by 11 ft
  B 21 ft by 4 ft
  ✳C 9 ft by 9 ft
  D 11 ft by 11 ft

14 Which set of numbers shows the least variability?
  J {2, 4, 6, 10}
  ✳K {2, 3, 5, 7}
  L {3, 9, 18, 27}
  M {3, 7, 8, 16}

Answer rows   7 Ⓐ Ⓑ Ⓒ ●   9 Ⓐ Ⓑ ● Ⓓ   11 ● Ⓑ Ⓒ Ⓓ   13 Ⓐ Ⓑ ● Ⓓ
              8 ● Ⓚ Ⓛ Ⓜ   10 Ⓙ ● Ⓛ Ⓜ   12 Ⓙ Ⓚ Ⓛ ●   14 Ⓙ ● Ⓛ Ⓜ   47

Directions: For questions 15–32, choose the answer that is the best estimate of the exact answer.

15 Speed of sound = 1088 feet per second
      60 seconds = 1 minute

   The closest estimate of how far sound travels in a minute is _____.
   A   60 feet
   B   600 feet
   C   6,000 feet
 * D   60,000 feet

16 $149.95 × 28 is _____.
   J   less than $3,000
   K   more than $4,500
   L   between $3,000 and $4,000
 * M   between $4,000 and $4,500

17 Fabric costs $4.97 per yard. Ms. Lazio spent $31.13 on fabric for a parade float. The number of yards of fabric she purchased is _____.
   A   less than 5
   B   between 5 and 6
 * C   between 6 and 7
   D   more than 7

18 The closest estimate of 59.7 ÷ 3.12 is _____.
   J   0.19
   K   1.9
 * L   19
   M   190

19 June bought a paint scraper for $4.89, a flashlight for $6.95, and electrical tape for 97¢ at a hardware store. The cost of the three items above is _____.
   A   less than $12.00
   B   more than $13.00
   C   between $12.00 and $12.50
 * D   between $12.50 and $13.00

20 The closest estimate of 26,728 + 14,301 + 8,962 is _____.
   J   500
   K   5,000
 * L   50,000
   M   500,000

 GO

48   Answer rows   15 Ⓐ Ⓑ Ⓒ ●   17 Ⓐ Ⓑ ● Ⓓ   19 Ⓐ Ⓑ Ⓒ ●
              16 Ⓙ Ⓚ Ⓛ ●   18 Ⓙ Ⓚ ● Ⓜ   20 Ⓙ Ⓚ ● Ⓜ

21 A car is $3\frac{1}{7}$ meters long. A driveway is 17 meters long. The closest estimate of the number of cars that will fit in the driveway is _____.

   A 3
   B 4
*C 5
   D 6

22 The closest estimate of $19\frac{7}{8} + 13\frac{1}{5} + 7\frac{1}{2} + 4\frac{2}{9}$ is _____.

   J 42
*K 45
   L 46
   M 47

23 Five people all share appetizers at a restaurant. The food costs $14.67 in all. The closest estimate of each person's share is _____.

   A $2.50
*B $3.00
   C $3.50
   D $4.00

24 The closest estimate of $36{,}215 - 7{,}797$ is _____.

*J 28,000
   K 29,000
   L 30,000
   M 31,000

25 Mr. Matthews runs 4 times a week. There are 52 weeks in a year. The closest estimate of the number of times Mr. Matthews runs in 10 years is _____.

   A 200
*B 2,000
   C 20,000
   D 200,000

26 $23.91 × 4 is _____.

   J less than $80
   K more than $100
   L between $80 and $90
*M between $90 and $100

GO

Answer rows **21** Ⓐ Ⓑ ● Ⓓ **23** Ⓐ ● Ⓒ Ⓓ **25** Ⓐ ● Ⓒ Ⓓ
               22 Ⓙ ● Ⓛ Ⓜ **24** ● Ⓚ Ⓛ Ⓜ **26** Ⓙ Ⓚ Ⓛ ●

49

Say It's time to stop. You have finished the Test Yourself lesson. Check to see that you have completely filled in your answer circles. Make sure that any marks for answers that you changed have been completely erased.

Go over the lesson with the students. Ask if they had enough time to finish the lesson. Did they work carefully on scratch paper? Which questions required them to guess? What were some of the problems they experienced? Work through any problems that caused difficulty.

Have the students indicate completion of the lesson by entering their score for this activity on the progress chart at the beginning of the book. If necessary, provide additional practice problems similar to the ones in this unit.

 Unit 6 **Test Yourself: Math Concepts and Estimation**

27 The closest estimate of $3.6 \times 3.1 \times 0.9$ is _____.
  A 1.0
  B 9.0
* C 10.0
  D 16.0

28 $36.138 - 14.961$ is between _____.
* J 21 and 22
  K 22 and 23
  L 23 and 24
  M 24 and 25

29 There are 197,000 people living in Madison, Wisconsin. There 42,000 people living in Verona, Wisconsin. What is the closest estimate of how many more people live in Madison than Verona?
  A 140,000
  B 150,000
* C 160,000
  D 170,000

30 The closest estimate of $4\frac{3}{4} + 5\frac{1}{3}$ is _____.
  J 8
  K 9
* L 10
  M 11

31 **Annette's Gift Shop**

  Postcards $0.85 each
  Envelopes $3.75/box
  Pens $1.20 each

  The cost of the three items above is _____.
  A less than $5.00
  B more than $6.00
  C between $5.00 and $5.50
* D between $5.50 and $6.00

32 The closest estimate of $4,852 + 6,206 + 12,691$ is _____.
  J 200
  K 2,000
* L 20,000
  M 200,000

 STOP

50   **Answer rows**   27 Ⓐ Ⓑ ● Ⓓ   29 Ⓐ Ⓑ ● Ⓓ   31 Ⓐ Ⓑ Ⓒ ●
                        28 ● Ⓚ Ⓛ Ⓜ   30 Ⓙ Ⓚ ● Ⓜ   32 Ⓙ Ⓚ ● Ⓜ

Background

This unit contains five lessons that deal with math problem solving and data interpretation skills.

• **In Lessons 10a and 10b,** students solve word problems. They work methodically, indicate that the correct answer is not given, and practice converting items to a workable format. They also identify and use key words, numbers and pictures and take the best guess when unsure of the answer.

• **In Lessons 11a and 11b,** students solve problems involving data interpretation. Students practice finding the answer without computing, evaluating answer choices, transferring numbers accurately, performing the correct operation, and computing carefully. They work methodically, use charts and graphs, and restate questions.

• **In the Test Yourself lesson,** the math problem solving, data interpretation, and test-taking skills introduced in Lessons 10a through 11b are reinforced and presented in a format that gives students the experience of taking an achievement test. Techniques for managing time effectively when taking a standardized test are reinforced.

Instructional Objectives

Lesson 10a	**Math Problem Solving**	Given a word problem, students identify which of three answer choices is correct or indicate that the correct answer is not given.
Lesson 10b	**Math Problem Solving**	
Lesson 11a	**Data Interpretation**	Given a problem involving a chart, diagram or graph, students identify which of three answer choices is correct or indicate that the correct answer is not given.
Lesson 11b	**Data Interpretation**	
	Test Yourself	Given questions similar to those in Lessons 10a through 11b, students utilize problem solving, data interpretation, and test-taking strategies on achievement test formats.

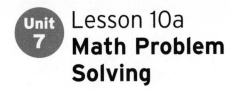

Unit 7 Lesson 10a
Math Problem Solving

Focus

Mathematics Skill
• solving word problems

Test-taking Skills
• indicating that the correct answer is not given
• working methodically
• converting items to a workable format

Samples A and B

Distribute scratch paper to the students.

Say Turn to Lesson 10a on page 51. In this lesson you will solve word problems. Read the directions at the top of the page to yourself.

Allow time for the students to read the directions.

Say Find Sample A. Read the question to yourselves. *(pause)* Which answer choice is correct? You may use scratch paper to find the answer. *(answer A)* **Yes, answer A is correct.** *Grant has exactly enough money.* Mark answer A for Sample A in the answer rows. Make sure the circle is completely filled in with a dark mark.

Check to see that the students have filled in the correct answer circle.

Say Now we'll do Sample B. Read the question to yourself. Choose the answer you think is correct. *(pause)* Which answer is correct? *(answer K)* Answer K is correct because *3 buses* would be needed. Fill in answer K for Sample B in the answer rows at the bottom of the page. Be sure you fill in the circle with a dark mark.

Check to see that the students have filled in the correct answer circle. If necessary elaborate on the solutions to the sample items.

Math Problem Solving and Data Interpretation
Lesson 10a **Math Problem Solving**

Directions: Read each mathematics problem. Choose the best answer.

Sample A Grant has $20. He wants to buy a baseball glove that normally costs $25 but is on sale for 20% off. Does he have enough money?
* A Yes, he has exactly enough.
  B Yes, he has more than enough.
  C No, he needs $4 more.
  D No, he needs $5 more.

Sample B If a school bus holds 45 people, how many buses would be needed for 100 people?
  J 2
* K 3
  L 4
  M 5

TIPS
• Read the question carefully. Think about what operation you should use to solve the problem.
• Set the problem up on scratch paper. Transfer numbers carefully and then solve the problem.

1 Bella is saving money to buy her father a birthday present. She saved $5 a month for 6 months, and her mother gave her $20. How much did she have in all?
  A $25
  B $30
* C $50
  D Not given

2 The tie Bella wants to buy normally costs $25. It is on sale for 20% off. What is the sale price of the tie?
  J $5
  K $10
  L $15
* M Not given

3 Bella and her mother are having a surprise party for her father. They have a recipe for punch that serves 12 people. They expect 36 people. What should they do to prepare enough punch for the party?
* A Multiply the recipe ingredients by 3.
  B Divide the recipe ingredients by 3.
  C Add 36 to the recipe ingredients.
  D Subtract 12 from 36 and multiply the recipe by the result.

4 The cake that Bella's mother wants to buy costs $18. She also bought 2 loaves of bread. She paid for everything with $40 and received $16 change. How much did each loaf of bread cost?
  J $1
  K $2
* L $3
  M Not given

 STOP

Answer rows A ●ⒷⒸⒹ 1 ⒶⒷ●Ⓓ 3 ●ⒷⒸⒹ
             B ⒥●ⓁⓂ 2 ⒥ⓀⓁ● 4 ⒥Ⓚ●Ⓜ

51

TIPS

Say Now let's look at the tips

Have a volunteer read the tips aloud to the group.

Say When you solve word problems, be sure to read them carefully. Think about the operation you should use to solve the problem. Use scratch paper, if necessary, and be sure to set the numbers up correctly.

Solve the two sample items on the chalkboard, demonstrating how to set the problems up correctly on scratch paper.

Practice

Say We are ready for Practice. You are going to do more problems in the same way that we did the samples. Do not write anything except your answer choices in your book. If you think it will help, you may do your work on scratch paper. When you have finished working a problem, fill in the circle for your answer in the answer rows at the bottom of the page. If the answer you find is not one of the choices, choose the last answer, Not given. Make sure that the circles for your answer choices are completely filled in with dark marks. Completely erase any marks for answers that you change. Work until you come to the STOP sign at the bottom of the page. Do you have any questions? Start working now.

Allow time for the students to fill in their answers.

Say You may stop working now. You have finished Lesson 10a.

Review the answers with the students. If any problems caused particular difficulty, work through each of the answer choices. It may be helpful to have volunteers solve each problem at the chalkboard and discuss the strategy they used.

Have the students indicate completion of the lesson by entering their score for this activity on the progress chart at the beginning of the book.

 Unit 7

Math Problem Solving and Data Interpretation

Lesson 10a **Math Problem Solving**

Directions: Read each mathematics problem. Choose the best answer.

 Sample A   Grant has $20. He wants to buy a baseball glove that normally costs $25 but is on sale for 20% off. Does he have enough money?
* A   Yes, he has exactly enough.
  B   Yes, he has more than enough.
  C   No, he needs $4 more.
  D   No, he needs $5 more.

Sample B   If a school bus holds 45 people, how many buses would be needed for 100 people?
  J   2
* K   3
  L   4
  M   5

 TIPS

• Read the question carefully. Think about what operation you should use to solve the problem.

• Set the problem up on scratch paper. Transfer numbers carefully and then solve the problem.

1   Bella is saving money to buy her father a birthday present. She saved $5 a month for 6 months, and her mother gave her $20. How much did she have in all?
  A $25
  B $30
* C $50
  D   Not given

2   The tie Bella wants to buy normally costs $25. It is on sale for 20% off. What is the sale price of the tie?
  J $5
  K $10
  L $15
* M   Not given

3   Bella and her mother are having a surprise party for her father. They have a recipe for punch that serves 12 people. They expect 36 people. What should they do to prepare enough punch for the party?
* A   Multiply the recipe ingredients by 3.
  B   Divide the recipe ingredients by 3.
  C   Add 36 to the recipe ingredients.
  D   Subtract 12 from 36 and multiply the recipe by the result.

4   The cake that Bella's mother wants to buy costs $18. She also bought 2 loaves of bread. She paid for everything with $40 and received $16 change. How much did each loaf of bread cost?
  J $1
  K $2
* L $3
  M   Not given

 STOP

Answer rows   A ●ⒷⒸⒹ   1 ⒶⒷ●Ⓓ   3 ●ⒷⒸⒹ
              B ⒥●ⓁⓂ   2 ⒿⓀⓁ●   4 ⒿⓀ●Ⓜ

51

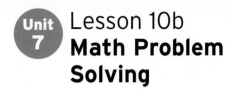

Lesson 10b
Math Problem Solving

Focus

Mathematics Skill
• solving word problems

Test-taking Skills
• working methodically
• identifying and using key words, numbers, and pictures
• indicating that the correct answer is not given
• taking the best guess when unsure of the answer

Samples A and B

Distribute scratch paper to the students.

Say Turn to Lesson 10b on page 52. In this lesson you will solve more word problems. Read the directions at the top of the page to yourself.

Allow time for the students to read the directions.

Say Find Sample A. Read the question to yourselves and find the answer. You may use scratch paper to solve the problem. If your answer is not one of the choices, choose the last answer, Not given. (pause) Which answer choice is correct? (answer B) Answer B is correct because Mr. Parker will use *112 ounces* of seed in 2 weeks. Mark answer B for Sample A in the answer rows. Make sure the circle is completely filled in with a dark mark.

Check to see that the students have filled in the correct answer circle.

Say Now do Sample B. Read the problem to yourself. Think about the process you should use before you solve the problem. (pause) Which answer is correct? (answer M) Answer M is correct because the correct answer to the problem, 12, is *not given*. Fill in answer M for Sample B in the answer rows at the bottom of the page. Be sure you fill in the circle with a dark mark.

Math Problem Solving and Data Interpretation
Lesson 10b **Math Problem Solving**

Directions: Read each mathematics problem. Choose the best answer.

Sample A Mr. Parker puts 8 ounces of seed in his bird feeder each day. There are 7 days in a week. How many ounces of seed will he put in his feeder in 2 weeks?

  A 100
*B 112
  C 278
  D Not given

Sample B If a restaurant uses 3 eggs in an omelette, how many omelettes can they make with 3 dozen eggs?

  J 10
  K 13
  L 30
*M Not given

TIPS
• If you solve the problem and it is not one of the answers, work it again before you choose "Not given."

Directions: The Sports Mart is going out of business. They placed this ad in the newspaper. Use the ad to answer questions 1–4.

REGULAR PRICE	
Bowling balls	$60.00
Baseballs	$9.00
Basketballs	$28.00
Footballs	$36.00
Tennis balls (can of 3)	$4.00
Golf balls (per dozen)	$24.00
Soccer balls	$30.00
Volleyballs	$20.00

Cross-training shoes were $60, now only $24.

Good customer bonus. Take an additional 10% off all orders of more than $50!

Special sale for school teams. All uniforms 60% off. Minimum purchase of $500.

1 How many golf balls can you buy on sale for $72?
  A 36
  B 48
  C 60
*D 72

2 What is the sale price of a bowling ball?
  J $10
  K $20
*L $30
  M Not given

3 The sale price of cross-training shoes is what percent of the regular price?
  A 24%
*B 40%
  C 46%
  D 60%

4 Which of the orders below qualifies for the good customer discount?
*J 2 basketballs and 2 footballs
  K 8 baseballs
  L 3 soccer balls
  M 1 volleyball and 5 cans of tennis balls

STOP

52   **Answer rows** A Ⓐ●ⒸⒹ 1 ⒶⒷⒸ● 3 Ⓐ●ⒸⒹ
              B ⒿⓀⓁ● 2 ⒿⓀ●Ⓜ 4 ●ⓀⓁⓂ

Check to see that the students have filled in the correct answer circle. If necessary elaborate on the solutions to the sample items.

★TIPS

Say Now let's look at the tip.

Have a volunteer read the tip aloud to the group.

Say Remember, the solution to the problem might not be one of the choices. When this happens, fill in the last answer, Not given. And don't forget, you should look for important words and numbers in a problem. They will help you find the answer.

Practice

Say We are ready for Practice. You are going to do more problems in the same way that we did the samples. Do not write anything except your answer choices in your book. If you think it will help, you may do your work on scratch paper. If you are not sure which answer is correct, take your best guess. When you have finished working a problem, fill in the circle for your answer in the answer rows at the bottom of the page. Make sure that the circles for your answer choices are completely filled in with dark marks. Completely erase any marks for answers that you change. Work until you come to the STOP sign at the bottom of the page. Do you have any questions? Start working now.

Allow time for the students to fill in their answers.

Say You may stop working now. You have finished Lesson 10b.

Review the answers with the students. If any problems caused particular difficulty, work through each of the answer choices. It may be helpful to have volunteers solve each problem at the chalkboard and discuss the strategy they used.

Have the students indicate completion of the lesson by entering their score for this activity on the progress chart at the beginning of the book.

 Unit 7

Math Problem Solving and Data Interpretation

Lesson 10b **Math Problem Solving**

Directions: Read each mathematics problem. Choose the best answer.

 Sample A
Mr. Parker puts 8 ounces of seed in his bird feeder each day. There are 7 days in a week. How many ounces of seed will he put in his feeder in 2 weeks?
A 100
∗ B 112
C 278
D Not given

Sample B
If a restaurant uses 3 eggs in an omelette, how many omelettes can they make with 3 dozen eggs?
J 10
K 13
L 30
∗ M Not given

TIPS
• If you solve the problem and it is not one of the answers, work it again before you choose "Not given."

Directions: The Sports Mart is going out of business. They placed this ad in the newspaper. Use the ad to answer questions 1–4.

Going Out of Business
Everything at least 50% off regular price.

REGULAR PRICE	
Bowling balls	$60.00
Baseballs	$9.00
Basketballs	$28.00
Footballs	$36.00
Tennis balls (can of 3)	$4.00
Golf balls (per dozen)	$24.00
Soccer balls	$30.00
Volleyballs	$20.00

Good customer bonus. Take an additional 10% off all orders of more than $50!

Cross-training shoes were $60, now only $24.

Special sale for school teams. All uniforms 60% off. Minimum purchase of $500.

1 How many golf balls can you buy on sale for $72?
A 36
B 48
C 60
∗ D 72

2 What is the sale price of a bowling ball?
J $10
K $20
∗ L $30
M Not given

3 The sale price of cross-training shoes is what percent of the regular price?
A 24%
∗ B 40%
C 46%
D 60%

4 Which of the orders below qualifies for the good customer discount?
∗ J 2 basketballs and 2 footballs
K 8 baseballs
L 3 soccer balls
M 1 volleyball and 5 cans of tennis balls

 STOP

52 Answer rows
A Ⓐ●ⒸⒹ 1 ⒶⒷⒸ● 3 Ⓐ●ⒸⒹ
B Ⓙ ⒦ Ⓛ● 2 Ⓙ ⒦●Ⓜ 4 ●ⓀⓁⓂ

Unit 7 Lesson 11a
Data Interpretation

Focus

Mathematics Skill
- interpreting tables and graphs

Test-taking Skills
- finding the answer without computing
- evaluating answer choices
- performing the correct operation
- computing carefully
- using charts and graphs
- transferring numbers accurately
- restating a question

Sample A

Distribute scratch paper to the students.

Say Turn to Lesson 11a on page 53. In this lesson you will solve problems involving a graph or chart. Read the directions at the top of the page to yourself.

Allow time for the students to read the directions.

Say Find Sample A. Look at the graph and read the question for Sample A to yourselves. Use the information in the graph to find the answer. *(pause)* Which answer choice is correct? *(answer B)* Yes, answer B is correct. About *30%* of the students preferred camping. Mark answer B for Sample A in the answer rows. Make sure the circle is completely filled in with a dark mark.

Check to see that the students have filled in the correct answer circle.

★**TIPS**

Say Now let's look at the tips.

Have a volunteer read the tips aloud to the group.

Unit 7 Math Problem Solving and Data Interpretation

Lesson 11a Data Interpretation

Directions: Read each mathematics problem. Choose the best answer.

Sample A Hal asked the students in his class which mountain activities they liked best. This graph shows the results of his survey. About what percentage of students preferred camping?

A	20%
*B	30%
C	50%
D	60%

TIPS
- Look at the graph or chart for each problem.
- If a problem seems complicated, try to say it to yourself in words you can understand better.

Directions: This graph shows the financial profile of a store that sells CDs. Use the graph to answer questions 1–4.

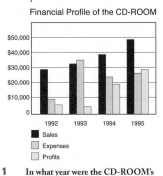

Financial Profile of the CD-ROOM

1 In what year were the CD-ROOM's profits the lowest?
- A 1992
- *B 1993
- C 1994
- D 1995

2 In 1992, the sales figure for the CD-ROOM was
- J $9,000.
- *K $29,000.
- L $32,000.
- M $34,000.

3 In which year were the CD-ROOM's expenses higher than the sales?
- A 1992
- *B 1993
- C 1994
- D 1995

4 How much did profits increase from 1994 to 1995?
- J $1,000
- K $5,000
- L $6,000
- *M $10,000

STOP

Answer rows   A ⊗●©D   1 ⊗●©D   2 ⊙●LM   3 ⊗●©D   4 ⊙⊗L●   53

Say Be sure to use the chart or graph to find the answer. Sometimes you will have to compute to find the answer, but other times you can answer a question just by using the information in the chart or graph. If a problem seems complicated, think about the problem and try to say it to yourself in words you understand better. This will help you avoid confusion.

Practice

Say We are ready for Practice. You are going to do more problems in the same way that we did the sample. Be sure to look at the graph when you solve the problems. Do not write anything except your answer choices in your book. If you think it will help, you may do your work on scratch paper. When you have finished working a problem, fill in the circle for your answer in the answer rows at the bottom of the page. Make sure that the circles for your answer choices are completely filled in with dark marks. Completely erase any marks for answers that you change. Work until you come to the STOP sign at the bottom of the page. Do you have any questions? Start working now.

Allow time for the students to fill in their answers.

Say You may stop working now. You have finished Lesson 11a.

Review the answers with the students. If any problems caused particular difficulty, work through each of the answer choices. It may be helpful to have volunteers solve each problem at the chalkboard and discuss the strategy they used. You may also want to review the information in the graph to be sure the students understand how to use them.

Have the students indicate completion of the lesson by entering their score for this activity on the progress chart at the beginning of the book.

 Unit 7

Math Problem Solving and Data Interpretation

Lesson 11a Data Interpretation

Directions: Read each mathematics problem. Choose the best answer.

Sample A Hal asked the students in his class which mountain activities they liked best. This graph shows the results of his survey. About what percentage of students preferred camping?

A 20%
* B 30%
C 50%
D 60%

 TIPS

- Look at the graph or chart for each problem.
- If a problem seems complicated, try to say it to yourself in words you can understand better.

Directions: This graph shows the financial profile of a store that sells CDs. Use the graph to answer questions 1–4.

Financial Profile of the CD-ROOM

(bar graph with values $10,000 to $50,000 for years 1992, 1993, 1994, 1995; legend: ■ Sales, Expenses, Profits)

1 In what year were the CD-ROOM's profits the lowest?
A 1992
* B 1993
C 1994
D 1995

2 In 1992, the sales figure for the CD-ROOM was
J $9,000.
* K $29,000.
L $32,000.
M $34,000.

3 In which year were the CD-ROOM's expenses higher than the sales?
A 1992
* B 1993
C 1994
D 1995

4 How much did profits increase from 1994 to 1995?
J $1,000
K $5,000
L $6,000
* M $10,000

 STOP

Answer rows A Ⓐ ● Ⓒ Ⓓ 1 Ⓐ ● Ⓒ Ⓓ 2 Ⓙ ● Ⓛ Ⓜ 3 Ⓐ ● Ⓒ Ⓓ 4 Ⓙ Ⓚ Ⓛ ●

53

Lesson 11b
Data Interpretation

Focus

Mathematics Skill
• interpreting tables and diagrams

Test-taking Skills
• working methodically
• finding the answer without computing
• using charts and graphs

Sample A

Say Turn to Lesson 11b on page 54. In this lesson you will solve problems involving a chart. Read the directions at the top of the page to yourself.

Allow time for the students to read the directions.

Say Find Sample A. Look at the table and read the question to yourselves. Use the information in the table to find the answer. *(pause)* Which answer choice is correct? *(answer C, 19)* Mark answer C for Sample A in the answer rows. Make sure the circle is completely filled in with a dark mark.

Check to see that the students have filled in the correct answer circle. Discuss the solution to the problem, pointing out that the solution involves using information from the chart and subtraction.

★ **TIPS**

Say Now let's look at the tip.

Have a volunteer read the tip aloud to the group.

Say When you solve the problems in this lesson, always use the information in the chart. Sometimes you may have to compute to find the answer, but the numbers that you need will always be found in the chart.

 Unit 7

Math Problem Solving and Data Interpretation

Lesson 11b **Data Interpretation**

Directions: Read each mathematics problem. Choose the best answer.

 Sample A

Basketball	27
Baseball	38
Football	46
Soccer	29

The table on the left shows how many students tried out for different teams. How many more students tried out for football than basketball?
A   9
B   11
∗ C   19
D   Not given

 TIPS

• The chart, table, or graph will always have the information you need to solve the problem.

Directions: Use the table below to answer questions 1–2.

Miller County Fish Caught in Cedar and Tyson River by Fish Type				
Fish Type	Cedar River	Tyson River	Total	Percent of Total Fish
Salmon	5,289	1,942	7,231	29.3
Trout	2,432	1,058	3,490	14.1
Bass	1,005	732	1,737	7.0
Steelhead	2,264	1,173	3,437	13.9
Sturgeon	292	68	360	1.5
Perch	1,893	884	2,777	11.2
Carp	1,578	743	2,321	9.4
Walleye	2,019	1,011	3,030	12.3
Catfish	233	89	322	1.3
Total	17,005	7,700	24,705	100.0

1 Which of the following statements about the relationship between trout and steelhead caught in Miller County is true?
A   A larger number of steelhead were caught.
B   More steelhead than trout were caught in the Cedar River.
∗ C   More steelhead than trout were caught in the Tyson River.
D   Steelhead make up a larger percent of the total fish.

2 About how many salmon are caught in the Cedar River for each one caught in the Tyson River?
J   1.0
∗ K   2.5
L   10
M   25

 STOP

54   Answer rows   A ⒶⒷ●Ⓓ   1 ⒶⒷ●Ⓓ   2 Ⓙ●ⓁⓂ

Practice

Say We are ready for Practice. You are going to do more problems in the same way that we did the sample. Be sure to look at the chart when you solve the problems. Do not write anything except your answer choices in your book. If you think it will help, you may do your work on scratch paper. When you have finished working a problem, fill in the circle for your answer in the answer rows at the bottom of the page. Make sure that the circles for your answer choices are completely filled in with dark marks. Completely erase any marks for answers that you change. Work until you come to the STOP sign at the bottom of the page. Do you have any questions? Start working now.

Allow time for the students to fill in their answers.

Say You may stop working now. You have finished Lesson 11b.

Review the answers with the students. If any problems caused particular difficulty, work through each of the answer choices. It may be helpful to have volunteers solve each problem and discuss the strategy they used.

Have the students indicate completion of the lesson by entering their score for this activity on the progress chart at the beginning of the book.

Unit 7

Math Problem Solving and Data Interpretation

Lesson 11b **Data Interpretation**

Directions: Read each mathematics problem. Choose the best answer.

Sample A

Basketball	27
Baseball	38
Football	46
Soccer	29

The table on the left shows how many students tried out for different teams. How many more students tried out for football than basketball?

A   9
B   11
✳ C   19
D   Not given

TIPS
- The chart, table, or graph will always have the information you need to solve the problem.

Directions: Use the table below to answer questions 1–2.

Miller County Fish Caught in Cedar and Tyson River by Fish Type				
Fish Type	Cedar River	Tyson River	Total	Percent of Total Fish
Salmon	5,289	1,942	7,231	29.3
Trout	2,432	1,058	3,490	14.1
Bass	1,005	732	1,737	7.0
Steelhead	2,264	1,173	3,437	13.9
Sturgeon	292	68	360	1.5
Perch	1,893	884	2,777	11.2
Carp	1,578	743	2,321	9.4
Walleye	2,019	1,011	3,030	12.3
Catfish	233	89	322	1.3
Total	17,005	7,700	24,705	100.0

1 Which of the following statements about the relationship between trout and steelhead caught in Miller County is true?
A   A larger number of steelhead were caught.
B   More steelhead than trout were caught in the Cedar River.
✳ C   More steelhead than trout were caught in the Tyson River.
D   Steelhead make up a larger percent of the total fish.

2 About how many salmon are caught in the Cedar River for each one caught in the Tyson River?
J   1.0
✳ K   2.5
L   10
M   25

 STOP

54   Answer rows   A ⒶⒷ●Ⓓ   1 ⒶⒷ●Ⓓ   2 Ⓙ●ⓁⓂ

Focus

Mathematics Skills
- solving word problems
- interpreting tables and graphs

Test-taking Skills
- managing time effectively
- following printed directions
- indicating that the correct answer is not given
- working methodically
- converting items to a workable format
- identifying and using key words, numbers, and pictures
- taking the best guess when unsure of the answer
- finding the answer without computing
- evaluating answer choices
- performing the correct operation
- computing carefully
- using charts and graphs
- transferring numbers accurately
- restating a question

Unit 7

Test Yourself: Math Problem Solving and Data Interpretation

Directions: Read each mathematics problem. Choose the best answer.

Sample A Nancy and Tim deliver newspapers in their neighborhood. Newspapers come in bundles of 25 on most days, but on Sunday they come in bundles of 15. The children are allowed to return the papers they do not sell.

Nancy and Tim have 143 customers for the daily paper. How many bundles of papers do they need on a weekday?
- A 4
- B 5
- ∗ C 6
- D Not given

1 Louis and his family are going on a 4-week trip in a camper they will rent. The camper costs $300 a week to rent, and gasoline will cost about $80 a week. How much will they spend in all to rent the camper and buy gasoline?
- A $1,200
- B $1,280
- C $1,420
- ∗ D Not given

2 During the first two days, the family drove through 2 states. On the first day, they traveled 230 miles. On the second day, they drove twice as far. How far did they drive in the first two days?
- J 460 miles
- ∗ K 690 miles
- L 920 miles
- M Not given

3 One-fourth of the food the family brought is canned goods. The canned goods weigh 20 pounds. How many pounds of food did the family bring all together?
- A 24 pounds
- B 40 pounds
- ∗ C 80 pounds
- D 100 pounds

4 Louis and his sister Tamara want to find the percentage of each state's total area that is land rather than water. They know the land area and the water area. How can they find the percentage that is land?
- ∗ J Add the land and water areas to find the total area. Divide the land area by the total area.
- K Add the land and water areas to find the total area. Divide the total area by the land area.
- L Divide the land area by the water area.
- M Divide the water area by the land area.

Answer rows A Ⓐ Ⓑ ● Ⓓ 1 Ⓐ Ⓑ Ⓒ ● 2 Ⓙ ● Ⓛ Ⓜ 3 Ⓐ Ⓑ ● Ⓓ 4 ● Ⓚ Ⓛ Ⓜ 55

This lesson simulates an actual test-taking experience. Therefore, it is recommended that the directions be read verbatim and that the suggested procedures and time allowances be followed.

Directions

Administration Time: approximately 20 minutes

Distribute scratch paper to the students.

Say Turn to the Test Yourself lesson on page 55.

Point out to the students that this Test Yourself lesson is timed like a real test, but that they will score it themselves to see how well they are doing. Encourage them to read each question carefully, to think about what they are supposed to do, and to work carefully on scratch paper when necessary.

They should skip difficult problems and return to them later and take the best guess when they are unsure of the answer.

Say This lesson will check how well you can solve mathematics problems like the ones we practiced before. Remember to make sure that the circles for your answer choices are completely filled in. Press your pencil firmly so that your marks come out dark. Completely erase any marks for answers that you change. Do not write anything except your answer choices in your books.

Look at Sample A. Read the story, the question, and the answer choices. Mark the circle for the answer you think is correct.

Allow time for the students to fill in their answers.

Say The circle for answer C should be filled in. Nancy and Tim will need 6 *bundles* of newspapers. If you chose another answer, erase yours and fill in circle C now.

Check to see that the students have filled in the correct answer circle.

Say Now you will do more mathematics problems. You may use the scratch paper I gave you. When you come to the GO sign at the bottom of a page, turn the page and continue working. Work until you come to the STOP sign at the bottom of page 57. Make sure that the circles for your answer choices are completely filled in with dark marks. Be sure to fill in the circle in the answer row for the problem you are working on. Completely erase any marks for answers that you change. You will have 15 minutes to solve the problems. You may begin.

Allow 15 minutes.

 Test Yourself: Math Problem Solving and Data Interpretation

Directions: Use the list below to answer questions 5–11. Do not allow for sales tax.

Community Cycling Center	
Pedals	$11.00 per pair
Light	$7.90
Reflector	$.98
Seat	$12.00
Chain	$4.54
Helmet	$27.00
Water bottle	$2.02 per bottle
Tube	$3.25 per tube
Box of patches	$6.00
Pump	$19.56

5 Mrs. Elder bought 4 water bottles for her children. She had $10. How much did the four water bottles cost?
A $1.92
B $7.98
C $8.02
∗D   Not given

6 Amir spent $9.05 for a chain, a tube, and spokes. How much did the spokes cost?
J $1.21
∗K $1.26
L $4.26
M   Not given

7 One pedal costs $5.80. How much did Haley save by buying a pair of pedals instead of 2 individual pedals?
∗A   60¢
B $5.20
C $11.60
D   Not given

8 It costs 50¢ to buy a single tire patch. How much money is saved by buying a box of patches that has 20 patches in it instead of buying the patches separately?
∗J $4.00
K $5.50
L $10.00
M   Not given

9 Steve wanted to buy 3 water bottles and 2 reflectors. He has $9. Did he have enough money?
A   No, he did not have enough money.
B   Yes, and he had $6.00 left over.
∗C   Yes, and he had 98¢ left over.
D   Yes, he had exactly the right amount.

10 Water bottles cost $2.02 each. A case contains 12 water bottles and costs $20. Coach Evelyn bought 4 cases of water bottles. Which of the following is not necessary to figure out what each water bottle cost Coach Evelyn?
J   She bought the bottles by the case.
K   A case costs $20.00.
L   A case holds 12 bottles.
∗M   Single bottles cost $2.02.

11 Coach Evelyn needed to buy some equipment for her cycling camp. She bought 7 chains from Community Cycling Center. She estimated the total cost by rounding the price of each chain to the nearest half-dollar. Which statement about their estimate is true?
A   Her estimate is $28.
B   Her estimate will be higher than the actual price.
∗C   Her estimate will be lower than the actual price.
D   Her estimate is $42.

56   Answer rows   5 Ⓐ Ⓑ Ⓒ ●   7 ● Ⓑ Ⓒ Ⓓ   9 Ⓐ Ⓑ ● Ⓓ   11 Ⓐ Ⓑ ● Ⓓ
6 Ⓙ ● Ⓛ Ⓜ   8 ● Ⓚ Ⓛ Ⓜ   10 Ⓙ Ⓚ Ⓛ ●

Say It's time to stop. You have finished the Test Yourself lesson. Check to see that you have completely filled in your answer circles. Make sure that any marks for answers that you changed have been completely erased.

Go over the lesson with the students. Ask if they had enough time to finish the lesson. Did they work carefully on scratch paper? Which questions required them to guess? What were some of the problems they experienced? Work through any problems that caused difficulty.

Have the students indicate completion of the lesson by entering their score for this activity on the progress chart at the beginning of the book. If necessary, provide additional practice problems similar to the ones in this unit.

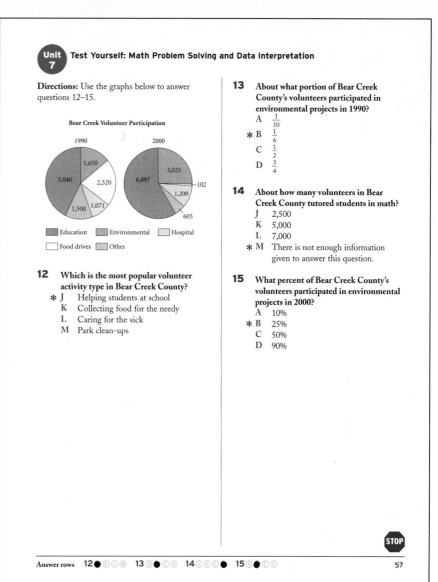

Unit 7 Test Yourself: Math Problem Solving and Data Interpretation

Directions: Use the graphs below to answer questions 12–15.

Bear Creek Volunteer Participation

1990 — 1,650; 5,040; 2,520; 1,500; 1,071

2000 — 3,025; 6,897; 102; 1,200; 605

Education Environmental Hospital
Food drives Other

12 Which is the most popular volunteer activity type in Bear Creek County?
* J Helping students at school
  K Collecting food for the needy
  L Caring for the sick
  M Park clean-ups

13 About what portion of Bear Creek County's volunteers participated in environmental projects in 1990?
  A $\frac{1}{10}$
* B $\frac{1}{6}$
  C $\frac{1}{2}$
  D $\frac{3}{4}$

14 About how many volunteers in Bear Creek County tutored students in math?
  J 2,500
  K 5,000
  L 7,000
* M There is not enough information given to answer this question.

15 What percent of Bear Creek County's volunteers participated in environmental projects in 2000?
  A 10%
* B 25%
  C 50%
  D 90%

STOP

Answer rows 12 ●ⓀⓁⓂ 13 Ⓐ●ⒸⒹ 14 ⒥ⓀⓁ● 15 Ⓐ●ⒸⒹ

57

Unit 8

Background

This unit contains five lessons that deal with math computation skills.

• **In Lessons 12a and 12b,** students solve problems involving addition and subtraction of whole numbers, fractions, and decimals. Students practice performing the correct operation, computing carefully, and transferring numbers accurately. They indicate that the correct answer is not given, convert items to a workable format, work methodically, and take the best guess when unsure of the answer.

• **In Lessons 13a and 13b,** students solve problems involving multiplication and division. In addition to reviewing the test-taking skills introduced in the previous lessons, students learn to skip difficult items and return to them later.

• **In the Test Yourself lesson,** the math computation skills and test-taking skills introduced in Lessons 12a through 13b are reinforced and presented in a format that gives students the experience of taking an achievement test. Techniques for managing time effectively when taking a standardized test are reinforced.

Instructional Objectives

| Lesson 12a | **Adding and Subtracting** | Given a problem involving adding or subtracting, students identify which of three answer choices is correct or indicate that the correct answer is not given. |
| Lesson 12b | **Adding and Subtracting** | |

| Lesson 13a | **Multiplying and Dividing** | Given a problem involving multiplying or dividing, students identify which of three answer choices is correct or indicate that the correct answer is not given. |
| Lesson 13b | **Multiplying and Dividing** | |

| | **Test Yourself** | Given questions similar to those in Lessons 12a through 13b, students utilize computation and test-taking strategies on achievement test formats. |

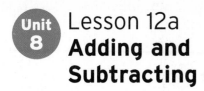

Lesson 12a
Adding and Subtracting

Focus

Mathematics Skill
- adding and subtracting whole numbers, fractions, and decimals

Test-taking Skills
- performing the correct operation
- computing carefully
- transferring numbers accurately
- indicating that the correct answer is not given
- converting items to a workable format
- working methodically

Samples A and B

Distribute scratch paper to the students.

Say Turn to Lesson 12a on page 58. In this lesson you will solve addition and subtraction problems. Read the directions at the top of the page to yourself while I read them out loud.

Read the directions out loud to the students.

Say Let's do Sample A. Read the problem and find the answer. You may work on the scratch paper I gave you. If you do work on scratch paper, be sure to transfer numbers accurately and compute carefully. *(pause)* Which answer choice is correct? *(answer B, 429)* What operation did you use to get this answer? *(addition)* Mark answer circle B for Sample A in the answer rows at the bottom of the page. Make sure the circle is completely filled in with a dark mark.

Check to see that the students have filled in the correct answer circle.

Say Do Sample B yourself. Read the problem and choose the answer you think is correct. If the correct answer is not one of the choices, choose the last answer, *N*. *(pause)* What is the correct answer choice? *(answer M)* Yes, the correct solution, *129*, is not one of the choices.

Math Computation
Lesson 12a Adding and Subtracting

Directions: Solve each problem. Choose the answer you think is correct. If the correct answer is not given, fill in the space for the last answer, *N*.

Sample A	148 +281	A 349 *B 429 C 439 D 529	Sample B	220 −91	J 99 K 109 L 119 *M N

 TIPS
- Look at the numbers and the operation sign carefully.
- Work the problem on scratch paper before you look at the answer choices.

1	500 −139	A 351 *B 361 C 639 D N	5	0.421 −0.407	A 0.0014 B 0.0041 *C 0.014 D N
2	72 205 13 +149	J 349 *K 439 L 440 M N	6	0.044 + 0.3009 =	J 0.03449 *K 0.3449 L 0.4439 M N
3	0.275 − 0.254 =	A 0.0021 *B 0.021 C 0.21 D N	7	$\frac{4}{50}$ $+\frac{16}{50}$	A $\frac{1}{5}$ B $\frac{3}{10}$ *C $\frac{2}{5}$ D N
4	1.7 8.0 2.4 +1.9	J 13.9 *K 14.0 L 14.2 M N	8	7 −0.57	J 5.57 K 6.33 *L 6.43 M N

STOP

58   Answer rows   A Ⓐ●ⒸⒹ   1 Ⓐ●ⒸⒹ   3 Ⓐ●ⒸⒹ   5 ⒶⒷ●Ⓓ   7 ⒶⒷ●Ⓓ
                       B ⒥ⓀⓁ●   2 ⒥●ⓁⓂ   4 ⒥●ⓁⓂ   6 ⒥●ⓁⓂ   8 ⒥Ⓚ●Ⓜ

Fill in circle M for Sample B in the answer rows. Make sure it is completely filled in with a dark mark.

Check to see that the students have filled in the correct answer circle.

⭐**TIPS**

Say Now let's look at the tips.

Have a volunteer read the tips aloud to the group.

Say Be sure you read the problem carefully, look at the numbers, and think about the operation you are supposed to perform. Be extra careful if the problem involves fractions or decimals. It's easier to make a mistake with these than with whole numbers.

Unit 8 **Lesson 12a Adding and Subtracting**   81

Practice

Say We are ready for Practice. You are going to do more problems in the same way that we did the samples. Do not write anything in your book except your answer choices. If you need to, use scratch paper to work the problems. Transfer numbers accurately to scratch paper and be sure to compute carefully. Pay careful attention to the operation sign for each problem. If the answer you find is not one of the choices, choose the last answer, N. Work until you come to the STOP sign at the bottom of the page. Make sure that the circles for your answer choices are completely filled in with dark marks. Erase any marks for answers that you change. You may begin.

Allow time for the students to fill in their answers.

Say It's time to stop. You have finished Lesson 12a.

Review the answers with the students. If any problems caused particular difficulty, work through each of the answer choices. Be sure to demonstrate each computation process in detail.

Have the students indicate completion of the lesson by entering their score for this activity on the progress chart at the beginning of the book.

 Unit 8

Math Computation
Lesson 12a **Adding and Subtracting**

Directions: Solve each problem. Choose the answer you think is correct. If the correct answer is not given, fill in the space for the last answer, *N*.

Sample A	148 + 281	A 349 ∗ B 429 C 439 D 529	Sample B	220 − 91	J 99 K 109 L 119 ∗ M N

 TIPS

- Look at the numbers and the operation sign carefully.
- Work the problem on scratch paper before you look at the answer choices.

1   500
      − 139

   A 351
∗ B 361
   C 639
   D N

2   72
      205
       13
     + 149

   J 349
∗ K 439
   L 440
   M N

3 0.275 − 0.254 =

   A 0.0021
∗ B 0.021
   C 0.21
   D N

4   1.7
       8.0
       2.4
     + 1.9

   J 13.9
∗ K 14.0
   L 14.2
   M N

5   0.421
      − 0.407

   A 0.0014
   B 0.0041
∗ C 0.014
   D N

6 0.044 + 0.3009 =

   J 0.03449
∗ K 0.3449
   L 0.4439
   M N

7 $\frac{4}{50}$
      + $\frac{16}{50}$

   A $\frac{1}{5}$
   B $\frac{3}{10}$
∗ C $\frac{2}{5}$
   D N

8   7
      − 0.57

   J 5.57
   K 6.33
∗ L 6.43
   M N

STOP

58   Answer rows   A ⓐ●ⓒⓓ   1 ⓐ●ⓒⓓ   3 ⓐ●ⓒⓓ   5 ⓐⓑ●ⓓ   7 ⓐⓑ●ⓓ
                B ⓙⓚⓛ●   2 ⓙ●ⓛⓜ   4 ⓙ●ⓛⓜ   6 ⓙ●ⓛⓜ   8 ⓙⓚ●ⓜ

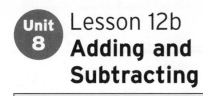

Focus

Mathematics Skill
- adding and subtracting whole numbers, fractions, and decimals

Test-taking Skills
- performing the correct operation
- computing carefully
- transferring numbers accurately
- indicating that the correct answer is not given
- taking the best guess when unsure of the answer

Samples A and B

Distribute scratch paper to the students.

Say Turn to Lesson 12b on page 59. In this lesson you will solve more addition and subtraction problems. Read the directions at the top of the page to yourself while I read them out loud.

Read the directions out loud to the students.

Say Let's do Sample A. Read the problem and find the answer. You may work on the scratch paper I gave you. *(pause)* Which answer choice is correct? *(answer B, three-fourths)* Mark answer circle B for Sample A in the answer rows at the bottom of the page. Make sure the circle is completely filled in with a dark mark.

Check to see that the students have filled in the correct answer circle.

Say Do Sample B yourself. Read the problem and choose the answer you think is correct. *(pause)* What is the correct answer? *(answer M)* Yes, answer M is correct because the solution to the problem, 488, is not one of the choices. Fill in circle M for Sample B in the answer rows. Make sure it is completely filled in with a dark mark.

Check to see that the students have filled in the correct answer circle.

Math Computation
Lesson 12b Adding and Subtracting

Directions: Solve each problem. Choose the answer you think is correct. If the correct answer is not given, fill in the space for the last answer, *N*.

Sample A	$\frac{1}{3} + \frac{5}{12} =$		A	$\frac{3}{5}$	Sample B	585		J	388
		*	B	$\frac{3}{4}$		$- 97$		K	412
			C	1				L	588
			D	N			*	M	N

 • Set problems up carefully on scratch paper. When you are finished working the problem, cross it out so it doesn't confuse you when you do another problem.

1	$\frac{2}{5} + \frac{4}{15} =$		A	$\frac{1}{3}$	5	$\frac{7}{10} - \frac{1}{5} =$		A	$\frac{1}{5}$
		*	B	$\frac{2}{3}$			*	B	$\frac{1}{2}$
			C	1				C	$\frac{9}{10}$
			D	N				D	N

2	324		J	139	6	$0.257 - 0.124 =$		J	0.00133
	$- 85$	*	K	239				K	0.0133
			L	339			*	L	0.133
			M	N				M	N

3	8.2	*	A	28.2	7	$\frac{2}{3} + \frac{1}{6} + \frac{5}{6} + \frac{1}{6} =$		A	$1\frac{1}{3}$
	11.3		B	28.4				B	$1\frac{2}{3}$
	2.0		C	38.2				C	2
	$+ 6.7$		D	N			*	D	N

4	831		J	129	8	$0.0474 + 0.286 =$		J	0.33334
	$- 659$		K	168				K	0.76
		*	L	172				L	0.334
			M	N			*	M	N

STOP

Answer rows
A Ⓐ●ⒸⒹ 1 Ⓐ●ⒸⒹ 3 ●ⒷⒸⒹ 5 Ⓐ●ⒸⒹ 7 ⒶⒷⒸ●
B ⒿⓀⓁ● 2 Ⓙ●ⓁⓂ 4 ⒿⓀ●Ⓜ 6 ⒿⓀ●Ⓜ 8 ⒿⓀⓁ●

59

⭐TIPS

Say Now let's look at the tip.

Have a volunteer read the tip aloud to the group.

Say Be sure to transfer the correct numbers to scratch paper and set it up carefully. When you have finished with a problem, cross it out. This will make it less likely that you will be confused when you solve the next problem.

Solve the sample problems on the chalkboard. Emphasize working neatly and discuss in detail the processes needed to solve the problem. When you have finished solving each problem, cross it out.

Practice

Say We are ready for Practice. You are going to do more problems in the same way that we did the samples. Do not write anything in your book except your answer choices. If necessary, use scratch paper to work the problems. Pay careful attention to the operation sign for each problem, and rearrange the problem on scratch paper in a way that will help you solve it. If you are not sure which answer is correct, be sure to take your best guess. Work until you come to the STOP sign at the bottom of the page. Make sure that the circles for your answer choices are completely filled in with dark marks. Erase any marks for answers that you change. You may begin.

Allow time for the students to fill in their answers.

Say It's time to stop. You have finished Lesson 12b.

Review the answers with the students. If any problems caused particular difficulty, work through each of the answer choices.

Have the students indicate completion of the lesson by entering their score for this activity on the progress chart at the beginning of the book.

 Unit 8

Math Computation
Lesson 12b Adding and Subtracting

Directions: Solve each problem. Choose the answer you think is correct. If the correct answer is not given, fill in the space for the last answer, *N*.

| Sample A | $\frac{1}{3} + \frac{5}{12} =$ | A $\frac{3}{5}$
 *B $\frac{3}{4}$
 C 1
 D N | Sample B | 585
 $- 97$ | J 388
 K 412
 L 588
 *M N |

 TIPS
- Set problems up carefully on scratch paper. When you are finished working the problem, cross it out so it doesn't confuse you when you do another problem.

1 $\frac{2}{5} + \frac{4}{15} =$
  A $\frac{1}{3}$
  *B $\frac{2}{3}$
  C 1
  D N

2 324
  $- 85$
  J 139
  *K 239
  L 339
  M N

3 8.2
  11.3
  2.0
  $+ 6.7$
  *A 28.2
  B 28.4
  C 38.2
  D N

4 831
  $- 659$
  J 129
  K 168
  *L 172
  M N

5 $\frac{7}{10} - \frac{1}{5} =$
  A $\frac{1}{5}$
  *B $\frac{1}{2}$
  C $\frac{9}{10}$
  D N

6 $0.257 - 0.124 =$
  J 0.00133
  K 0.0133
  *L 0.133
  M N

7 $\frac{2}{3} + \frac{1}{6} + \frac{5}{6} + \frac{1}{6} =$
  A $1\frac{1}{3}$
  B $1\frac{2}{3}$
  C 2
  *D N

8 $0.0474 + 0.286 =$
  J 0.33334
  K 0.76
  L 0.334
  *M N

 STOP

59

Answer rows A Ⓐ●ⒸⒹ 1 Ⓐ●ⒸⒹ 3 ●ⒷⒸⒹ 5 Ⓐ●ⒸⒹ 7 ⒶⒷⒸ●
B Ⓙ🅚🅛● 2 Ⓙ●ⓁⓂ 4 ⒿⓀ●Ⓜ 6 Ⓙ🅚●Ⓜ 8 Ⓙ🅚🅛●

Lesson 13a
Multiplying and Dividing

Focus

Mathematics Skill
- multiplying and dividing whole numbers, fractions, and decimals

Test-taking Skills
- performing the correct operation
- computing carefully
- transferring numbers accurately
- indicating that the correct answer is not given
- converting items to a workable format
- working methodically

Samples A and B

Distribute scratch paper to the students.

Say Turn to Lesson 13a on page 60. In this lesson you will solve multiplication and division problems. Read the directions at the top of the page to yourself while I read them out loud.

Read the directions out loud to the students.

Say Let's do Sample A. Read the problem and find the answer. You may work on the scratch paper I gave you. *(pause)* Which answer choice is correct? *(answer C, 24 remainder 1)* Mark answer circle C for Sample A in the answer rows at the bottom of the page. Make sure the circle is completely filled in with a dark mark.

Check to see that the students have filled in the correct answer circle.

Say Do Sample B yourself. Read the problem and choose the answer you think is correct. *(pause)* What is the correct answer? *(answer J)* Yes, answer J is correct because the solution to the problem is *15 and nine-tenths*. Fill in circle J for Sample B in the answer rows. Make sure it is completely filled in with a dark mark.

Check to see that the students have filled in the correct answer circle.

Math Computation
Lesson 13a Multiplying and Dividing

Directions: Solve each problem. Choose the answer you think is correct. If the correct answer is not given, fill in the space for the last answer, *N*.

Sample A $5\overline{)121}$	A 22
	B 22 r1
	*C 24 r1
	D N

Sample B $\frac{3}{10} \times 53 =$	*J $15\frac{9}{10}$
	K $16\frac{3}{10}$
	L 159
	M N

 TIPS

- Set the problem up on scratch paper carefully.
- Pay attention to the operation you should perform in each problem.

1 $28 \div 10 =$
A 0.28
B 2.08
C 280
*D N

2 $0.6\overline{)0.72}$
J 0.12
K 0.16
*L 1.2
M N

3 $\frac{1}{2} \times \frac{1}{4} =$
*A $\frac{1}{8}$
B $\frac{1}{6}$
C $\frac{3}{8}$
D N

4 385
$\times 11$
J 396
K 4,010
L 38,511
*M N

5 $0.225 \times 40 =$
A 0.8
B 8
C 80
*D N

6 $5.4 \div 30 =$
*J 0.18
K 1.8
L 18
M N

7 $\frac{2}{9}$
$\times 9$
A 1
*B 2
C 18
D N

8 $296\overline{)37}$
J 0.0125
K 1.25
L 12.5
*M N

 STOP

60   Answer rows   A ⒜Ⓑ●Ⓓ 1 ⒜ⒷⒸ● 3 ●ⒷⒸⒹ 5 ⒜ⒷⒸ● 7 ⒜●ⒸⒹ
                   B ●ⓀⓁⓂ 2 ⒿⓀ●Ⓜ 4 ⒿⓀⓁ● 6 ●ⓀⓁⓂ 8 ⒿⓀⓁ●

⭐ **TIPS**

Say Now let's look at the tips.

Have a volunteer read the tips aloud to the group.

Say Be sure to transfer the correct numbers to scratch paper and compute carefully. It's easy to make a mistake if you don't take your time and work carefully. Pay attention to the operation you should perform and work neatly. It is easy to make a mistake if you don't take your time.

Solve the sample problems on the chalkboard. Set the problems up carefully and describe each step of the solution process.

Practice

Say We are ready for Practice. You are going to do more problems in the same way that we did the samples. Do not write anything in your book except your answer choices. If you need to, use scratch paper to work the problems. Pay careful attention to the operation sign for each problem, and rearrange the problem on scratch paper in a way that will help you solve it. If you are not sure which answer is correct, be sure to take your best guess. Work until you come to the STOP sign at the bottom of the page. Make sure that the circles for your answer choices are completely filled in with dark marks. Erase any marks for answers that you change. You may begin.

Allow time for the students to fill in their answers.

Say It's time to stop. You have finished Lesson 13a.

Review the answers with the students. If any problems caused particular difficulty, work through each of the answer choices.

Have the students indicate completion of the lesson by entering their score for this activity on the progress chart at the beginning of the book.

 Unit 8

Math Computation
Lesson 13a **Multiplying and Dividing**

Directions: Solve each problem. Choose the answer you think is correct. If the correct answer is not given, fill in the space for the last answer, *N*.

Sample A $5\overline{)121}$

  A 22
  B 22 r1
 *C 24 r1
  D N

Sample B $\frac{3}{10} \times 53 =$

 *J $15\frac{9}{10}$
  K $16\frac{3}{10}$
  L 159
  M N

 TIPS

• Set the problem up on scratch paper carefully.

• Pay attention to the operation you should perform in each problem.

1 $28 \div 10 =$

  A 0.28
  B 2.08
  C 280
 *D N

2 $0.6\overline{)0.72}$

  J 0.12
  K 0.16
 *L 1.2
  M N

3 $\frac{1}{2} \times \frac{1}{4} =$

 *A $\frac{1}{8}$
  B $\frac{1}{6}$
  C $\frac{3}{8}$
  D N

4 385
   $\times\,11$

  J 396
  K 4,010
  L 38,511
 *M N

5 $0.225 \times 40 =$

  A 0.8
  B 8
  C 80
 *D N

6 $5.4 \div 30 =$

 *J 0.18
  K 1.8
  L 18
  M N

7 $\frac{2}{9}$
   $\times\,9$

  A 1
 *B 2
  C 18
  D N

8 $296\overline{)37}$

  J 0.0125
  K 1.25
  L 12.5
 *M N

 STOP

60 **Answer rows** A Ⓐ Ⓑ ● Ⓓ 1 Ⓐ Ⓑ Ⓒ ● 3 ● Ⓑ Ⓒ Ⓓ 5 Ⓐ Ⓑ Ⓒ ● 7 Ⓐ ● Ⓒ Ⓓ
              B ● Ⓚ ● Ⓜ 2 Ⓙ Ⓚ ● Ⓜ 4 Ⓙ Ⓚ Ⓛ ● 6 ● Ⓚ Ⓛ Ⓜ 8 Ⓙ Ⓚ Ⓛ ●

Focus

Mathematics Skill
- multiplying and dividing whole numbers, fractions, and decimals

Test-taking Skills
- performing the correct operation
- computing carefully
- transferring numbers accurately
- indicating that the correct answer is not given
- converting items to a workable format
- working methodically
- skipping difficult items and returning to them later

Samples A and B

Distribute scratch paper to the students.

Say Turn to Lesson 13b on page 61. In this lesson you will solve more multiplication and division problems. Read the directions at the top of the page to yourself while I read them out loud.

Read the directions out loud to the students.

Say Let's do Sample A. Read the problem and find the answer. You may work on the scratch paper I gave you. *(pause)* Which answer choice is correct? *(answer A)* Mark answer circle A for Sample A in the answer rows at the bottom of the page. Make sure the circle is completely filled in with a dark mark.

Check to see that the students have filled in the correct answer circle.

Say Do Sample B yourself. Read the problem and choose the answer you think is correct. *(pause)* What is the correct answer? *(answer J)* Yes, answer J is correct. Fill in circle J for Sample B in the answer rows. Make sure it is completely filled in with a dark mark.

Check to see that the students have filled in the correct answer circle.

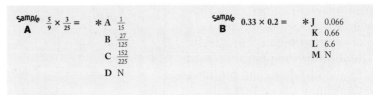

Math Computation
Lesson 13b Multiplying and Dividing

Directions: Solve each problem. Choose the answer you think is correct. If the correct answer is not given, fill in the space for the last answer, *N*.

Sample A $\frac{5}{9} \times \frac{3}{25} =$ *A $\frac{1}{15}$
     B $\frac{27}{125}$
     C $\frac{152}{225}$
     D   N

Sample B $0.33 \times 0.2 =$ *J   0.066
     K   0.66
     L   6.6
     M   N

TIPS • Pay extra attention when you multiply or divide fractions and decimals.

1 $47\overline{)768}$ A   10 r2
     B   10 r29
     C   11
   *D   N

2 $9,000 \times 20 =$ J   18,000
   *K   180,000
     L   1,800,000
     M   N

3 $4 \times \frac{5}{9}$ *A $2\frac{2}{9}$
     B $4\frac{5}{9}$
     C $7\frac{1}{5}$
     D   N

4 $0.6\overline{)0.48}$ J   0.08
   *K   0.8
     L   8
     M   N

5 $\begin{array}{r} 39 \\ \times\ 73 \\ \hline \end{array}$ A   1,267
     B   1,647
   *C   2,847
     D   N

6 $12.24 \div 4 =$ J   0.36
   *K   3.06
     L   3.60
     M   N

7 $\begin{array}{r} 0.027 \\ \times\ 300 \\ \hline \end{array}$ A   0.081
   *B   8.1
     C   81
     D   N

8 $\frac{3}{7} \div 5 =$ *J $\frac{3}{35}$
     K $2\frac{1}{7}$
     L $11\frac{2}{3}$
     M   N

STOP

Answer rows   A ●ⒷⒸⒹ   1 ⒶⒷⒸ●   3 ●ⒷⒸⒹ   5 ⒶⒷ●Ⓓ   7 Ⓐ●ⒸⒹ
         B ●ⒻⓁⓂ   2 Ⓙ●ⓁⓂ   4 Ⓙ●ⓁⓂ   6 Ⓙ●ⓁⓂ   8 ●ⓀⓁⓂ   61

⭐**TIPS**

Say Now let's look at the tip.

Have a volunteer read the tip aloud to the group.

Say When you solve problems involving fractions and decimals, pay extra attention. It is easy to make mistakes if you are not careful.

Solve the sample items on the chalkboard. Emphasize each step of the solution, particularly those associated with multiplying fractions and decimals.

Practice

Say We are ready for Practice. You are going to do more problems in the same way that we did the samples. Do not write anything in your book except your answer choices. If you need to, use scratch paper to work the problems. Pay careful attention to the operation sign for each problem, and rearrange the problem on scratch paper in a way that will help you solve it. If an item seems difficult, skip it and come back to it later. Work until you come to the STOP sign at the bottom of the page. Make sure that the circles for your answer choices are completely filled in with dark marks. Erase any marks for answers that you change. You may begin.

Allow time for the students to fill in their answers.

Say It's time to stop. You have finished Lesson 13b.

Review the answers with the students. If any problems caused particular difficulty, work through each of the answer choices. Pay extra attention to the items involving fractions and decimals.

Have the students indicate completion of the lesson by entering their score for this activity on the progress chart at the beginning of the book.

Math Computation

Lesson 13b **Multiplying and Dividing**

Directions: Solve each problem. Choose the answer you think is correct. If the correct answer is not given, fill in the space for the last answer, *N*.

Sample A $\frac{5}{9} \times \frac{3}{25} =$
 * A $\frac{1}{15}$
 B $\frac{27}{125}$
 C $\frac{152}{225}$
 D N

Sample B $0.33 \times 0.2 =$
 * J 0.066
 K 0.66
 L 6.6
 M N

- Pay extra attention when you multiply or divide fractions and decimals.

1 $47\overline{)768}$
 A 10 r2
 B 10 r29
 C 11
 * D N

2 $9,000 \times 20 =$
 J 18,000
 * K 180,000
 L 1,800,000
 M N

3 $4 \times \frac{5}{9}$
 * A $2\frac{2}{9}$
 B $4\frac{5}{9}$
 C $7\frac{1}{5}$
 D N

4 $0.6\overline{)0.48}$
 J 0.08
 * K 0.8
 L 8
 M N

5 39
 $\times 73$
 A 1,267
 B 1,647
 * C 2,847
 D N

6 $12.24 \div 4 =$
 J 0.36
 * K 3.06
 L 3.60
 M N

7 0.027
 $\times 300$
 A 0.081
 * B 8.1
 C 81
 D N

8 $\frac{3}{7} \div 5 =$
 * J $\frac{3}{35}$
 K $2\frac{1}{7}$
 L $11\frac{2}{3}$
 M N

STOP

Answer rows A ●ⒷⒸⒹ 1 ⒶⒷⒸ● 3 ●ⒷⒸⒹ 5 ⒶⒷ●Ⓓ 7 Ⓐ●ⒸⒹ
             B ●ⓀⓁⓂ 2 Ⓙ●ⓁⓂ 4 Ⓙ●ⓁⓂ 6 Ⓙ●ⓁⓂ 8 ●ⓀⓁⓂ

61

Focus

Mathematics Skill
- adding, subtracting, multiplying, and dividing whole numbers, fractions, and decimals

Test-taking Skills
- managing time effectively
- performing the correct operation
- computing carefully
- transferring numbers accurately
- indicating that the correct answer is not given
- converting items to a workable format
- working methodically
- taking the best guess when unsure of the answer
- skipping difficult items and returning to them later

This lesson simulates an actual test-taking experience. Therefore, it is recommended that the directions be read verbatim and that the suggested procedures and time allowances be followed.

Unit 8 Test Yourself: Math Computation

Directions: Solve each problem. Choose the answer you think is correct. If the correct answer is not given, fill in the space for the last answer, N.

Sample A $23 \times 47 =$
- *A 1,081
- B 1,085
- C 1,181
- D N

Sample B $8)\overline{3,412}$
- J 424
- K 425 r6
- *L 426 r4
- M N

1 $800)\overline{20}$
- A 2.5
- B 0.25
- *C 0.025
- D N

2 22.37 $\times$ 3.40
- J 25.77
- K 75.058
- *L 76.058
- M N

3 $3 - 0.57 =$
- A 0.54
- *B 2.43
- C 2.57
- D N

4 $\frac{1}{9} \div \frac{2}{6} =$
- *J $\frac{1}{3}$
- K $\frac{5}{11}$
- L $\frac{8}{9}$
- M N

5 $\frac{12}{16} + \frac{8}{16} =$
- A $\frac{1}{4}$
- B $\frac{5}{16}$
- C $\frac{5}{8}$
- *D N

6 $\frac{2}{3} + \frac{3}{9} + \frac{1}{6} =$
- J $\frac{6}{18}$
- *K $1\frac{1}{6}$
- L $1\frac{1}{3}$
- M N

7 7,314 $- 2,796$
- *A 4,518
- B 4,528
- C 4,818
- D N

8 $0.58 - 0.3 =$
- J 0.028
- K 0.35
- L 0.55
- *M N

GO

62 Answer rows A ●⒝©Ⓓ 1 ⒜⒝●Ⓓ 3 ⒜●©Ⓓ 5 ⒜⒝©● 7 ●⒝©Ⓓ
B ⒥⒦●Ⓜ 2 ⒥⒦●Ⓜ 4 ●⒦⒧Ⓜ 6 ⒥●⒧Ⓜ 8 ⒥⒦⒧●

Directions

Administration Time: approximately 15 minutes

Distribute scratch paper to the students.

Say Turn to the Test Yourself lesson on page 62.

Point out to the students that this Test Yourself lesson is timed like a real test, but that they will score it themselves to see how well they are doing. Encourage them to read each question carefully, to think about what they are supposed to do, and to work carefully on scratch paper when necessary. They should skip difficult problems and return to them later and take the best guess when they are unsure of the answer.

Say This lesson will check how well you can solve computation problems. Remember to make sure that the circles for your answer choices are completely filled in. Press your pencil firmly so that your marks come out dark. Completely erase any marks for answers that you change. Do not write anything except your answer choices in your books.

Look at Sample A. Read the question and the answer choices. Mark the circle for the answer you think is correct.

Allow time for the students to fill in their answers.

Say The circle for answer A should be filled in. If you chose another answer, erase yours and fill in circle A now.

Check to see that the students have filled in the correct answer circle.

Say Now do Sample B. Solve the problem and fill in the circle for the answer you think is correct.

Allow time for the students to fill in their answers.

Say The circle for answer L should be filled in. If you chose another answer, erase yours and fill in circle L now.

Check to see that the students have filled in the correct answer circle.

Say Now you will do more mathematics problems. You may use the scratch paper I gave you. Remember, for some items, the correct answer is not given. When this happens, choose the last answer. When you come to the GO sign at the bottom of the page, continue working. Work until you come to the STOP sign at the bottom of page 63. Make sure that the circles for your answer choices are completely filled in with dark marks. Be sure to fill in the circle in the answer row for the problem you are working on. Completely erase any marks for answers that you change. You will have 10 minutes to solve the problems. You may begin.

Allow 10 minutes.

Say It's time to stop. You have finished the Test Yourself lesson. Check to see that you have completely filled in your answer circles. Make sure that any marks for answers that you changed have been completely erased.

Go over the lesson with the students. Ask if they had enough time to finish the lesson. Did they work carefully on scratch paper? Which questions required them to guess? What were some of the problems they experienced? Work through any problems that caused difficulty.

Have the students indicate completion of the lesson by entering their score for this activity on the progress chart at the beginning of the book. If necessary, provide additional practice problems similar to the ones in this unit.

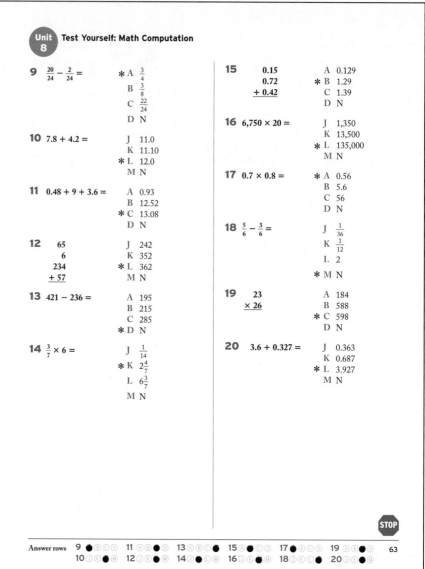

Background

This unit contains seven lessons that deal with study skills.

• **In Lessons 14a and 14b,** students answer questions about a chart, diagram, or map. They work methodically, refer to a reference source, skim a reference source, and reread questions.

• **In Lessons 15a through 16b,** students answer questions about the Dewey decimal system, a dictionary, and an index. They differentiate among reference sources and use key words. In addition to reviewing the test-taking skills introduced in earlier lessons, the students compare and eliminate answer sources. They take the best guess when unsure of the answer and skip difficult items and return to them later.

• **In the Test Yourself lesson,** the study skills and test-taking skills introduced and used in Lessons 14a through 16b are reinforced and presented in a format that gives students the experience of taking an achievement test. Techniques for managing time effectively when taking a standardized test are reinforced.

Instructional Objectives

Lesson 14a **Maps and Diagrams** Lesson 14b **Maps and Diagrams**	Given a question about a map or diagram, students identify which of four answer choices is correct.
Lesson 15a **Reference Materials** Lesson 15b **Reference Materials** Lesson 16a **Reference Materials** Lesson 16b **Reference Materials**	Given a question about a reference source, index, dictionary, key words, or the Dewey decimal classification system, students identify which of four answer choices is correct.
Test Yourself	Given questions similar to those in Lessons 14a through 16b, students utilize study skills and test-taking strategies on achievement test formats.

Lesson 14a
Maps and Diagrams

Unit 9

Focus

Reference Skills
- understanding a map
- using a chart

Test-taking Skills
- working methodically
- rereading a question
- referring to a reference source

Sample A

Say Turn to Lesson 14a on page 64. In this lesson you will practice using maps and charts. Read the directions at the top of the page to yourself.

Allow time for the students to read the directions.

Say Look at the chart at the top of the page and read the question for Sample A. What is the correct answer to the question? *(pause)* Answer D is correct. Mark circle D for Sample A in the answer rows at the bottom of the page. Make sure the circle is completely filled in. Press your pencil firmly so that your mark comes out dark.

Check to see that the students have filled in the correct answer circle. Discuss with the students how to find the answer using the information in the chart.

★**TIPS**

Say Now let's look at the tip.

Have a volunteer read the tip aloud.

Say When you find it hard to understand a question, try this strategy. Read the question, read the answer choices, then read the question again. This will often help you understand the question. It is also important that you use the chart, map, or other reference source to answer questions on an achievement test. The answer will always be found in the reference source.

Maps, Diagrams, and Reference Materials

Unit 9

Lesson 14a **Maps and Diagrams**

Directions: Read each question. Choose the best answer.

Sample A

Item	Regular Price	Warehouse Price	Minimum Purchase
Chicken	$1.99	$1.69	10 pounds
Bread	$.89	$.59	5 loaves
Tuna	$1.89	$1.59	12 cans
Corn	$1.29	$.99	12 cans
Noodles	$12.29	$9.99	10-pound box

Which of these is less than the minimum purchase amount?
A 1 box of noodles
B 12 cans of tuna
C 10 loaves of bread
✳D 5 pounds of chicken

TIPS
- If a question is difficult, read the question, read the answer choices, then read the question again. Look at any reference material, look at the answer choices, and then choose the one you think is correct.

Directions: A camping supplies store made this chart to help its customers select the right tent for their needs. Use the chart to answer questions 1–8.

Model	Price	Sleeps	Weight (in Pounds)	Fabric	Frame Type	Storm Flaps	Set-up Time (minutes)	Durability (years)	Consumer Rating
Pitch-It I	$	1	10	nylon	metal	✓	12	• •	*
Skip I	$$	1	10	nylon	metal	✓	15	• •	*
Star I	$$	1	7	nylon	fiberglass	–	20	• •	**
Sport I	$$	1	12	cotton	fiberglass	✓	18	•	*
Canopy II	$$	2–4	6	nylon	wood	–	15	• •	***
Roughy II	$$	2–4	5	nylon	metal	–	10	•	**
Meteor III	$$	5	30	canvas	metal	✓	45	•	***
Tip-Top III	$$	5	15	cotton	wood	✓	45	•	***
Leer IV	$$$	4	25	canvas	metal	✓	20	•	**
Trooper IV	$$$	6	35	canvas	metal	✓	30	•	*

Legend
$= $50 or less $$ = $50 to $100 $$$ = $100 or more   • = 5 years
The Roman numerals stand for tent type:
I = A-Frame   II = Dome and Hoop   III = Umbrella   IV = Wall

GO

64   **Answer rows**   A Ⓐ Ⓑ Ⓒ ●

---

92   **Unit 9** Lesson 14a **Maps and Diagrams**

Practice

Say Let's do the Practice items now. Read the directions for each section and answer the questions. Think about what the questions are asking and be sure to refer to the chart or map to answer the questions. When you come to the GO sign at the bottom of a page, continue working. Work until you come to the STOP sign at the bottom of page 66. Remember to make sure that your answer circles are completely filled in with dark marks. Completely erase any marks for answers that you change. Any questions? Start working now.

Allow time for the students to mark their answers.

 Unit 9 Lesson 14a **Maps and Diagrams**

1 Which of these has the shortest set-up time and can sleep a family of five?
A Tip-Top
∗ B Trooper
C Leer
D Meteor

2 How are the dome and hoop tents different from the other tents?
J They cost more.
K They have storm flaps.
∗ L They weigh less.
M They have a higher rating.

3 How are the Star and the Leer similar?
A In how much they cost
B In how long they last
C In how many they sleep
∗ D In how long they take to set up

4 Which of these seems to be most affected by a tent's fabric?
∗ J Weight
K Durability
L Cost
M Rating

5 Which tent lasts the longest and has the highest rating?
A Tip-Top
B Star
C Pitch-It
∗ D Canopy

6 How is this chart organized?
J By sleeping capacity
K By price range
∗ L By tent type
M By consumer rating

7 Which of these tents has cotton fabric and a fiberglass frame?
A Pitch-It
B Meteor
∗ C Sport
D Leer

8 Of the tents that require the shortest amount of set-up time, which is the least costly?
J Skip
K Roughy
∗ L Pitch-It
M Canopy

GO

Answer rows 1 Ⓐ●ⒸⒹ 3 ⒶⒷⒸ● 5 ⒶⒷⒸ● 7 Ⓐ●ⒸⒹ   65
2 ⒿⓀ●Ⓜ 4 ●ⓀⓁⓂ 6 ⒿⓀ●Ⓜ 8 ⒿⓀ●Ⓜ

Say It's time to stop. You have finished Lesson 14a.

Review the answers with the students. If any questions caused particular difficulty, work through each of the answer choices.

Have the students indicate completion of the lesson by entering their score for this activity on the progress chart at the beginning of the book.

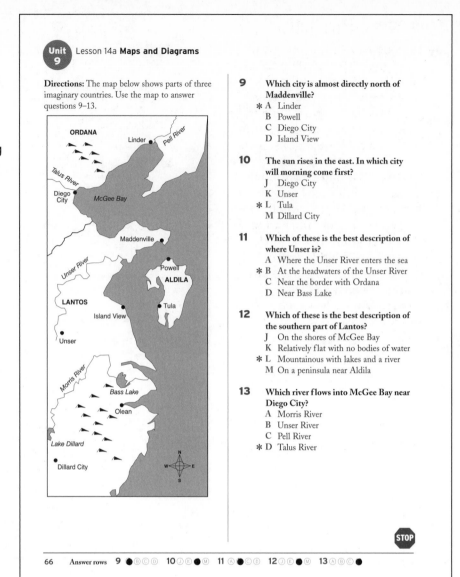

Directions: The map below shows parts of three imaginary countries. Use the map to answer questions 9–13.

9 Which city is almost directly north of Maddenville?
∗ A Linder
   B Powell
   C Diego City
   D Island View

10 The sun rises in the east. In which city will morning come first?
   J Diego City
   K Unser
∗ L Tula
   M Dillard City

11 Which of these is the best description of where Unser is?
   A Where the Unser River enters the sea
∗ B At the headwaters of the Unser River
   C Near the border with Ordana
   D Near Bass Lake

12 Which of these is the best description of the southern part of Lantos?
   J On the shores of McGee Bay
   K Relatively flat with no bodies of water
∗ L Mountainous with lakes and a river
   M On a peninsula near Aldila

13 Which river flows into McGee Bay near Diego City?
   A Morris River
   B Unser River
   C Pell River
∗ D Talus River

STOP

66   Answer rows   9 ●ⒷⒸⒹ   10 ⒿⓀ●Ⓜ   11 Ⓐ●ⒸⒹ   12 ⒿⓀ●Ⓜ   13 ⒶⒷⒸ●

Lesson 14b
Maps and Diagrams

Focus

Reference Skills
- understanding a map
- understanding a diagram

Test-taking Skills
- skimming a reference source
- working methodically
- referring to a reference source

Say Turn to Lesson 14b on page 67. In this lesson you will answer more questions about maps and diagrams. Read the directions at the top of the page to yourself.

Allow time for the students to read the directions.

Practice

Say Let's do the Practice items now. They are very much like the items you did in lesson 14a. Skim the map or diagram and then read the questions. Think about what the questions are asking and be sure to refer to the reference source to answer the questions. When you come to the GO sign at the bottom of the page, turn the page and continue working. Work until you come to the STOP sign at the bottom of page 68. Remember to make sure that your answer circles are completely filled in with dark marks. Completely erase any marks for answers that you change. Any questions? Start working now.

Allow time for the students to mark their answers.

Maps, Diagrams, and Reference Materials

Lesson 14b **Maps and Diagrams**

Directions: A historic-park tourism book features this information and map of structures that once made up a Pueblo community. Use them to answer questions 1–5.

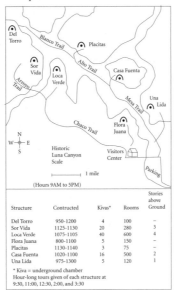

Historic Luna Canyon Scale

(Hours 9AM to 5PM)

Structure	Contructed	Kivas*	Rooms	Stories above Ground
Del Torro	950-1200	4	100	–
Sor Vida	1125-1130	20	280	3
Loca Verde	1075-1105	40	600	4
Flora Juana	800-1100	5	150	–
Placitas	1130-1140	3	75	–
Casa Fuenta	1020-1100	16	500	2
Una Lida	975-1300	5	120	1

* Kiva = underground chamber
Hour-long tours given of each structure at
9:30, 11:00, 12:30, 2:00, and 3:30

1 Which trail leads north to the largest Pueblo structure?
A Arroyo Trail
∗ B Chaco Trail
C Mesa Trail
D Blanco Trail

2 Which is the oldest of the structures?
∗ J Flora Juana
K Del Torro
L Casa Fuenta
M Loca Verde

3 How are structures Flora Juana and Del Torro similar?
A In their number of kivas
B In their number of rooms
∗ C In their underground structure
D In the years they were built

4 If you arrived at the park when it opened and left when it closed, how many different tours could you take in one day?
J Three
∗ K Five
L Seven
M Nine

5 Which of the structures would be best to visit if a tour group could not go far on foot?
A Del Torro
B Placitas
∗ C Flora Juana
D Una Lida

 GO

Answer rows 1 Ⓐ ● Ⓒ Ⓓ   2 ● Ⓚ Ⓛ Ⓜ   3 Ⓐ Ⓑ ● Ⓓ   4 Ⓙ ● Ⓛ Ⓜ   5 Ⓐ Ⓑ ● Ⓓ   67

Say It's time to stop. You have finished Lesson 14b.

Review the answers with the students. If any questions caused particular difficulty, work through each of the answer choices.

Have the students indicate completion of the lesson by entering their score for this activity on the progress chart at the beginning of the book.

Directions: The students in a wood-shop class used this diagram to make a five-shelf bookshelf. The numbers shown are in inches. Use the diagram to answer questions 6–11.

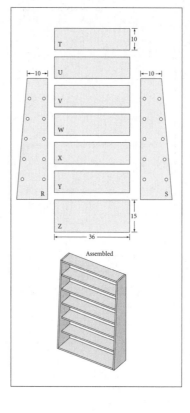

Assembled

6 What is the purpose of the holes in pieces R and S?
   J To use for looking through
   K To hang the bookshelf on the wall
 ∗ L To put posts in to hold up the shelves
   M To allow room for more shelves

7 When the bookshelf is assembled, which two pieces would not be nailed to each other?
   A Pieces T and R
   B Pieces S and T
   C Pieces Z and S
 ∗ D Pieces T and Z

8 Which of these is the smallest piece of wood from which piece Y could be made?
   J 10″ × 15″
   K 10″ × 30″
 ∗ L 15″ × 40″
   M 15″ × 45″

9 If the top of side piece R is 10″ wide, how wide is its bottom?
   A 5″
   B 10″
 ∗ C 15″
   D 20″

10 Which of these could be the first step in assembling the bookshelf?
   J Nail piece T to piece U
 ∗ K Nail piece T to piece R
   L Nail piece R to piece S
   M Nail piece Z to piece Y

11 Which part of the bookshelf is part Z?
   A The top
   B The front
   C The side
 ∗ D The bottom

68 Answer rows 6 Ⓙ Ⓚ ● Ⓜ   8 Ⓙ Ⓚ ● Ⓜ   10 Ⓙ ● Ⓛ Ⓜ
              7 Ⓐ Ⓑ Ⓒ ●   9 Ⓐ Ⓑ ● Ⓓ   11 Ⓐ Ⓑ Ⓒ ●

Unit 9 Lesson 15a
Reference Materials

Focus

Reference Skills
- using guide words
- differentiating among reference sources

Test-taking Skills
- working methodically
- comparing answer choices
- eliminating answer choices
- referring to a reference source

Sample A

Say Turn to Lesson 15a on page 69. In this lesson you will practice different study skills. Read the directions at the top of the page to yourself.

Allow time for the students to read the directions.

Say Look at the guide words for Sample A. Guide words tell you which words are on a dictionary page. Now look at the question. Which answer is correct? *(pause)* Yes, answer A is correct because *holiday* would be found on *page 631*. Mark circle A for Sample A in the answer rows at the bottom of the page. Make sure the circle is completely filled in. Press your pencil firmly so that your mark comes out dark.

Check to see that the students have filled in the correct answer circle.

 TIPS

Say Now let's look at the tips.

Have a volunteer read the tips aloud.

Unit 9 Maps, Diagrams, and Reference Materials

Lesson 15a Reference Materials

Directions: Read each question. Choose the best answer.

 Sample A

hold	•	hollow	631
holly	•	holy	632
homage	•	homework	633
homey	•	homonym	634

On which page would you find the word *holiday*?
* A 631
  B 632
  C 633
  D 634

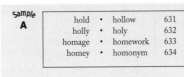
- Look carefully at any reference material that is part of a question.
- Compare the answer choices with one another and the question.
- Eliminate answer choices you know are wrong.

Directions: The Dewey decimal classification system arranges nonfiction books in ten major categories according to subject. Use the categories below to answer questions 1–3.

000-099	**General works** (encyclopedias, magazines, newspapers)
100-199	**Philosophy** (psychology, ethics)
200-299	**Religion** (world religions, mythology)
300-399	**Social sciences** (customs, law, economics, government, education)
400-499	**Languages** (dictionaries, grammars)
500-599	**Pure sciences** (math, biology, chemistry, physics)
600-699	**Applied sciences** (medicines, business, engineering, farming, homemaking)
700-799	**Arts and recreation** (music, sports, painting, dance)
800-899	**Literature** (poetry, plays, essays)
900-999	**History** (biography, travel, geography)

1 Where would a book about cooking be found?
  A 500–599
* B 600–699
  C 700–799
  D 900–999

2 Which category would contain a book of funny poems?
  J 000–099
  K 300–399
* L 800–899
  M 900–999

3 Where would a book about Olympic athletes from around the world be found?
  A 600–699
* B 700–799
  C 800–899
  D 900–999

GO

Answer rows A ●ⒷⒸⒹ 1 Ⓐ●ⒸⒹ 2 ⒿⓀ●Ⓜ 3 Ⓐ●ⒸⒹ

69

Say It is important that you read the directions for each part of this lesson. Be sure to refer to the reference material to answer the questions. Compare the answer choices with one another and with the question, and if you are sure an answer choice is not correct, you can eliminate it and concentrate on the other answers. Remember, you should only eliminate an answer choice if you are sure it is wrong.

Practice

Say Let's do the Practice items now. Read the questions and use the reference source to find the answer. When you come to the GO sign at the bottom of a page, turn the page and continue working. Work until you come to the STOP sign at the bottom of page 70. Remember to make sure that your answer circles are completely filled in with dark marks. Completely erase any marks for answers that you change. Any questions? Start working now.

Allow time for the students to mark their answers.

Say It's time to stop. You have finished Lesson 15a.

Review the answers with the students. If any questions caused particular difficulty, work through each of the answer choices.

Have the students indicate completion of the lesson by entering their score for this activity on the progress chart at the beginning of the book.

 Unit 9 Lesson 15a **Reference Materials**

Directions: Questions 4–13 are about using reference materials you might find in a library. For each question, choose the answer you think is best.

4 Which of these would help you find out what an *obelisk* is?
  J   An almanac
* K   A dictionary
  L   A thesaurus
  M   An anthology

5 Which of these should you use to find pictures of different kinds of trees?
  A   A glossary
  B   A dictionary
* C   An encyclopedia
  D   A thesaurus

6 Which of these would most likely feature an article comparing several brands of swimming goggles?
  J   *People*
  K   *Sports Illustrated*
  L   *National Geographic*
* M   *Consumer Reports*

7 Where could you find a list of the Pulitzer Prize winners from different countries?
* A   An almanac
  B   A thesaurus
  C   A history book
  D   A travel magazine

8 Which of these should you use to find a list of words that have almost the same meaning as *travail*?
  J   An encyclopedia
  K   A glossary
* L   A thesaurus
  M   An atlas

9 How could you find out which of Gary Soto's books of short stories are available at the local library?
  A   Look in the G section of biographies
  B   Look in the S section of fiction
  C   Search in the catalog system for "Short Stories" as a topic
* D   Search in the catalog system for "Soto" as an author

10 You would most likely find the book *A Life of Courage: The Wilma Rudolph Story*, by Gertrude Flavin, on a shelf with which label?
  J   Autobiography
  K   Sports
* L   Biography
  M   Mythology

11 Which of these would you be most likely to find in an encyclopedia?
  A   How to pronounce the word *penicillin*
  B   Which drugstores carry penicillin
  C   The companies that make penicillin
* D   The story of the discovery of penicillin

12 Suppose your teacher asked you to find synonyms for words you overused in a composition. Which of these should you use?
* J   A thesaurus
  K   An almanac
  L   A dictionary
  M   An English grammar book

13 Which of these would probably contain a story about a train ride through Mexico's Copper Canyon?
  A   *Reader's Digest*
* B   *National Geographic*
  C   *Business Week*
  D   *Scientific American*

70   Answer rows   4 Ⓙ⬤ⓁⓂ   6 Ⓙ🔵Ⓛ⬤   8 Ⓙ🔵⬤Ⓜ   10 Ⓙ🔵⬤   12 ⬤ⓀⓁⓂ
5 Ⓐ🔵⬤🔵   7 ⬤ⒷⒸⒹ   9 Ⓐ🔵🔵⬤   11 Ⓐ🔵Ⓒ⬤   13 Ⓐ⬤ⒸⒹ

Focus

Reference Skills
• using a dictionary
• using key words

Test-taking Skills
• working methodically
• referring to a reference source
• taking the best guess when unsure of the answer

Sample A

Say Turn to Lesson 15b on page 71. In this lesson you will show how well you can use different reference sources. Read the directions at the top of the page to yourself.

Allow time for the students to read the directions.

Say Look at the part of a dictionary and the questions for Sample A. Which answer is correct? *(pause)* Yes, answer C is correct because the word *profit* would most likely be used by a *businessperson*. Mark circle C for Sample A in the answer rows at the bottom of the page. Make sure the circle is completely filled in. Press your pencil firmly so that your mark comes out dark.

Check to see that the students have filled in the correct answer circle.

Practice

Say Let's do the Practice items now. Read the questions and choose the answers you think are best. If you are not sure which answer is correct, take your best guess. When you come to the GO sign at the bottom of the page, turn the page and continue working. Work until

you come to the STOP sign at the bottom of page 72. Remember to make sure that your answer circles are completely filled in with dark marks. Completely erase any marks for answers that you change. Any questions? Start working now.

Allow time for the students to mark their answers.

 Maps, Diagrams, and Reference Materials

Lesson 15b **Reference Materials**

Directions: Read each question. Choose the best answer.

Sample A

prof•it (prof'it) *n.* 1. gain coming from an investment or business 2. benefit or advantage –*v.* 3. to gain an advantage 4. to make money on an investment or business

You would be most likely to use the word *profit* if you were
A a fisherman.
B a gardener.
✳ C a businessperson.
D a runner.

me•sa (mā′sə) *n.* a land formation having a flat top and steep rock walls

mesh (měsh) *n.* one of the open spaces in a net or screen

mes•mer•ize (měz′mə rīz′) *v.* 1. to hypnotize 2. to fascinate

mess (měs) *n.* 1. a dirty or untidy condition 2. an unpleasant situation 3. a group of people who regularly eat together –*v.* 3. to make dirty or untidy

mess hall (měs hôll) *n.* a place where a group of people eat, especially in a military camp

met•al (mět′əl) *n.* any of the hard crystalline elementary substances such as iron or gold

1. Pronunciation Guide:

ă	sat	ŏ	lot	ə	represents
ā	day	ō	so		a in alone
ä	calm	ŏŏ	look		e in open
â	pare	ōō	root		i in easily
ě	let	ô	ball		o in gallop
ē	me	ŭ	cut		u in circus
ĭ	sit	û	purr		
ī	lie				

2. Abbreviations: *n.*, noun; *v.*, verb; *adj.*, adjective; *pl.*, plural

Directions: Use the dictionary and the guides on the left to answer questions 1–4.

1 How would you spell the word that means "to fascinate"?
A mezmerize
B mezmarize
✳ C mesmerize
D mesmarise

2 The *e* in *mesa* sounds like the
J *e* in *let.*
K *e* in *me.*
L *i* in *lie.*
✳ M *a* in *day.*

3 Which word fits best in the sentence "I know it sounds funny, but my aunt says she has lunch with her _____"?
✳ A mess   C mesa
B mess hall   D mesh

4 What is the plural of *metal*?
J metales   L metalies
✳ K metals   M metal

Answer rows A Ⓐ Ⓑ ● Ⓓ 1 Ⓐ Ⓑ ● Ⓓ 2 Ⓙ Ⓚ Ⓛ ● 3 ● Ⓑ Ⓒ Ⓓ 4 Ⓙ ● Ⓛ Ⓜ   71

Say It's time to stop. You have finished Lesson 15b.

Review the answers with the students. If any questions caused particular difficulty, work through each of the answer choices.

Have the students indicate completion of the lesson by entering their score for this activity on the progress chart at the beginning of the book.

 Unit 9 Lesson 15b **Reference Materials**

Directions: At the top of each page in a dictionary, there are two guide words. They are the first and last words on that page of the dictionary. Use the guide words and page numbers below to answer questions 5–9.

seep •	seizure	921
seldom •	self-contained	922
self-control •	sell	923
selvage •	seminary	924
Seminole •	senator	925

5 On which page would you find the word *self-centered*?
A 921 ∗B 922 C 923 D 924

6 On which page would you find the word *senary*?
J 922 K 923 L 924 ∗M 925

7 On which page would you find the word *segment*?
∗A 921 B 922 C 923 D 924

8 On which page would you find the word *selenium*?
∗J 922 K 923 L 924 M 925

9 On which page would you find the word *seer*?
∗A 921 B 922 C 923 D 924

Directions: Before you use certain reference materials, you need to decide exactly which word or phrase to use to find the information you want. We call this word or phrase the *key term*. In questions 10–14, select the best key term.

10 In 1926, Edna Ferber wrote a book called *Showboat* that became a successful Broadway musical. Which key term should you use to find other books she wrote?
J 1926 L *Showboat*
K Broadway ∗M Ferber

11 Which key term should you use to find out how to prepare a garden for corn, tomatoes, and other vegetables?
∗A Gardening C Corn
B Vegetables D Preparing

12 Which key term should you use to find the rules for the game of tennis?
J Rules L Games
∗K Tennis M Sports

13 Which key term should you use to find out how the space shuttle is protected against heat when it returns through the atmosphere?
∗A Space Shuttle C Protect
B Heat D Atmosphere

14 Which key term should you use to find the names of insects that might damage houseplants?
J Insects ∗L Plants, house
K Names M Damage, might

 STOP

72 Answer rows 5 Ⓐ●ⒸⒹ 7 ●ⒷⒸⒹ 9 ●ⒷⒸⒹ 11 ●ⒷⒸⒹ 13 ●ⒷⒸⒹ
6 ⒿⓀⓁ● 8 ●ⓀⓁⓂ 10 ⒿⓀⓁ● 12 Ⓙ●ⓁⓂ 14 ⒿⓀ●Ⓜ

Unit 9 Lesson 16a
Reference Materials

Focus

Reference Skills
- differentiating among reference sources
- understanding the Dewey decimal classification system
- using a dictionary

Test-taking Skills
- working methodically
- skimming a reference source
- skipping difficult items and returning to them later

Samples A and B

Say Turn to Lesson 16a on page 73. In this lesson you will show how well you understand how to use different reference sources. Read the directions at the top of the page to yourself.

Allow time for the students to read the directions.

Say Read the question for Sample A. Which answer is correct? *(pause)* Answer B is correct because information about what an author wrote would be found in *the card catalog*. Mark circle B for Sample A in the answer rows at the bottom of the page. Make sure the circle is completely filled in. Press your pencil firmly so that your mark comes out dark.

Check to see that the students have filled in the correct answer circle.

Say Now do Sample B. Read the question and decide which answer is correct. *(pause)* Answer K is correct because *an atlas* is the best source for maps. Mark circle K for Sample B in the answer rows at the bottom of the page. Make sure the circle is completely filled in. Press your pencil firmly so that your mark comes out dark.

Check to see that the students have filled in the correct answer circle.

Unit 9 Maps, Diagrams, and Reference Materials

Lesson 16a **Reference Materials**

Directions: Read each question. Choose the best answer.

Sample A Which of these would help you find out which books J.R.R. Tolkien wrote? A *Reader's Digest* ✱ B The card catalog C *Readers' Guide to Periodical Literature* D A history textbook	**Sample B** Which of these would contain the best selection of maps of the large cities in the United States? J An encyclopedia ✱ K An atlas L A thesaurus M A dictionary

- Before you mark your answer, be sure to match the item number with the answer number. This will help you avoid careless mistakes.

Directions: The Dewey decimal classification system arranges nonfiction library books in ten major categories according to subject. Use the categories below to answer questions 1–4.

000-099	**General works** (encyclopedias, magazines, newspapers)
100-199	**Philosophy** (psychology, ethics)
200-299	**Religion** (world religions, mythology)
300-399	**Social sciences** (customs, law, economics, government, education)
400-499	**Languages** (dictionaries, grammars)
500-599	**Pure sciences** (math, biology, chemistry, physics)
600-699	**Applied sciences** (medicine, business, engineering, farming, homemaking)
700-799	**Arts and recreation** (music, sports, painting, dance)
800-899	**Literature** (poetry, plays, essays)
900-999	**History** (biology, travel, geography)

1 How would a book about the national parks in America be shelved?
A   100–199   C   700–799
B   200–299   ✱ D   900–999

2 How would the book *Spanish for Business Travelers* be categorized?
J   200–299   L   600–699
✱ K   400–499   M   900–999

3 Where would a book of the collected poetry of Robert Frost be shelved?
A   100–199   C   700–766
B   300–399   ✱ D   800–899

4 Where would a book about the first canal built in the United Staes be shelved?
J   200–299   L   800–899
K   300–399   ✱ M   900–999

GO ➡

Answer rows   A Ⓐ●ⒸⒹ   1 ⒶⒷⒸ●   3 ⒶⒷⒸ●
                          B Ⓙ●ⓁⓂ   2 Ⓙ●ⓁⓂ   4 ⒿⓀⓁ●

73

★ TIPS

Say Now let's look at the tip.

Have a volunteer read the tip aloud.

Say Be sure to match the item number on which you are working with the answer row you fill in. It is easy to make a mistake on a test if you don't do this.

Practice

Say Let's do the Practice items now. There are different kinds of items in this lesson, so be sure to read the directions for each section. Think about what the questions are asking, and if there is a reference source, be sure to refer to it to find the answers. Skip difficult items and return to them after you have tried the the other items. When you come to a GO sign at the bottom of the page, turn the page and continue working. Work until you come to the STOP sign at the bottom of page 75. Remember to make sure that your answer circles are completely filled in with dark marks. Completely erase any marks for answers that you change. Any questions? Start working now.

Allow time for the students to mark their answers.

 Unit 9 Lesson 16a **Reference Materials**

Directions: Questions 5–8 are about using library materials. Choose the best answer for each question.

5 Which of these should you use to find books about starting your own business?
A *Reader's Digest*
B The card catalog
C *Readers' Guide to Periodical Literature*
∗D A business textbook

6 Which of these would help you learn about the histories of India and China?
∗J An encyclopedia
K An atlas
L A thesaurus
M A dictionary

7 Which of these would probably contain a story about the vice president of the United States?
A *National Geographic*
∗B *Newsweek*
C *TV Guide*
D *Consumer Reports*

8 How could you find out which books by Wallace Stegner were in your school library?
J Look in the encyclopedia in the S section.
K Look in the W section of the fiction shelf.
L Search in the catalog system for "Wallace" as an author.
∗M Search in the catalog system for "Stegner" as an author.

74   Answer rows   5 Ⓐ Ⓑ Ⓒ ● 6 ● Ⓚ Ⓛ Ⓜ 7 Ⓐ ● Ⓒ Ⓓ 8 Ⓙ Ⓚ Ⓛ ●

Say It's time to stop. You have finished Lesson 16a.

Review the answers with the students. If any questions caused particular difficulty, work through each of the answer choices.

Have the students indicate completion of the lesson by entering their score for this activity on the progress chart at the beginning of the book.

---

pal•pa•ble (păl′ pə bəl) *adj.* readily or plainly seen, heard, or perceived −*n.* **palpability, palpableness** −*adv.* **palpably**

par•af•fin (păr′ ə fĭn) *n.* a white or colorless, tasteless, odorless substance obtained from petroleum and used primarily in candles

par•a•pet (păr′ ə pət, -pĕt) *n.* a defensive wall or elevation of earth or stone; a fortification

par•o•dy (păr′ ə dē) *n., pl.* -**dies** a humorous or satirical imitation of a certain piece of literature or writing

par•ti•cu•late (pər tĭk′ yə lĭt) *adj.* 1. of, or pertaining to or composed of, distinct particles −*n.* 2. a separate and distinct particle

pas•sé (pă′ sā) *adj.* no longer fashionable or in wide use; out of date

pas•to•ral (păs′ tər əl) *adj.* having the simplicity, charm, and serenity generally attributed to the countryside

pa•tri•ar•ch•y (pā′ trē är′ kē) *n., pl.* -**chies** a social organization in which the father is the supreme authority

1. Pronunciation Guide:

ă	sat	ŏ	lot	ə	represents
ā	day	ō	so		a in alone
ä	calm	o͞o	look		e in open
â	pare	o͞o	root		i in easily
ĕ	let	ô	ball		o in gallop
ē	me	ŭ	cut		u in circus
ĭ	sit	û	purr		
ī	lie				

2. Abbreviations: *n.*, noun; *v.*, verb; *adj.*, adjective; *pl.*, plural

---

Directions: Use the dictionary and the guides on the left to answer questions 9–13.

9 How should you spell the word that means "a substance used mostly in candles"?
  A parafin
✽ B paraffin
  C parrafin
  D parraffin

10 The *e* in *passé* sounds like the first *a* in
  J parapet.
  K pastoral.
✽ L patriarchy.
  M palpable.

11 How do the two pronunciations of *parapet* differ?
✽ A The *e* is pronounced differently.
  B The *t* is silent in one and not the other.
  C The first *a* is pronounced differently.
  D The accent is on different syllables.

12 What is the plural of *parody*?
  J parodes
  K parodys
✽ L parodies
  M parodosis

13 In which sentence is a form of the word *particulate* used correctly?
  A I am very particulate about keeping my room neat and tidy.
✽ B My father studies the particulates found in air pollution.
  C When giving a speech, it is important to be particulate.
  D No one can know about the particulates of my situation yet.

Answer rows   9 Ⓐ●ⒸⒹ   10 ⒿⓀ●Ⓜ   11 ●ⒷⒸⒹ   12 ⒿⓀ●Ⓜ   13 Ⓐ●ⒸⒹ

75

Lesson 16b
Reference Materials

Focus

Reference Skill
• using an index

Test-taking Skills
• working methodically
• comparing answer choices
• skimming a reference source
• referring to a reference source

Sample A

Say Turn to Lesson 16b on page 76. In this lesson you will practice using an index. Read the directions at the top of the page to yourself.

Allow time for the students to read the directions.

Say Look at the index and the question for Sample A. Which answer is correct? *(pause)* Yes, answer B is correct because this page talks about styles of fences. Mark circle B for Sample A in the answer rows at the bottom of the page. Make sure the circle is completely filled in. Press your pencil firmly so that your mark comes out dark.

Check to see that the students have filled in the correct answer circle.

⭐**TIPS**

Say Now let's look at the tip.

Have a volunteer read the tip aloud.

Say Don't spend too much time looking at a reference source. Just skim it and then look back at the reference source when you answer questions. You should also compare the answers to the reference source to decide which one is correct.

 Maps, Diagrams, and Reference Materials

Lesson 16b **Reference Materials**

Directions: Read each question. Choose the best answer.

Sample A fence
basket-weave, 29; gate on, 84; cleaning, 71; design of, 7, 47; extending an existing, 68-70; plywood, 29; repair, 75-77; styles of, 20-34

Which page would help you decide which style of fence you wanted?
A 7
✳ B 27
C 71
D 76

 • Skim the reference source. Look back at it to find the answer.

INDEX
Additions, 404-435; *diagrams*, 404-409; blueprint symbols, 405; foundations for, 404, 410-413; roofs for, 426; walls for, 419-425
Building codes, 130-147; and additions, 144-147; and new construction, 135-143
Cabinets, 234-238; *diagrams*, 236-237; installing, 234-236
Doors, 302-319; converting windows to, 310-314; insulating around, 315-317
Electricity, 270-299; *diagrams*, 272-277; ground fault circuit interrupt, 298; in the home, 278-283; outdoors, 284-292; safety, 270-271; wiring, 293-299
Flooring, 87-104; hardwood, 89-93; tile, 94-98; underlay, 99-101
Ground Fault Circuit Interrupt. *See* Electricity
Heating, 252-269; by baseboard, 254-256; forced-air system, 257-259; hot water system, 260-265; fireplaces, 266-268

This is part of an index from a book called *Home Repairs and Improvements*. Use the index to answer questions 1–3.

1 Which page would show you a diagram of a new room that was added onto an existing house?
A 146 ✳ C 404
B 236 D 410

2 Which page would tell you about ground fault circuit interrupts?
J 277 L 299
✳ K 298 M 314

3 Which page contains information about removing a window and replacing it with a door?
A 234 ✳ C 312
B 302 D 319

 STOP

76   Answer rows   A Ⓐ●ⒸⒹ   1 ⒶⒷ●Ⓓ   2 Ⓙ●ⓁⓂ   3 ⒶⒷ●Ⓓ

Practice

Say Let's do the Practice items now. Read the questions and answer choices carefully, and be sure to use the reference source to find the answers. Work until you come to the STOP sign at the bottom of the page. Remember to make sure that your answer circles are completely filled in with dark marks. Completely erase any marks for answers that you change. Any questions? Start working now.

Allow time for the students to mark their answers.

Say It's time to stop. You have finished Lesson 16b.

Review the answers with the students. If any questions caused particular difficulty, work through each of the answer choices.

Have the students indicate completion of the lesson by entering their score for this activity on the progress chart at the beginning of the book.

Maps, Diagrams, and Reference Materials

Lesson 16b **Reference Materials**

Directions: Read each question. Choose the best answer.

Sample A fence
basket-weave, 29; gate on, 84; cleaning, 71; design of, 7, 47; extending an existing, 68-70; plywood, 29; repair, 75-77; styles of, 20-34

Which page would help you decide which style of fence you wanted?
A 7
✳ B 27
C 71
D 76

• Skim the reference source. Look back at it to find the answer.

INDEX

Additions, 404-435; *diagrams*, 404-409; blueprint symbols, 405; foundations for, 404, 410-413; roofs for, 426; walls for, 419-425
Building codes, 130-147; and additions, 144-147; and new construction, 135-143
Cabinets, 234-238; *diagrams*, 236-237; installing, 234-236
Doors, 302-319; converting windows to, 310-314; insulating around, 315-317
Electricity, 270-299; *diagrams*, 272-277; ground fault circuit interrupt, 298; in the home, 278-283; outdoors, 284-292; safety, 270-271; wiring, 293-299
Flooring, 87-104; hardwood, 89-93; tile, 94-98; underlay, 99-101
Ground Fault Circuit Interrupt. *See* Electricity
Heating, 252-269; by baseboard, 254-256; forced-air system, 257-259; hot water system, 260-265; fireplaces, 266-268

This is part of an index from a book called *Home Repairs and Improvements*. Use the index to answer questions 1–3.

1 Which page would show you a diagram of a new room that was added onto an existing house?
A 146   ✳ C 404
B 236   D 410

2 Which page would tell you about ground fault circuit interrupts?
J 277   L 299
✳ K 298   M 314

3 Which page contains information about removing a window and replacing it with a door?
A 234   ✳ C 312
B 302   D 319

76   Answer rows   A ⒜●©ⓓ   1 ⒜Ⓑ●ⓓ   2 ⒥●ⓛⓜ   3 ⒜Ⓑ●ⓓ

Focus

Reference Skills
- using an index
- understanding a map
- using a chart
- using a dictionary
- using key words
- understanding the Dewey decimal classification system
- alphabetizing words or names
- differentiating among reference sources
- using an encyclopedia

Test-taking Skills
- managing time effectively
- following printed directions
- working methodically
- comparing answer choices
- eliminating answer choices
- referring to a reference source
- taking the best guess when unsure of the answer
- skimming a reference source
- skipping difficult items and returning to them later

Unit 9

Test Yourself:
Maps, Diagrams, and Reference Materials

Directions: Read each question. Choose the best answer.

Sample A

INDEX

Additions, 404–435; *diagrams,* 404–409; blueprint symbols, 405; foundations for, 404, 410–413; roofs for, 426; walls for, 419–425
Building codes, 130–147; and additions, 144–147; and new construction, 135–143

Which page would discuss how to build walls for an addition?
A 144
B 404
C 418
∗ D 420

Directions: This map shows an imaginary continent with several countries. Use the map to answer questions 1–3.

1 Which country does not share a border with Urtan?
A Pardy
B Liam
C North Ortis
∗ D South Ortis

2 If you were flying to the island from the south, which country would you fly over first?
J Kendar
∗ K Brinden
L Sauron
M Liam

3 The sun sets in the west. In which country would you have the best view of the sunset?
∗ A Sauron
B Pardy
C Urtan
D North Ortis

Answer rows   A ⒶⒷⒸ●   1 ⒶⒷⒸ●   2 ⓙ●ⓁⓂ   3 ●ⒷⒸⒹ

77

This lesson simulates an actual test-taking experience. Therefore it is recommended that the directions be read verbatim and that the suggested procedures and time allowances be followed.

Directions

Administration Time: approximately 40 minutes

Say Turn to the Test Yourself lesson on page 77.

Point out to the students that this Test Yourself lesson is timed like a real test, but that they will score it themselves to see how well they are doing. Remind the students to work quickly and not to spend too much time on any one item. Encourage them to compare their answers with the reference material and to take the best guess when they are unsure of the answer.

Say This lesson will check how well you learned the reference skills you practiced in other lessons. Remember to make sure that the circles for your answer choices are completely filled in. Press your pencil firmly so that your marks come out dark. Completely erase any answers that you change. Do not write anything except your answer choices in your books.

Look at the index and question for Sample A. What is the correct answer to the question? Mark the circle for your answer.

Allow time for the students to mark their answers.

Say The circle for answer D should have been filled in. If you chose another answer, erase yours and fill in circle D now.

Check to see that the students have marked the correct answer circle.

Say Now you will do more items. Do not spend too much time on any one question and pay attention to the directions for each section of the lesson. If you are not sure of an answer, take your best guess and mark the circle for the answer you think might be right. When you come to the GO sign at the bottom of a page, turn the page and continue working. Work until you come to the STOP sign at the bottom of page 83. When you have finished, you can check over your answers to this lesson. Then wait for the rest of the group to finish. Do you have any questions? You will have 35 minutes. Begin working now.

Allow 35 minutes.

Directions: The map below is a part of a larger map. Use this map to answer questions 4–8.

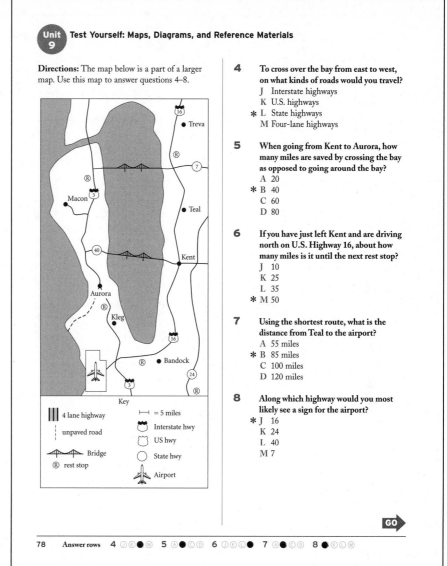

4   To cross over the bay from east to west, on what kinds of roads would you travel?
  J   Interstate highways
  K   U.S. highways
  * L   State highways
  M   Four-lane highways

5   When going from Kent to Aurora, how many miles are saved by crossing the bay as opposed to going around the bay?
  A   20
  * B   40
  C   60
  D   80

6   If you have just left Kent and are driving north on U.S. Highway 16, about how many miles is it until the next rest stop?
  J   10
  K   25
  L   35
  * M   50

7   Using the shortest route, what is the distance from Teal to the airport?
  A   55 miles
  * B   85 miles
  C   100 miles
  D   120 miles

8   Along which highway would you most likely see a sign for the airport?
  * J   16
  K   24
  L   40
  M   7

GO

Directions: This chart was made to help students who are studying endangered and threatened animal species. Use the chart to answer questions 9–15.

Group	Endangered		Threatened		Total	Recovery Plan
	U.S.	Foreign	U.S.	Foreign		
Mammals	56	252	7	16	331	39
Birds	75	178	15	6	274	74
Reptiles	14	65	18	14	111	30
Amphibians	9	8	7	1	25	11
Fish	65	11	40	—	119	74
Snails	15	1	7	—	23	18
Clams	56	2	6	—	64	44
Crustaceans	15	—	3	—	18	6
Insects	24	4	9	—	37	21
Arachnids	5	—	—	—	5	4

9 Of the animals that have the greatest numbers of endangered species, which has the fewest recovery plans?

✱A Mammals
B Birds
C Crustaceans
D Amphibians

10 Which group has endangered species in the U.S. but not anywhere else?

J Fish
K Clams
L Insects
✱M Arachnids

11 Which group has fewer endangered species in the U.S. than in other places?

✱A Reptiles
B Fish
C Snails
D Insects

12 How are the bird and fish groups similar?

J In the number of U.S. endangered species
K In the number of foreign threatened species numbers
L In the total number of endangered species
✱M In the number of recovery plans

13 Which of these groups is the most threatened?

✱A Mammals
B Amphibians
C Snails
D Arachnids

14 How many species of reptiles are threatened or endangered?

J 14
K 65
L 79
✱M 111

15 How is this chart organized?

A By animal size
B By country name
✱C By total listings
D By recovery plan

GO

Directions: The map below shows a continent and several islands on a planet like Earth. Use this map to answer questions 16–22.

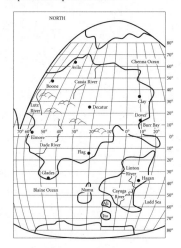

16 Which cities are probably located in different time zones?
J Clay and Dover
K Decatur and Flag
L Hagan and Clay
∗ M Elmore and Hagan

17 Where is the origin of the Dade River?
∗ A 15°N and 44°W
B 15°S and 54°E
C 54°S and 15°W
D 25°N and 40°E

18 When it is midnight in Flag, what time is it on the island of Namu?
J Noon
∗ K Midnight
L Three hours later
M Three hours earlier

19 Where is the point 55°S, 20°E located?
A Near Hagan
B On the island of Ali
∗ C In the Ladd Sea
D Near the island of Namu

20 Which of these probably has a climate most favorable for snow-related sporting activities?
J Clay
∗ K Avila
L Boone
M Glades

21 Which river flows northeast?
A Lutz
B Dade
C Linton
∗ D Cayuga

22 How many degrees north is Flag from Hagan?
∗ J About 25°
K About 35°
L About 45°
M About 100°

GO

Directions: At the top of each page in a dictionary, there are two *guide words*. They are the first and last words on that page of the dictionary. Use the guide words and page numbers below to answer questions 23–27.

ebullient	• echolocation	320
ecology	• ectoblast	321
ectoderm	• edutainment	322
Edwardian	• egocentric	323
egotism	• eightpenny	324

23   On which page would you find the word *Egypt*?
    A   321
    B   322
    C   323
  * D   324

24   On which page would you find the word *ecru*?
    J   320
  * K   321
    L   322
    M   323

25   On which page would you find the word *Ecuador*?
    A   320
    B   321
  * C   322
    D   323

26   On which page would you find the word *effigy*?
    J   320
    K   321
    L   322
  * M   323

27   On which page would you find the word *eddy*?
    A   321
  * B   322
    C   323
    D   324

Directions: Before you use certain reference materials, you need to decide exactly which word or phrase to use to find the information you want. We call this word or phrase the *key term*. In questions 28–30, select the best key term.

28   Which key term should you use to find information about Yuri Gagarin, the Russian cosmonaut who was the first person into space?
    J   Russian
    K   Person, first
    L   Cosmonaut
  * M   Gagarin, Yuri

29   Which key term should you use to find out how concrete is made from sand, lime, portland cement, and other ingredients?
    A   Ingredients, other
  * B   Concrete
    C   Lime
    D   Portland

30   A *glacier* is body of ice and snow that doesn't melt during the summer. Glaciers are found in mountain ranges and cold areas around the world. Which key term should you use to find pictures of a glacier?
    J   Regions, cold
    K   Ice and snow
  * L   Glacier
    M   Mountains

de•mean•or (dĭ mē´ nər) *n.* 1. conduct or behavior 2. facial appearance

de•mure (dĭ myŏŏr´) *adj.* characterized by shyness and modesty —*adv.* **demurely** —*n.* **demureness**

den•i•zen (dĕn´ ĭ zən) *n.* an inhabitant or resident, a person who goes somewhere frequently

de•plore (dĭ plôr, plōr´) *v.* 1. to regret deeply or strongly. 2. to disapprove of

de•scent (dĭ sĕnt´) *n.* a downward inclination or slope

di•ag•no•sis (dī əg nō´sĭs) *n., pl.* **-no•ses** the act of determining the nature of a disease or condition

di•dac•tic (dĭ dăc´ tĭk) *adj.* intended for instruction

di•plo•ma•t (dĭp´ lə măt) *n.* a person appointed by a national government to conduct official relations with another country —*adj.* **diplomatic** —*n.* **diplomacy**

1. Pronunciation Guide:

ă	sat	ŏ	lot	ə	represents
ā	day	ō	so	a	in alone
ä	calm	ŏŏ	look	e	in open
â	pare	ōō	root	i	in easily
ĕ	let	ô	ball	o	in gallop
ē	me	ŭ	cut	u	in circus
ĭ	sit	û	purr		
ī	lie				

2. Abbreviations: *n.*, noun; *v.*, verb; *adj.*, adjective; *pl.*, plural

Directions: Use the dictionary and the guides on the left to answer questions 31–36.

31 How should you spell the word that means "a person goes to the same place often"?
  A denizin
  B denezin
  C denezen
✱ D denizen

32 The first *e* in *descent* sounds like the
  J *y* in *diplomacy*.
  K *e* in *denizen*.
✱ L *e* in *deplore*.
  M *ea* in *demeanor*.

33 How do the two pronunciations of *deplore* differ?
  A The first *e* is pronounced differently.
✱ B The *o* is pronounced differently.
  C The second *e* is silent in one but not the other.
  D The accent is on different syllables.

34 What is the plural of *diagnosis*?
  J diagnosis
  K diagnosies
✱ L diagnoses
  M diagnoseses

35 Which word fits best in this sentence? "Kiersten spent several years in France when her father worked there as a foreign _____."
  A diplomacy
  B diplomatic
  C diploma
✱ D diplomat

36 Which word fits best in this sentence? "The kindergarten teacher had a warm and gentle _____ that attracted children."
✱ J demeanor
  K demure
  L diagnosis
  M didactic

GO

82   Answer rows   **31** Ⓐ Ⓑ Ⓒ ●   **33** Ⓐ ● Ⓒ Ⓓ   **35** Ⓐ Ⓑ Ⓒ ●
                   32 Ⓙ Ⓚ ● Ⓜ   **34** Ⓙ Ⓚ ● Ⓜ   **36** ● Ⓚ Ⓛ Ⓜ

Say It's time to stop. You have finished the Test Yourself lesson. Check to see that you have completely filled in your answer circles with dark marks. Make sure that any marks for answers that you changed have been completely erased.

Go over the lesson with the students. Ask them if they had enough time to finish the lesson. Did they remember to take their best guess when unsure of an answer? Did they refer to the reference sources to answer the questions?

Work through any questions that caused difficulty. If necessary, provide additional practice questions similar to the ones in this unit.

Have the students indicate completion of the lesson by entering their score for this activity on the progress chart at the beginning of the book.

 Unit 9 Test Yourself: Maps, Diagrams, and Reference Materials

Directions: The Dewey decimal classification system arranges nonfiction books in ten major categories according to subject. Use the categories below to answer questions 37–39.

000-099	**General works** (encyclopedias, magazines, newspapers)
100-199	**Philosophy** (psychology, ethics)
200-299	**Religion** (world religions, mythology)
300-399	**Social sciences** (customs, law, economics, government, education)
400-499	**Languages** (dictionaries, grammars)
500-599	**Pure sciences** (math, biology, chemistry, physics)
600-699	**Applied sciences** (medicines, business, engineering, farming, homemaking)
700-799	**Arts and recreation** (music, sports, painting, dance)
800-899	**Literature** (poetry, plays, essays)
900-999	**History** (biography, travel, geography)

37 How would a book about becoming a lawyer be categorized?
A Philosophy
B Religion
∗ C Social sciences
D Languages

38 Where would a book about important archeological discoveries be found?
J 000–099
K 300–399
L 600–699
∗ M 900–999

39 Where would the book *Heroes, Monsters, and Gods of the Ancient Greeks* be shelved?
A 000–099
B 100–199
∗ C 200–299
D 300–399

Directions: Questions 40–44 are about using library materials. Choose the best answer for each question.

40 Which of these would you use to find information on U.S. state capitol buildings?
J An index
K A thesaurus
L A book of quotations
∗ M An encyclopedia

41 Which of the following would most likely contain information about recent election results on the East Coast?
∗ A *U.S. News and World Report*
B *National Geographic*
C *Consumer Reports*
D *Sports Illustrated*

42 Where would you find information on average personal income for the people in different countries?
J In a topographical atlas
K In a history book
∗ L In an almanac
M In an autobiography

43 Which of these would you find in an anthology of essays?
∗ A A collection of nonfiction opinion pieces
B A list of songs arranged by genre
C The table of periodic elements
D A group of short stories

44 Which of these would help you find synonyms and antonyms for the word *whimsy*?
∗ J A thesaurus
K A newspaper
L An almanac
M An encyclopedia

 STOP

Answer rows   37 Ⓐ Ⓑ ● Ⓓ   39 Ⓐ Ⓑ ● Ⓓ   41 ● Ⓑ Ⓒ Ⓓ   43 ● Ⓑ Ⓒ Ⓓ   83
38 Ⓙ Ⓚ Ⓛ ●   40 Ⓙ Ⓚ Ⓛ ●   42 Ⓙ Ⓚ ● Ⓜ   44 ● Ⓚ Ⓛ Ⓜ

Unit 10

Background

This unit contains three lessons that deal with science skills.

• In Lessons 17a and 17b, students answer questions about science. They refer to a passage to answer questions and work methodically. Students analyze answer choices, identify and use key words, numbers and pictures, and eliminate answer choices.

• In the Test Yourself lesson, the science skills and test-taking skills introduced in Lessons 17a and 17b are reinforced and presented in a format that gives students the experience of taking an achievement test. Techniques for managing time effectively when taking a standardized test are reinforced.

Instructional Objectives

Lesson 17a	**Science Skills**	Given a question about science, the student identifies which of four answer choices is correct.
Lesson 17b	**Science Skills**	
	Test Yourself	Given questions similar to those in Lessons 17a and 17b, the student utilizes science skills and test-taking strategies on achievement test formats.

Focus

Science Skills
- recognizing states, properties, and composition of matter
- understanding plant and animal behaviors and characteristics
- understanding gravity, inertia, and friction
- understanding characteristics of bodies of water
- understanding scientific instruments, measurement, and processes
- understanding life cycles and reproduction
- understanding magnetism
- recalling characteristics and functions of the human body
- differentiating plants and animals
- understanding the history and language of science
- recalling characteristics of Earth and bodies in space
- using illustrations, charts, and graphs
- recognizing importance of environmentally sound practices

Test-taking Skills
- referring to a passage to answer questions
- working methodically
- analyzing answer choices

Samples A and B

Say Turn to Lesson 17a on page 84. In this lesson you will answer questions about science. Read the directions at the top of the page to yourself.

Allow time for the students to read the directions.

Say Look at Sample A and read the question. Which answer demonstrates that energy can change the physical state of matter? *(pause)* Answer D is correct because *the energy of sunlight causes solid ice to change to a liquid.*

Science
Lesson 17a **Science Skills**

Directions: Read each question. Choose the best answer.

Sample A Which of these demonstrates that energy can change the physical state of matter?
A Plants using carbon dioxide in photosynthesis
B Fire burning wood
C Rust developing on iron
∗ D Ice melting on a sunny day

Sample B The bright colors of some flowers help the flowers because they
J please humans.
∗ K attract insects.
L make food.
M absorb moisture.

TIPS
- If a passage is needed to answer a question, read it carefully. You might even want to write important information from the passage on scratch paper.
- Read the question and try to understand it. Think about the question while you look at the answer choices.

1 An example of gravity affecting matter in nature is
A a lightning strike hitting a tree.
B a leaf changing color in the fall.
∗ C a landslide.
D a pond freezing.

2 Stripes benefit zebras by helping them
∗ J hide from animals that prey on them.
K keep cool in hot weather.
L attract birds which eat the insects that bother the zebra.
M make other animals think they are dangerous.

GO

84   Answer rows   A Ⓐ Ⓑ Ⓒ ●   B Ⓙ ● Ⓛ Ⓜ   1 Ⓐ Ⓑ ● Ⓓ   2 ● Ⓚ Ⓛ Ⓜ

Mark circle D for Sample A in the answer rows at the bottom of the page. Make sure the circle is completely filled in. Press your pencil firmly so that your mark comes out dark.

Check to see that the students have filled in the correct answer circle.

Say Move over to Sample B. Read the question and answer choices. What is the correct answer to the question? *(pause)* Answer K is correct because colorful flowers *attract insects*. Mark circle K for Sample B in the answer rows at the bottom of the page. Make sure the circle is completely filled in. Press your pencil firmly so that your mark comes out dark.

Check to see that the students have filled in the correct answer circle. Review the answers to the sample items, if necessary.

Say Now let's look at the tips.

Have a volunteer read the tips aloud.

Say Sometimes a short passage appears on a science test. One or more items ask about information in the passage. It is important that you read the passage before trying to answer the questions that are about it. You might even want to write important information from the passage on scratch paper so you will remember it. And when you read a question, do your best to understand it. Think about the question while you look at the answer choices and pick the answer that makes the most sense with the question.

Practice

Say Let's do the Practice items now. Read the questions and answer choices carefully. Be sure to read the passage that relates to some items. When you come to the GO sign at the bottom of a page, continue working. Work until you come to the STOP sign at the bottom of page 89. Remember to make sure that your answer circles are completely filled in with dark marks. Completely erase any marks for answers that you change. Any questions? Start working now.

Allow time for the students to mark their answers.

 Unit 10 Lesson 17a **Science Skills**

3 What causes streams to move faster or slower?
  A Decreases in the number of fish in the stream
  B Variations in the direction that the wind is blowing
  C Increases in the magnetic field near the stream
  * D Changes in the slope of the ground under the stream

4 Some people have garden soil that is too acidic. They add lime to the soil to reduce the acidity. This suggests that
  J all plants grow better when lime is added to the soil.
  * K some plants don't grow well in acidic soil.
  L lime makes plants a greener color.
  M vegetable plants add their own lime to the soil.

5 Two geraniums are in pots next to one another. One of them has red flowers and the other one has white flowers. If neither red flowers nor white flowers are a dominant trait over the other, what will happen if the two plants are crossbred?
  A The flowers of the offspring will all be red.
  B The flowers of the offspring will all be white.
  * C The flowers of the offspring will all be pink.
  D There will not be any flowers in the offspring.

6 Which tool can best be used to separate plastic paperclips from metal ones in a container with a mixture of both?
  J Tweezers
  * K A magnet
  L Tape
  M A computer

7 Which of these is most helpful in forming clots in blood?
  * A Platelets
  B White blood cells
  C Antibiotics
  D DNA

 GO

Answer rows   3 ⒶⒷⒸ●   4 Ⓙ●ⓁⓂ   5 ⒶⒷ●Ⓓ   6 Ⓙ●ⓁⓂ   7 ●ⒷⒸⒹ   85

Directions: Use this information to answer questions 8 and 9.

Don was experimenting with a chocolate chip cookie recipe. He used half of the baking powder the recipe called for, but followed the recipe exactly in every other way. When the cookies were done, they were much flatter and more crisp than another batch he had made when he followed the recipe and used the full amount of baking powder.

8   Why might Don want to repeat what he had done even if he doesn't want his cookies to be flat and crisp?
* ∗ J   To see if he gets the same results again
  K   To make sure the oven temperature was different
  L   To see if he measured the flour incorrectly
  M   To try a different cookie tray

9   If Don has only half of the correct amount of baking powder but wants his cookies to turn out plump and chewy, what should he do?
  A   Use just half of all of the other ingredients, and cut the cooking time in half.
  B   Use the same amounts of other ingredients that the recipe calls for, but cut the cooking time in half.
* ∗ C   Use just half of all of the other ingredients and use the same cooking time.
  D   Double all of the other ingredients to make up for the lack of baking powder.

10   If a living thing makes its own food, it is probably a
* ∗ J   plant.
  K   vertebrate.
  L   amphibian.
  M   fish.

11   Which of these does <u>not</u> describe the action of a force?
  A   A book falling over when a person bumps it
  B   A person dropping a book on the floor
  C   A person turning the pages of a book
* ∗ D   A book resting on a table

12   Cora and Willie saw the sun set behind the ocean. Then they ran up a hill behind the beach. From where they were standing, the sun still hadn't completely set. What did this demonstrate?
  J   Gravity was bending the rays of light.
  K   Sunlight was being reflected off the surface of the water.
* ∗ L   The surface of Earth is curved.
  M   You can see the sun through the water.

GO ➜

Directions: Use the information below to answer questions 13–16.

Susan noticed that cars traveling past her house went faster at certain times of the day. She recorded the speeds of the cars at four different times of day and calculated the average of these speeds for each time of day. She also recorded the length of time it took for fifty cars to go past her house. The results appear in the table below.

Time of Day	Average Speed (mph)	Elapsed Time for 50 Cars to Pass
8:00 A.M.	20	8 minutes
12:00 noon	30	23 minutes
4:00 P.M.	27	20 minutes
10:00 P.M.	35	30 minutes

13 **What was changed on purpose so its effect could be studied?**
* A The time of day the speeds were measured
  B The average speeds of the cars
  C The number of cars that passed Susan's house
  D The length of time it took for fifty cars to pass Susan's house

14 **What is the reason for recording the length of time it took for fifty cars to go by the house?**
* J To see if the number of cars on the road affected speed
  K To make sure that cars were slower in the morning
  L To see if it took longer for cars to reach high speed
  M To predict how fast cars will be at any given time of day

15 **At what time of day did the cars travel past Susan's house the most quickly?**
  A 8:00 A.M.
  B 12:00 noon
  C 4:00 P.M.
* D 10:00 P.M.

16 **What conclusion can be made with Susan's data?**
  J Cars go faster in the daytime.
  K When more cars are on the road, they travel faster.
* L The greatest number of cars passed the house at 8:00 A.M.
  M A higher speed limit will affect how many cars pass the house.

17 Over a long time, birds learned to migrate to follow food sources. This is an example of

* A adaptation.
B reproduction.
C digestion.
D erosion.

18 Why is it better to recycle plastic rather than to put it in a landfill?

J Plastic breaks down fairly easily into its raw materials.
K When plastic is in a landfill, it is more likely to burn and cause toxic fumes in the air.
L Plastic is an essential byproduct of living things.
* M It takes less energy to make new plastic from old plastic than raw materials.

19 Which is most responsible for a balloon bursting?

A Temperature
B Mass
* C Pressure
D Gravity

20 In a canyon, the oldest layers of rock are usually found

* J near the bottom.
K near the top.
L halfway up the canyon wall.
M wherever the plant life is least abundant.

21 An animal that scavenges for food on the bottom of the ocean

* A usually blends into its surroundings.
B requires very sharp teeth to eat its food.
C has no natural enemies.
D is very fast so it can catch food more easily.

GO

Say It's time to stop. You have finished Lesson 17a.

Review the answers with the students. If any questions caused particular difficulty, work through each of the answer choices. Check to be sure that the students read the passages needed to answer some of the items.

Have the students indicate completion of the lesson by entering their score for this activity on the progress chart at the beginning of the book.

Directions: Use the information below to answer questions 22–25.

A scientist thought she had discovered a substance that could lessen a person's reaction to a mosquito bite. She used thirty subjects who had recently been bitten by mosquitoes and measured the size of the welts the bites had created.

She gave ten of the subjects a paste containing the substance, and they applied it to the mosquito bite. A second group of ten subjects applied a similar paste without the substance. The third group received no treatment. After one hour, she measured the size of each welt. She found that the size of the welts had decreased in seven of the ten people who had received the substance in the paste, and that only one out of the ten people in each of the other two groups showed a decrease in the size of their welts.

22 **Why did the scientist give one group of subjects the paste without the substance?**

  J To show that the paste could lessen a welt even if it didn't contain the substance

  K To show that the paste did not contain something that would increase the size of the welts

  L To show that a reaction to a mosquito bite can lessen over time

  * M To show that the reaction was lessened by the substance and not the paste it was in

23 **Why did the scientist measure the welts before she had the subjects apply the paste?**

  A To help her decide which group to put the subjects in

  * B So she could measure a change in the size of the welts after treatment

  C To be sure every mosquito bite made the same size welt

  D In order to determine how long it had been since the person had been bitten

24 **Of the ten subjects who received the substance in the paste, three did not show a decrease in the size of their mosquito bite welts. What should the scientist do about these results?**

  J Repeat the study, only give these subjects the paste without the substance.

  K Repeat the study, but increase the length of time between application of the paste and measurement of the welts.

  * L Examine other factors that might account for the results.

  M Ignore the results from these subjects.

25 **Suppose the size of the welts did not decrease after an hour in any of the scientist's subjects. What should she do?**

  A Have them apply more paste but only if they were in the group that applied the paste with the substance in it.

  B Start over again and measure the size of the welts after half an hour.

  C Start over again and use twice the amount of the substance in the paste.

  * D Wait another hour and measure the size of the welts again.

Focus

Science Skills
- recognizing states, properties, and composition of matter
- understanding plant and animal behaviors and characteristics
- understanding electricity and circuits
- classifying things based on characteristics
- understanding scientific instruments, measurement, and processes
- using illustrations, charts, and graphs
- recognizing forms, sources, and principles of energy
- understanding properties of light
- recognizing chemical changes
- understanding characteristics of bodies of water
- recalling characteristics of Earth and bodies in space
- recalling characteristics and functions of the human body

Test-taking Skills
- identifying and using key words, numbers, and pictures
- eliminating answer choices

Samples A and B

Say Turn to Lesson 17b on page 90. In this lesson you will answer more questions about science. Read the directions at the top of the page to yourself.

Allow time for the students to read the directions.

Say Look at Sample A and read the question. How is water different from many other substances? (pause) **Answer B is correct.** Water *expands as it cools.* Mark circle B for Sample A in the answer rows at the bottom of the page. Make sure the circle is completely filled in. Press your pencil firmly so that your mark comes out dark.

Unit 10
Science
Lesson 17b **Science Skills**

Directions: Read each question and the answer choices. Choose the best answer.

Sample A Water is different from many substances because it	**Sample B** Which of these birds is a scavenger rather than a predator?
A has three physical forms.	J An owl
✳ B expands as it cools.	✳ K A vulture
C feels cold rather than warm.	L A hawk
D dissolves other substances.	M An osprey

TIPS
- Look for important words in the question and answer choices. These key words are especially important in science.
- Eliminate answer choices that don't make sense with the question.

1 A lightning rod protects structures. What is a lightning rod made of?
- ✳ A A conductor
- B A battery
- C A circuit
- D A vacuum

2 Which of the following is true about most reptiles?
- J The mother carries the babies inside a pouch.
- K Babies are born full-sized.
- ✳ L A reptile has many babies at one time.
- M Babies are cared for by their parents for a long period of time.

GO

90   Answer rows A Ⓐ●ⒸⒹ B Ⓙ●ⓁⓂ 1 ●ⒷⒸⒹ 2 ⒥Ⓚ●Ⓜ

Check to see that the students have filled in the correct answer circle.

Say Move over to Sample B. Read the question and answer choices. What is the correct answer to the question? (pause) **Answer K is correct.** *A vulture* is a scavenger, not a predator. Mark circle K for Sample B in the answer rows at the bottom of the page. Make sure the circle is completely filled in. Press your pencil firmly so that your mark comes out dark.

Check to see that the students have filled in the correct answer circle. Review the answers to the sample items, if necessary.

Say Now let's look at the tips.

Have a volunteer read the tips aloud.

Say Read the question and answer choices carefully. Look at every word, especially important words that might cause you to misunderstand a question. For some items, you may be able to eliminate answer choices you know are wrong.

Practice

Say Let's do the Practice items now. Read each question carefully. Look for key words in the question. When you come to the GO sign at the bottom of a page, continue working. Work until you come to the STOP sign at the bottom of page 95. Remember to make sure that your answer circles are completely filled in with dark marks. Completely erase any marks for answers that you change. Any questions? Start working now.

Allow time for the students to mark their answers.

 Unit 10 Lesson 17b **Science Skills**

Directions: Use the information below to answer questions 3–7.

While on a backpacking trip, Dale noticed that water heated to the boiling point faster on some days than on others. He decided to heat exactly one quart of water to its boiling point at his next three campsites, using the same camp stove and pan at each site. He made sure that the starting temperature of the water was the same at each site. He timed how long it took the water to boil at each site and recorded the elevation. His results are given in the table below.

Altitude	Time to Boil
3000 feet	15 minutes
4000 feet	12 minutes
5000 feet	10 minutes

3 **What question was Dale asking in his experiment?**
  A How can water be made to boil more quickly?
* B Does water boil more quickly at different altitudes?
  C What makes water boil?
  D Does water boil at different temperatures on different days?

4 **What did Dale change on purpose to see his results?**
  J The time of day he was conducting his experiment
  K The amount of water he used
  L The heat setting on the camp stove
* M The altitude at which he was boiling water

Answer rows   3 Ⓐ ● Ⓒ Ⓓ   4 Ⓙ Ⓚ Ⓛ ●   91

---

5 Based on the results, which of these is the best conclusion about the effects of altitude on the time it takes to boil water?

∗ A Water boils faster at higher altitudes.

B Water boils faster at lower altitudes.

C Altitude does not affect how long it takes to boil water.

D Water boils at a higher temperature at a higher altitude.

6 Dale also noticed that bubbles formed in the water more quickly along the sides of the pan than they did in the middle. Why is this?

J The water nearest the side of the pan was cooler.

K The pan created a magnetic field in the water.

L Water molecules in contact with the pan have greater friction.

∗ M The side of the pan conducted more heat to the water.

7 Suppose Dale changed the pot on one of the days. How will his results be changed?

A The water will boil more slowly.

B The water will boil at a higher temperature.

C The water will boil more evenly.

∗ D There is too little information to say.

8 The energy in the sun comes mostly from

J chemical reactions.

K an enormous magnetic field.

∗ L changes in the nuclei of atoms.

M the burning of a gas.

9 How does a telescope work?

A It divides rays of light.

B It absorbs rays of light.

∗ C It bends rays of light.

D It reflects rays of light.

 GO

Directions: Use the following information to answer questions 10–13.

Meredith purchased two identical philodendron plants and made sure each pot contained the same amount of soil. She placed one plant in a windowless basement room of her house and set it under a growing light. She placed the other plant on a sunny window sill. She was very careful to turn the growing light on at exactly sunrise every day and to turn it off at sunset. Each plant received the same amount of water at the same time, and the same amount of plant food. She measured each plant once a week for six weeks. The results are in the chart below.

Week	Height of Plant Under Lamp	Height of Plant in Sun
1	9.0 inches	10.0 inches
2	9.8 inches	11.1 inches
3	10.6 inches	11.9 inches
4	11.5 inches	12.9 inches
5	12.6 inches	14.0 inches
6	13.5 inches	15.2 inches

10 **Which question was this experiment designed to answer?**
J Do plants growing in sunlight need more water?
∗ K Do plants grow faster in natural or artificial light?
L Do plants exposed to a growing light need more food?
M Does plant food make a difference in how fast a plant grows?

11 **Why did Meredith turn on the growing light at sunrise and off at sunset?**
A Because the growing lamp got hot if it stayed on all of the time
B So that the leaves of the plant would not turn brown
C She thought it might help that plant grow straighter
∗ D So that each plant would be exposed to the same amount of light

12 **After week 2, Meredith realized that the basement room was cooler than the room where the other plant was being kept. She adjusted the thermostat of the basement room so that both rooms were the same temperature. How did this change affect her results?**
∗ J There is too little information to say.
K The plant in the cooler room grew faster.
L Temperature does not make a difference.
M Cooler temperatures cause plants to give off more gas.

13 **If one of these situations had occurred, which would have had the greatest effect on Meredith's results?**
A If she had used ivy plants instead of philodendrons
B If she had only measured the plants every two weeks
∗ C If she had given one plant more water than the other
D If she had taken measurements for two more weeks

Answer rows **10** Ⓙ ● Ⓛ Ⓜ **11** Ⓐ Ⓑ Ⓒ ● **12** ● Ⓚ Ⓛ Ⓜ **13** Ⓐ Ⓑ ● Ⓓ

14 **What causes iron to rust?**
  J Dust in the air coats the iron.
  *K Oxygen in the air combines with the iron.
  L The outer layer of iron decays to form the rust.
  M Sunlight damages the iron.

15 **People float in the ocean more easily than in fresh water because**
  *A the salt in the water makes floating easier.
  B the warmer water in the ocean makes floating easier.
  C they are swimming faster than they would be in a pool.
  D magnetic forces in the floor of the ocean push up on them.

16 **What might indicate that an earthquake is about to occur?**
  J Bodies of water in the area become calmer.
  *K Movement is detected under the surface of Earth.
  L A humidity gauge suddenly has a very high reading.
  M A string of severe thunderstorms hits the area.

17 **Which type of pan would a chef not want to use if she wanted to heat water on a stove?**
  *A Plastic
  B Glass
  C Iron
  D Copper

18 **Which helps to transport oxygen to all of the cells in the body?**
  J Strands of DNA
  K Lymph nodes
  *L Hemoglobin
  M White blood cells

GO

94   **Answer rows**   14 ⓙ ● ⓛ Ⓜ   15 ● Ⓑ ⓒ ⓓ   16 ⓙ ● ⓛ Ⓜ   17 ● Ⓑ ⓒ ⓓ   18 ⓙ Ⓚ ● Ⓜ

Say It's time to stop. You have finished Lesson 17b.

Review the answers with the students. If any questions caused particular difficulty, work through each of the answer choices. Review some of the key words in the questions.

Have the students indicate completion of the lesson by entering their score for this activity on the progress chart at the beginning of the book.

 Lesson 17b **Science Skills**

19 Which of these is <u>not</u> a form of energy?
A Heat
B Light
✳C Rain
D Electricity

20 How do spots help leopards living in a rainforest?
✳J They prevent the leopards from being seen by animals they are hunting.
K They keep the leopards cooler
L They allow young leopards to be seen by their mothers more easily.
M They help the leopards to survive in the low sunlight of the rainforest.

21 What happens when ocean waves reach shallow water?
A The sand absorbs the water.
✳B The waves break at the surface.
C The beach causes the waves to bend.
D The wind reduces the power of the waves.

22 Which of these is a form of a leaf?
J An apple
K A pine cone
L A kernel of corn
✳M A cactus spine

23 What shows that the surface of Earth is curved?
A Rocks roll down a hill.
B Tornadoes spin in circles.
C There are more hours of daylight in the summertime.
✳D You see more of a mountain as you get closer to it.

Answer rows 19 Ⓐ Ⓑ ● Ⓓ 20 ● Ⓚ Ⓛ Ⓜ 21 Ⓐ ● Ⓒ Ⓓ 22 Ⓙ Ⓚ Ⓛ ● 23 Ⓐ Ⓑ Ⓒ ●   95

Unit 10 Test Yourself: Science

Focus

Science Skills
- understanding characteristics of bodies of water
- understanding plant and animal behaviors and characteristics
- understanding magnetism
- recalling characteristics of Earth and bodies in space
- differentiating plants and animals
- understanding gravity, inertia, and friction
- understanding scientific instruments, measurement, and processes
- understanding form and function
- understanding weather, climate, and seasons
- using illustrations, charts, and graphs
- understanding life cycles and reproduction
- understanding the history and language of science
- understanding electricity and circuits
- recalling characteristics and functions of the human body

Test-taking Skills
- managing time effectively
- referring to a passage to answer questions
- working methodically
- analyzing answer choices
- identifying and using key words, numbers, and pictures
- eliminating answer choices

This lesson simulates an actual test-taking experience. Therefore it is recommended that the directions be read verbatim and that the suggested procedures and time allowances be followed.

Unit 10 Test Yourself: Science

Test Yourself: Science

Directions: Read each question and the answer choices. Choose the best answer.

Sample A Which of these statements about the ocean is true?
- A Only some oceans are salty.
- *B Ocean waves are caused mostly by wind.
- C It never gets cold enough for oceans to freeze.
- D Each ocean is completely surrounded by land.

Sample B Where do plants get their energy?
- J From moisture in the air
- K From minerals in the ground
- L From the wind
- *M From the sun

1 Which of the following statements about magnetism is true?
- A A magnet doesn't work in space.
- *B A magnet can lose its magnetism.
- C A magnet will attract plastic.
- D A magnet makes plants grow better.

2 Why are areas around the equator warmer than other parts of Earth?
- J The plants near the equator generate more heat than do plants in other places.
- *K The sun strikes the equator more directly than other areas.
- L There is more water around the equator.
- M The force of gravity is strongest at the equator.

3 What can a mouse do that a sunflower cannot?
- A Make its own food
- B Live without air
- C Produce offspring
- *D Move on its own

4 Which of these is an example of a force?
- *J Gravity
- K Temperature
- L Mass
- M Length

GO

96   Answer rows   A Ⓐ●ⒸⒹ B ⒿⓀⓁ● 1 Ⓐ●ⒸⒹ 2 Ⓙ●ⓁⓂ 3 ⒶⒷⒸ● 4 ●ⓀⓁⓂ

Directions

Administration Time: approximately 50 minutes

Say Turn to the Test Yourself lesson on page 96.

Point out to the students that this Test Yourself lesson is timed like a real test, but that they will score it themselves to see how well they are doing. Remind the students to work quickly and not to spend too much time on any one item.

Say This lesson will check how well you learned the science skills you practiced in other lessons. Remember to make sure that the circles for your answer choices are completely filled in. Press your pencil firmly so that your marks come out dark. Completely erase any answers that you change. Do not write anything except your answer choices in your books.

Look at Sample A. Read the question and answer choices. Mark the circle for the answer you think is correct.

Allow time for the students to mark their answers.

Say The circle for answer B should have been marked. If you chose another answer, erase yours and fill in circle B now.

Check to see that the students have marked the correct answer circle.

Say Move over to Sample B. Read question and answer choices. Mark the circle for the answer you think is correct.

Allow time for the students to mark their answers.

Say The circle for answer M should have been marked. If you chose another answer, erase yours and fill in circle M now.

Check to see that the students have marked the correct answer circle.

Say Now you will do more items. Do not spend too much time on any one question and pay attention to the directions. If you are not sure of an answer, take your best guess. Mark the circle for the answer you think might be right. When you come to the GO sign at the bottom of a page, continue working. Work until you come to the STOP sign at the bottom of page 105. When you have finished, you can check over your answers to this lesson. Then wait for the rest of the group to finish. Do you have any questions? You will have 45 minutes. Begin working now.

Allow 45 minutes.

 Unit 10 **Test Yourself: Science**

Directions: Use the information below to answer questions 5 and 6.

Nancy was making paste out of flour and water so that she could put up some wallpaper. She added two tablespoons of flour to one cup of water according to some instructions she had researched on the Internet. She mixed them and applied the paste to the wallpaper with a brush. She put up the wallpaper and allowed the paste to dry. After two days, the wallpaper fell off of the wall.

5 Why might Nancy want to repeat what she had done?
 A To try a different brand of flour
 B To try a different brush
 C To see if she measured the water incorrectly
* D To see if she gets the same results again

6 If Nancy wants to find out how the proportion of flour in the paste affects the ability of the paste to glue on wallpaper, what should she do?
* J Double the amount of flour only.
 K Double the amount of both the flour and the water.
 L Use half the amount of both the flour and the water.
 M Use half the amount of flour and double the amount of water.

7 Which of the following is true about most mammals?
 A A mammal has many babies at one time.
 B Mammals leave their babies soon after birth.
* C A baby mammal is much smaller than its parents.
 D The father carries the babies inside a pouch.

8 Some people like to run with snowshoes in the winter. How do snowshoes help a runner?
 J The weight of the snowshoes keeps the runner from falling.
* K The snowshoes keep the runner from sinking into the snow.
 L The snowshoes reduce the force of gravity on the runner's legs.
 M The snowshoes keep the runner's feet completely dry.

9 What might indicate that a hurricane is about to occur?
* A A large change in air pressure
 B Radiation from the sun increases
 C Movement under the surface of Earth
 D A full moon

GO

Answer rows 5   6   7  8   9   97

Directions: Use the information below to answer questions 10–13.

Carmen wanted to find out whether subjects could run faster after a large meal or after a small one. She had fourteen people run 400 meters around the track at her school and recorded how long it took each one to complete the distance. She gave seven of them a large meal of steak, potatoes with sour cream, and green beans. She gave the other seven a small salad topped with chunks of chicken and cheese and a slice of bread. After an hour, she had each subject run again. Of the seven subjects who had eaten a large meal, only one ran a faster lap, while four of the seven subjects who had eaten the smaller meal ran a faster lap.

10 **Which question was the experiment designed to answer?**
   J Do people need food from the four basic food groups to run fast?
✳ K Does the size of a meal a person eats affect running speed?
   L Is an hour after a meal long enough to wait before running fast?
  M Do people run faster one at a time or in a group?

11 **What is the most likely reason for having the subjects run before they eat?**
   A To give people a chance to warm up before eating
   B To make sure each one could run 400 meters
✳ C To find out how fast each person ran before eating
   D To put all of the fastest runners in the same group

12 **Which of these did Carmen probably do to be sure her study was fair?**
   J Cheer for all the runners
   K Make the fastest runners carry some weight
   L Put the slowest runners in one group
✳ M Assign people randomly to each group

13 **Which change to this experiment would make the results more difficult to interpret?**
✳ A Making one group of subjects run two laps
   B Having subjects run on an indoor 200 meter track
   C Letting subjects wait only half an hour after eating to run
   D Waiting for a rainy day to perform the experiment

Directions: Use the information below to answer questions 14–17.

Paul was observing the length of time it took for four trees of different varieties in his yard to lose their leaves after they began to change color in the autumn. He noted the date each tree began to have leaves that were changing color. He then recorded the number of days it took for all the leaves from each tree to fall to the ground. His results are listed in the table below.

Tree Type	Date of First Color Change	Number of Days for Leaves to Fall
Oak	September 30	46
Elm	September 25	35
Maple	October 2	32
Sycamore	September 27	36

14 **What was compared so its effect could be studied?**
* J The tree type
K The date Paul began checking for color changes
L The length of time it took for 100 leaves to fall from each tree
M The number of leaves to fall

15 **What could Paul have done to increase the confidence people would have in his results?**
A Record the time as well as date the leaves first changed color.
B Measure the temperature each day.
* C Observe several of each kind of tree.
D Count the number of leaves on each tree.

16 **Which type of tree lost its leaves the most quickly?**
J Oak
K Elm
L Sycamore
* M Maple

17 **Which of these conclusions can be made with Paul's data?**
A More leaves fall off of trees in September than any other time of year.
B Sycamore trees have more leaves than maple trees.
* C The elm tree was the first to show a color change.
D The maple tree was the first to lose all its leaves.

18 A fossil of an animal that has segmented body parts has been found. Which type of animal most likely made the fossil?

  J A fish

  K A bird

✱ L An insect

  M A mammal

19 What happens to plants after they die?

✱ A They break down and become nutrients for new plants.

  B A new plant sprouts out of the stem of some of the plants.

  C They need to be put in a landfill quickly because they cause disease.

  D Their leaves roll up, become seeds, and grow into new plants.

20 Which is most responsible for an apple falling from a tree?

  J Magnetism

✱ K Gravity

  L Pressure

  M Friction

21 Over thousands of years, a river may form a canyon. This is an example of

  A respiration.

  B evacuation.

  C adaptation.

✱ D erosion.

22 An animal that hunts zebras for food

  J is often brightly colored.

✱ K needs to run quickly.

  L has flat teeth for grinding.

  M does not need very good eyesight.

GO ▶

Directions: Use the information below to answer questions 23–26.

Two scientists thought they had discovered a substance that strengthened rubber. They tested their theory with the following experiment.

Out of a package of thirty balloons, fifteen were dipped into the substance and were then inflated from a helium tank with a pressure gauge. The other fifteen were inflated without having the substance applied to them. The scientists timed how long it took from when inflation of a balloon began until the balloon burst. Of the fifteen balloons that had been dipped in the substance, twelve still had not ruptured after ten seconds of inflation. Only five of the undipped balloons were still intact after ten seconds.

23 Which factor was purposefully changed so its effects could be observed?
A   The color of the balloons
B   The length of time it took for a balloon to burst
C   The number of balloons used in the study
∗ D   The application of the substance

24 Suppose none of the balloons in either group had burst after ten seconds of inflation time. What should the scientists do?
J   Repeat the study and apply a thicker layer of the substance to the balloons.
∗ K   Increase the inflation time to fifteen seconds.
L   Get a larger package of balloons.
M   Decrease the pressure of the helium in the tank.

25 What should the scientists do about the three balloons that were dipped in the substance and ruptured before ten seconds of inflation had occurred?
A   These results were mistakes and should be ignored.
B   Conduct the study again using fewer balloons.
∗ C   Explore other things besides pressure that cause balloons to burst.
D   Conduct the study again, but use carbon dioxide instead of helium gas.

26 One of the scientists thought that the white balloons took longer to burst than any other color of balloon. How can the experiment be changed to make balloon color less of a factor?
J   Dip the white balloons into the substance.
∗ K   Use only white balloons.
L   Inflate white balloons at a higher pressure.
M   Inflate the white balloons for seven seconds.

Answer rows   23 Ⓐ Ⓑ Ⓒ ●   24 Ⓙ ● Ⓛ Ⓜ   25 Ⓐ Ⓑ ● Ⓓ   26 Ⓙ ● Ⓛ Ⓜ   101

Directions: Use the information below to answer questions 27–30.

A group of forest rangers was given the task of counting the number of deer in four different herds within the same national park. The rangers noted the number of deer in each herd and also counted the number of berry bushes within a quarter of a mile radius of where the herd was located. Their findings are given in the table below.

Herd	Number of Deer	Number of Berry Bushes
1	27	27
2	35	22
3	17	30
4	40	54

27 Which question are the rangers most likely asking?
A Does it take a whole berry bush to feed one deer?
B Can data about this park show conditions in other parks?
C Do berry bushes tend to grow where there are deer?
∗ D Is the number of deer related to the number of berry bushes?

28 What, if anything, was changed so its effects could be studied?
J The national park in which the study was conducted
K How many deer lived in a quarter mile radius
L Which area of the park each herd occupied
∗ M Nothing was varied in this study

29 Based on the results in the table, what is the best conclusion that can be reached about the numbers of deer and berry bushes in this park?
∗ A There seems to be no relationship between the deer and berry bushes.
B Berry bushes grow larger when there are more deer in the area.
C When there are more deer in an area, there will be more berry bushes.
D Large herds of deer seem to cause fewer berry bushes.

30 What is the next step that the scientists who thought of this study will probably consider?
J Do the deer like the flavor of the berries on the bushes?
K Will more rain increase the number of berry bushes?
∗ L Is something else affecting the size of deer herds?
M Did the rangers do a good job counting the deer and bushes?

31 What can a deer do that a frog cannot?
A Blend into its surroundings
B Move to a new area if food becomes scarce
* C Regulate its own body temperature
D Live without water

32 Which of these is <u>not</u> a force?
J Gravity
K Friction
* L Mass
M Magnetism

33 Which of these organisms usually produces offspring with exactly the same genes?
A A dog
B A rosebush
* C A bacterium
D A worm

34 Which of these rods will best direct an electrical current into the ground?
* J Iron
K Glass
L Plastic
M Wooden

35 Which of these is made up of nucleotides that form the genetic code to make a new cell?
A Plasma
* B DNA
C Red blood cells
D White blood cells

 GO

Answer rows **31** Ⓐ Ⓑ ● Ⓓ **32** Ⓙ Ⓚ ● Ⓜ **33** Ⓐ Ⓑ ● Ⓓ **34** ● Ⓚ Ⓛ Ⓜ **35** Ⓐ ● Ⓒ Ⓓ   103

36 **Which of these is an example of how energy can change the state of matter?**
* J A pan of water on a stove begins to boil.
  K Leaves turn color in the fall.
  L Waves move sand on a beach
  M Ice forms on a highway and makes cars skid.

37 **Why are some male fish brightly colored?**
  A Bright colors keep the fish warmer than dull colors.
  B They cannot be seen as easily by bigger fish that hunt them.
  C Fish remove oxygen from water with their gills.
* D Bright colors attract mates more easily.

38 **An animal that has no natural enemies**
  J is usually very large.
  K can outrun anything that might hunt it.
  L only moves around at night.
* M is not eaten by other animals.

Directions: Use the information below to answer questions 39 and 40.

Dorothy wanted to make a pot of tea. She boiled one quart of water and poured it into a teapot that had a teabag in it. After exactly two minutes, she removed the teabag from the pot and tasted her tea. It was very weak.

39 **Which of these probably has the <u>least</u> effect on the strength of the tea Dorothy made?**
* A The kind of teapot she used
  B The kind of tea she used
  C The amount of water she used
  D The length of time the teabag was in the water

40 **Dorothy discovers that she has only one teabag left. What should she change about her tea formula so that she will have tea she might like better than the first pot?**
  J Use half the amount of water and remove the teabag after one minute.
  K Use more water to make up for the lack of tea.
* L Use half the amount of water and remove the teabag after two minutes.
  M Use twice the amount of water and remove the teabag after one minute.

GO

Say It's time to stop. You have finished the Test Yourself lesson. Check to see that you have completely filled in your answer circles with dark marks. Make sure that any marks for answers that you changed have been completely erased.

Go over the lesson with the students. Ask them if they had enough time to finish the lesson. Did they read the questions and answer choices carefully? Did they compare their answer with the other choices to be sure it was correct?

Work through any questions that caused difficulty. If necessary, provide additional practice questions similar to the ones in this unit.

Have the students indicate completion of the lesson by entering their score for this activity on the progress chart at the beginning of the book.

 Unit 10 **Test Yourself: Science**

41 How is a skunk different from a lilac bush?
  A A skunk can make its own food.
  * B A skunk breathes oxygen.
  C A lilac bush can live without water.
  D A lilac bush produces offspring.

42 What causes a lunar eclipse?
  * J The moon passes through Earth's shadow.
  K Earth passes through the moon's shadow.
  L The moon passes through the sun's shadow.
  M The sun passes through the moon's shadow.

43 Two purebred pea plants have been crossbred. The two plants are identical except that one plant has green peas and the other plant has yellow peas. If yellow is recessive, what color will the peas in the next generation be?
  A Half of the peas will be yellowish green.
  B Half of the peas will be yellow and half will be green.
  C All of the peas will be yellow.
  * D All of the peas will be green.

44 Which type of spoon should you use to keep from getting burned when you stir food in boiling water?
  J Stainless steel
  K Iron
  L Aluminum
  * M Plastic

45 Which system is responsible for moving substances to each cell in the body?
  A Digestive
  B Excretory
  * C Circulatory
  D Nervous

 STOP

Answer rows 41 Ⓐ●ⒸⒹ 42 ●ⓀⓁⓂ 43 ⒶⒷⒸ● 44 ⒿⓀⓁ● 45 ⒶⒷ●Ⓓ   105

 **Practice**

To the Teacher:

The Test Practice unit provides the students with an opportunity to apply the reading, spelling, language arts, mathematics, study skills, and test-taking skills practiced in the lessons of this book. It is also a final practice activity to be used prior to administering the Iowa Tests of Basic Skills®. By following the step-by-step instructions on the subsequent pages, you will be able to simulate the structured atmosphere in which achievement tests are given. Take time to become familiar with the administrative procedures before the students take the tests.

Preparing for the Tests

1. **Remove the Name and Answer Sheet from each student's book.**

2. **Put a "Testing—Do Not Disturb" sign on the classroom door to eliminate unnecessary interruptions.**

3. **Make sure the students are seated at comfortable distances from each other and that their desks are clear.**

4. **Provide each student sharpened pencils with erasers. Have an extra supply of pencils available. For the mathematics items, provide each student with scratch paper.**

5. **Distribute the students' books and answer sheets.**

6. **Instruct the students in filling out the identifying data on their Name and Answer Sheets. Instructions are given on the next page of this Teacher's Edition.**

7. **Encourage the students with a "pep talk."**

Scheduling the Tests

Allow 10–15 minutes for the students to complete the identifying data on the Name and Answer Sheet before beginning Test 1.

Each test may be administered in a separate session, or you may follow the schedule below that indicates the recommended testing sessions.

Two sessions may be scheduled for the same day if a sufficient break in time is provided between sessions.

Recommended Session	Test	Administration Time (minutes)
1	1 Vocabulary	20
	2 Reading Comprehension	30
2	3 Spelling	25
	4 Capitalization	20
	5 Punctuation	20
3	6 Part 1 Usage	15
	6 Part 2 Expression	25
4	7 Part 1 Math Concepts	25
	7 Part 2 Math Estimation	15
5	8 Part 1 Math Problem Solving	20
	8 Part 2 Data Interpretation	20
	9 Math Computation	20
6	10 Maps and Diagrams	25
	11 Reference Materials	25
7	12 Science	45

Administering the Tests

1. Follow the time limit provided for each test by using a clock or a watch with a second hand to ensure accuracy.

2. Read the "Say" copy verbatim to the students and follow all the instructions given.

3. Make sure the students understand the directions for each test before proceeding.

4. Move about the classroom during testing to see that the directions are being followed. Make sure the students are working on the correct page and are marking their answers properly.

5. Without distracting the students, provide test-taking tips at your discretion. If you notice a student is unable to answer a question, encourage him or her to skip the question and go on to the next one. If students finish the test before time is called, suggest they go back to any skipped questions within that part of the test. However, do not provide help with the content of any question.

Name and Answer Sheet

To the Student:

Now that you have completed the lessons in this book, you are on the way to scoring high! The test in this part of your *Scoring High on the ITBS* will give you a chance to put the tips you have learned to work.

A few reminders…
• Be sure you understand all the directions before you begin each test. You may ask the teacher questions about the directions if you do not understand them.

• Work as quickly as you can during each test.
• When you change an answer, be sure to erase your first mark completely.
• You can guess at an answer or skip difficult items and go back to them later.
• Use the tips you have learned whenever you can.
• It is okay to be a little nervous. You might even do better.

STUDENT'S NAME — SCHOOL — TEACHER — FEMALE / MALE — BIRTH DATE — MONTH DAY YEAR — GRADE 6 7 8 — Book 7 — Scoring High on the ITBS® — Copyright © 2007 by SRA/McGraw-Hill

107

Preparing the Name and Answer Sheet

Proper marking of the grids on a machine-scorable answer sheet is necessary for the correct listing of students' test results. Use the directions below to give the students practice in completing the identifying data on an answer sheet.

Say You have to fill in some information on your Name and Answer Sheet before you begin the Test Practice section. I am going to tell you how to do this.

Make sure your Name and Answer Sheet is facing up and the heading STUDENT'S NAME is above the boxes with circles. In the boxes under the word LAST, print your last name. Start at the left and put one letter in each box. Print as many letters of your last name as will fit before the heavy rule. In the boxes under

the word FIRST, print your first name. Put one letter in each box and print only as many letters of your first name as will fit before the heavy rule. If you have a middle name, print your middle initial in the box under MI.

Allow time for the students to print their names.

Say Look at the columns of letters under the boxes. In each column, fill in the space for the letter you printed in the box. Fill in only one space in each column. Fill in the empty space at the top of a column if there is no letter in the box.

Allow time for the students to fill in the spaces. Give help to individual students as it is needed.

Say Print the name of your school
after the word SCHOOL.

Print your teacher's last name
after the word TEACHER.

Fill in the space after the word
FEMALE if you are a girl. Fill in
the space after the word MALE
if you are a boy.

Look at the heading BIRTH
DATE. In the box under the
word MONTH, print the first
three letters of the month in
which you were born. In the
column of months under the
box, fill in the space for the
month you printed in the box.

In the box under the word DAY,
print the one or two numerals
of your birth date. In the
columns of numerals under the
box, fill in the spaces for the
numerals you printed in the
box. If your birth date has just
one numeral, fill in the space
with a zero in it in the column
on the left.

In the box under the word
YEAR, print the last two
numerals of your year of birth.
In the columns of numerals
under the box, fill in the spaces
for the numerals you printed in
the box.

Look at the heading GRADE. Fill
in the space for the numeral that stands for
your grade.

Check to see that the students have filled in all the
identifying data correctly. Then have them identify
the part of the Answer Sheet for each part of the
Test Practice section.

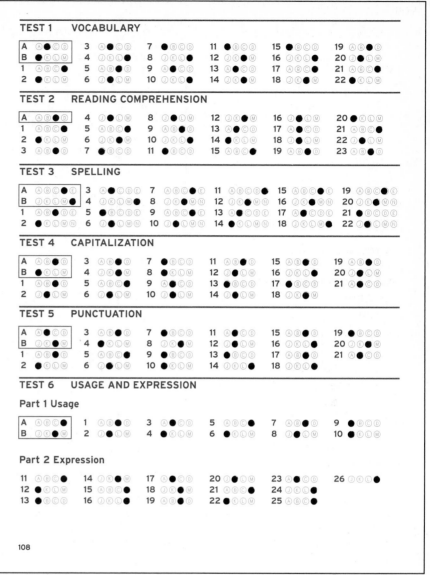

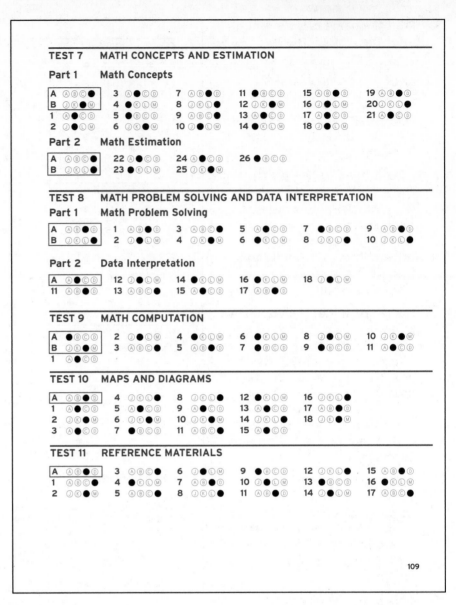

TEST 7   MATH CONCEPTS AND ESTIMATION

Part 1   Math Concepts

Part 2   Math Estimation

TEST 8   MATH PROBLEM SOLVING AND DATA INTERPRETATION

Part 1   Math Problem Solving

Part 2   Data Interpretation

TEST 9   MATH COMPUTATION

TEST 10   MAPS AND DIAGRAMS

TEST 11   REFERENCE MATERIALS

109

A Ⓐ ● Ⓒ Ⓓ
B Ⓙ Ⓚ ● Ⓜ

1 Ⓐ Ⓑ ● Ⓓ
2 Ⓙ ● Ⓛ Ⓜ
3 Ⓐ Ⓑ ● Ⓓ
4 Ⓙ Ⓚ Ⓛ ●
5 Ⓐ ● Ⓒ Ⓓ
6 Ⓙ Ⓚ Ⓛ ●

7 ● Ⓑ Ⓒ Ⓓ
8 Ⓙ ● Ⓛ Ⓜ
9 ● Ⓑ Ⓒ Ⓓ
10 Ⓙ ● Ⓛ Ⓜ
11 Ⓐ ● Ⓒ Ⓓ
12 ● Ⓚ Ⓛ Ⓜ
13 Ⓐ ● Ⓒ Ⓓ
14 Ⓙ Ⓚ Ⓛ Ⓜ

15 ● Ⓑ Ⓒ Ⓓ
16 Ⓙ Ⓚ Ⓛ ●
17 Ⓐ Ⓑ Ⓒ ●
18 ● Ⓚ Ⓛ Ⓜ
19 Ⓐ Ⓑ ● Ⓓ
20 Ⓙ Ⓚ ● Ⓜ
21 Ⓐ Ⓑ Ⓒ ●
22 Ⓙ Ⓚ ● Ⓜ

23 Ⓐ ● Ⓒ Ⓓ
24 Ⓙ Ⓚ ● Ⓜ
25 ● Ⓑ Ⓒ Ⓓ
26 Ⓙ Ⓚ Ⓛ ●
27 Ⓐ Ⓑ ● Ⓓ
28 Ⓙ Ⓚ ● Ⓜ
29 ● Ⓑ Ⓒ Ⓓ
30 Ⓙ Ⓚ Ⓛ ●

31 Ⓐ ● Ⓒ Ⓓ
32 Ⓙ Ⓚ Ⓛ Ⓜ
33 ● Ⓑ Ⓒ Ⓓ
34 Ⓙ Ⓚ Ⓛ ●
35 Ⓐ ● Ⓒ Ⓓ
36 Ⓙ Ⓚ ● Ⓜ
37 Ⓐ ● Ⓒ Ⓓ
38 Ⓙ Ⓚ ● Ⓜ

39 Ⓐ ● Ⓒ Ⓓ
40 Ⓙ Ⓚ Ⓛ ●
41 Ⓐ Ⓑ ● Ⓓ
42 ● Ⓚ Ⓛ Ⓜ
43 Ⓐ Ⓑ ● Ⓓ

Unit 11 Test 1 Vocabulary

Administration Time: 20 minutes

Say Turn to the Test Practice section of your book on page 111. This is Test 1, Vocabulary.

Check to see that the students have found page 111.

Say Look at your answer sheet. Find the part of the answer sheet called Test 1, Vocabulary. All your answers for this test should be marked on your answer sheet, not in your book.

Check to see that the students have found the correct part of the answer sheet.

Say This test will check how well you know vocabulary words. Remember to make sure that the circles for your answer choices are completely filled in. Press your pencil firmly so that your marks come out dark. Completely erase any marks for answers that you change.

Look at Sample A. Read the phrase and fill in the circle for the answer that means the same as the underlined word. Mark your answer in the row for Sample A on the answer sheet.

Allow time for the students to read the item and mark their answers.

Say You should have filled in answer circle B because *irritate* means about the same as *bother*. If you did not fill in answer B, erase your answer and fill in answer B now.

Check to see that the students have filled in the correct answer circle.

Say Do Sample B now. Read the phrase and fill in the circle for the answer that means the same as the underlined word. Mark your answer in the row for Sample B on the answer sheet.

Allow time for the students to read the item and mark their answers.

Unit 11 Test Practice
Test 1 Vocabulary

Directions: Read the phrase and the answer choices. Choose the answer that means the same as the underlined word.

Sample A To <u>irritate</u> my skin
- A soothe
- *B bother
- C cool
- D wet

Sample B An <u>unfit</u> choice
- *J poor
- K welcome
- L sudden
- M unanimous

1 An <u>accurate</u> description
- A long
- B humorous
- C scientific
- *D correct

2 They <u>detected</u> the problem.
- *J found
- K solved
- L avoided
- M described

3 Made a <u>slash</u>
- A knot
- *B cut
- C turn
- D stop

4 A <u>permanent</u> change
- J done quickly
- K successful
- L recent
- *M lasting forever

5 An <u>isolated</u> place
- A unknown
- B beautiful
- *C lonely
- D distant

6 To <u>expand</u> the school
- J visit
- *K make larger
- L make a drawing of
- M call

7 A <u>dismal</u> place
- *A unpleasant
- B swampy
- C windy
- D busy

8 Very nice <u>attire</u>
- J hair
- K manners
- L friends
- *M clothes

9 Send a <u>parcel</u>
- A message
- *B package
- C book
- D bill

10 Heard a <u>whimper</u>
- J long song
- K beep
- L honk
- *M soft sound

111

Say You should have filled in answer circle J because *unfit* means about the same as *poor* in this phrase. If you did not fill in answer J, erase your answer and fill in answer J now.

Check to see that the students have filled in the correct answer circle.

Say Now you will answer more questions. Read each item. Fill in the space for your answers on the answer sheet. Be sure the number of the answer row matches the item you are doing. Work by yourself. When you come to the GO sign at the bottom of the page, turn to the next page and continue working. Work until you come to the STOP sign at the bottom of page 112. When you have finished, you can check over your answers to this test. Then wait for the rest of the group to finish. Do you have any questions?

Answer any questions that the students have.

Say Start working now. You have 15 minutes.

Allow 15 minutes.

Say It's time to stop. You have completed Test 1. Check to see that you have completely filled in your answer circles with dark marks. Make sure that any marks for answers that you changed have been completely erased. Now you may close your books.

Review the items with the students. Have them indicate completion of the lesson by entering their score for this activity on the progress chart at the beginning of the book. Then collect the students' books and answer sheets if this is the end of the testing session.

Unit 11 Test 1 **Vocabulary**

11 A great famine
* A time of hunger
  B celebration
  C type of play
  D hotel

12 To reform a person
  J contact
  K cause trouble for
* L change for the better
  M warn

13 A mournful song
  A without words
* B sad
  C old
  D famous

14 Having problems from the outset
  J weather
  K neighbors
* L beginning
  M traffic

15 A frisky dog
* A energetic
  B long-haired
  C barking
  D well-trained

16 A wonderful narrator
  J artist
  K actor
  L photographer
* M storyteller

17 Humid day
  A breezy
  B frigid
  C fun-filled
* D damp

18 A small puncture
  J paragraph
  K book
* L hole
  M cave

19 Approach the city
  A explore
  B drive around
* C come near to
  D move to

20 The bellow of the bull
  J horn
* K loud noise
  L tail
  M sharp hooves

21 Durable furniture
  A old-fashioned
  B colorful
  C comfortable
* D long-lasting

22 To hasten to the park
* J hurry
  K march
  L walk in a group
  M ride in a carriage

STOP

112

Administration Time: 30 minutes

Say Turn to the Test Practice section of your book on page 113. This is Test 2, Reading Comprehension.

Check to see that the students have found page 113.

Say Look at your answer sheet. Find the part called Test 2, Reading Comprehension. All your answers for this test should be marked on your answer sheet, not in your book.

Check to see that the students have found the correct part of the answer sheet.

Say This test will check your reading comprehension. Remember to make sure that the circles for your answer choices are completely filled in. Press your pencil firmly so that your marks come out dark. Completely erase any marks for answers that you change.

Look at Sample A. Read the passage to yourself. Then read the question beside the passage. On your answer sheet, find the answer circles for Sample A. Mark the circle for the answer you think is right.

Allow time for the students to read the item and mark their answers.

Say You should have filled in answer circle C. You can figure out from the passage that *Jim Thorpe's accomplishments were extraordinary.* If you did not fill in answer C, erase your answer and fill in answer C now.

Check to see that the students have filled in the correct answer circle.

Test Practice

Unit 11 Test 2 Reading Comprehension

Directions: Read the passage and the answer choices. Choose the best answer.

Sample A	
The town of Jim Thorpe, Pennsylvania, is named after one of the greatest athletes of the twentieth century. A Native American, Thorpe was the star of the 1912 Olympics, where he won both the decathlon and pentathlon, a feat never achieved before or after.	**Jim Thorpe's accomplishment at the Olympics was** A common. B typical. * C extraordinary. D overrated.

The Bandit Squirrel

He steals scraps of my picnic lunch.
Then covers his mouth—crrruncchh.
He licks his hands and prances away.
"Thanks for the snack," he seems to say.
Slyly he scurries up the tree,
And I laugh at the bandit who stares down at me.

1 The narrator describes the squirrel by using
  A repeated words or phrases.
  B exaggeration.
  C comparisons.
  * D human qualities.

2 The squirrel appears to run up the tree to
  * J keep away from the narrator.
  K watch people passing by.
  L eat his food.
  M play with other squirrels.

3 How does the narrator regard the squirrel?
  A As friendly
  B As wild
  * C As unafraid
  D As intelligent

4 The narrator calls the squirrel "the bandit" because
  J the narrator watches him take food from someone.
  * K the squirrel takes some of the narrator's picnic lunch.
  L the squirrel runs away from people quickly.
  M the narrator likes to give names to animals he sees.

113

Say Now you will answer more questions. Read the passages and the questions that follow them. Fill in the space for your answers on the answer sheet. Be sure the number of the answer row matches the item you are doing. Work by yourself. When you come to the GO sign at the bottom of a page, turn to the next page and continue working. Work until you come to the STOP sign at the bottom of page 117. When you have finished, you can check over your answers to this test. Then wait for the rest of the group to finish. Do you have any questions?

Answer any questions that the students have.

Say Start working now. You have 25 minutes.

Allow 25 minutes.

The ukulele is a small four-stringed instrument that most people associate with Hawaii. If you speak Hawaiian, you might have an urge to giggle when you talk about the ukulele. That's because in Hawaiian, *ukulele* means "jumping flea." The name comes from the quick movement of a good ukulele player's fingers.

The ukulele has become part of everyone's image of Hawaii, along with hula dancing, grass skirts, and flower leis. Few people know it, but the ukulele is not actually a Hawaiian instrument. In the 1870s, a group of Portuguese immigrants arrived in Hawaii. They brought with them the *braguinha*, a small stringed instrument that they used to accompany folk songs. Hawaiians, including King David Kalakaua, fell in love with the *braguinha*. With the king's leadership, the instrument became very fashionable in Hawaii and received its new name.

On the mainland of the United States, the ukulele was often dismissed because of its small size. People saw it as suitable only for light, amusing music. In contrast, Hawaiians used the ukulele for traditional and classical music. In the twentieth century, several well-respected musicians, like Ohta-San and Eddie Kamae, began using the ukulele as a solo instrument instead of for accompaniment. Gradually, the ukulele has come to be accepted all over the world as a serious instrument. The popularity of the ukulele has varied somewhat over the years, but the "jumping flea" is definitely here to stay.

5 How was the Hawaiians' use of the ukulele different from the rest of the world?
  A The Hawaiians used it mostly for folk music and amateur entertainment.
  B The Hawaiians used it to welcome immigrants from Portugal.
  C The Hawaiians used it as an accompaniment for humorous songs.
*D The Hawaiians used it for formal music and as a solo instrument.

6 The ukulele's immediate popularity in Hawaii was influenced most by
  J its arrival with Portuguese immigrants.
  K its dismissal by serious mainland musicians.
*L King David Kalakaua's love of the instrument.
  M Eddie Kamae's interest in music composed for the ukulele.

7 Which of these is most like a ukulele?
*A A banjo
  B A drum
  C A clarinet
  D A piano

8 This passage was most likely taken from
  J an interview with Ohta-San.
*K a book about Hawaiian culture.
  L a travel brochure about vacations in Hawaii.
  M a collection of ukulele music.

GO

114

1 Language holds a deep fascination for me. I listen to my friend Trinh when she speaks a stream of musical words in Vietnamese to her mother. I practice Spanish with my teacher in awkward sentences. And while my mother does some shopping, I sit each Saturday and watch my thirteen-month-old twin brothers, Joey and Ralphie, speak a language entirely their own.

2 I didn't notice it at first. Their babble sounded like a chorus of church bells striking wrong chords, rising in pitch and tone, eventually reaching the level of empty noise. But as I watched, I noticed an exchange.

3 Joey stood next to the couch. As his little exploring fingers dug deep into the couch cushions, he triumphantly pulled out a comb that had been lost months ago. Grinning with delight, he walked over to Ralphie. He told Ralphie a warbled story, raising his eyebrows for emphasis, thrusting the comb high up in the air, and then ending his monologue with a victorious, high-pitched, "Dah!"

4 Ralphie watched with rapt attention, laughing at the appropriate moments. Next, Joey handed the comb to Ralphie. Ralphie squealed, "Dado!" and proceeded to explain what appeared to be rules for an unwritten game.

5 Joey clapped his hands with hearty agreement, and the two walked over to the bookshelf with determination and mutual understanding. Ralphie pulled out a book about dogs. He sat down, thumbed clumsily through the book, and found a page that must have been particularly interesting to him. He took the comb and buried it in the book. After closing the book, he placed it back on the shelf.

6 Now Joey had been observing with great skill and concentration. Ralphie sat down next to Joey, grunted a sort of permission to continue, and Joey stood up. He started at one end of the shelf and began to pull out every book. He held each book, pages down, and shook it violently, tossing it precariously over his shoulder and squealing "Deeeee!" before moving on to the next. He finally came to the dog book. He shook the book, the comb fell out, and the victor stomped his feet, yelling "Aaaaahhhhh!"

7 He picked up the comb and handed it to Ralphie. Ralphie gave him what sounded like praise for his achievement, clapping and waving the comb in the air.

8 When Mom walked in, I didn't know what to say. The books were strewn across the room. The twins were smiling, passing the missing comb back and forth to one another, and their big brother was sitting, mouth open, in awe and wonder.

 GO

115

9 In what way was Joey triumphant in paragraph 3?

A He pulled all the books from the shelf.

B He won the game.

∗C He found an object hidden in the couch.

D He tricked his twin.

10 In paragraph 2, what does it mean to say that the twins' babble sounded like "empty noise"?

J It was similar to how humans speak.

K It seemed to rhyme.

L It sounded like a song.

∗M It was loud and meaningless.

11 In paragraphs 4, 5, and 6, what appears to be the purpose of the twins' communication?

∗A They are playing a game.

B They are acting out a play.

C They are pretending to be grown-ups.

D They are trying to make their brother laugh.

12 In paragraph 5, what does *mutual* mean?

J Sympathetic

K Confused

∗L Shared

M Lazy

13 In paragraph 6, what is meant by Ralphie "grunted a sort of permission"?

A He gave Joey the comb to help explain the game.

∗B He showed Joey that it was his turn to play in the game.

C He pretended to speak another language to Joey.

D He made a noise that sounded like a football player being tackled.

14 What does the author emphasize about the twins?

∗J Their ability to understand each other

K Their awareness that their brother watches them

L Their interest in books

M Their enthusiasm for making a mess

15 How does the author help the reader understand his point of view?

A By summarizing all the sounds the twins made

B By describing the events of a typical day

C By explaining the twins' environment

∗D By telling about what he saw

16 What probably caused the narrator to sit with "mouth open, in awe and wonder"?

J He couldn't believe what a mess the twins made.

∗K He was shocked that the twins understood each other.

L He was concerned that his mother would be angry with him.

M He didn't understand the game that the twins played.

17 How did the narrator notice his twin brothers were communicating?

A He read a book that talked about babies babbling.

∗B He paid close attention to how they interacted.

C He observed them every Saturday for a class.

D He played with them while they communicated.

Say It's time to stop. You have completed Test 2. Check to see that you have completely filled in your answer circles with dark marks. Make sure that any marks for answers that you changed have been completely erased. Now you may close your books.

Review the items with the students. Have them indicate completion of the lesson by entering their score for this activity on the progress chart at the beginning of the book. Then collect the students' books and answer sheets if this is the end of the testing session.

Unit 11 Test 2 **Reading Comprehension**

1   The colorless, dry earth spans across the plains for miles in the West Texas Panhandle as the blue cloudless horizon stretches out above it. The wind, having nothing to restrain it, whips the dirt into a spindling swirl of brown. Sparse patches of green dot the dull ground of this arid region near Amarillo.

2   Then a spectacle leaps from the landscape. Brilliant colors—deep burnt orange, honey gold, and milk chocolate—and wild shapes wind through Palo Duro Canyon, interrupting the endless horizon. The canyon dives to a ravine 800 feet below and winds 110 miles beneath the West Texas sky.

3   Officially discovered in 1852 but long inhabited by Native Americans, the canyon offers a slice of geologic history. Wind and water erosion created the dramatic canyon at the fork where the Palo Duro Creek and Terra Blanca Creek meet, called the Prairie Dog Town Fork. Erosion chiseled through thousands of years of sediment to outline nature's work throughout the eras in geologic history.

4   Palo Duro Canyon became a state park in the 1930s and offers a glimpse of larger-than-life natural formations. Visitors to the park can hike, bike, and even camp in the canyon. A major attraction to the park in the summer months is the open-air theater built at the bottom of a 600-foot canyon wall. Here a dramatic musical performance called *Texas* offers viewers a walk through Texas history.

18   **What natural occurrence that formed the canyon is mentioned in paragraph 3?**
    J   Melted snow and glaciers
✱ K   Wind and water erosion
    L   Tornado
    M   Hurricane

19   **What makes the horizon appear endless in most of West Texas?**
    A   The farms spread over many acres.
    B   The soil is rich.
✱ C   The land is flat.
    D   The grass covers the fields.

20   **The author seems to feel that Palo Duro Canyon is**
✱ J   more beautiful than the land around it.
    K   difficult to find when driving.
    L   not as attractive as the Grand Canyon.
    M   not a place of historical significance.

21   **In paragraph 1, what does "the wind, having nothing to restrain it, whips the dirt" indicate?**
    A   Dry weather causes dirt to collect.
    B   Tornadoes often form in the canyon.
    C   There are many windmills.
✱ D   There are few trees or mountains.

22   **In paragraph 2, what does it mean to say that "a spectacle leaps from the landscape"?**
    J   Waterfalls seem to jump out of the canyon.
✱ K   The canyon is unusual because the land around it is flat.
    L   The play *Texas* is a dramatic musical about Texas history.
    M   Many lights from the nearby city can be seen from the canyon.

23   **Which word best describes Palo Duro Canyon's land formations?**
    A   new
    B   small
✱ C   unusual
    D   colorless

117

Unit 11 Test 3 Spelling

Administration Time: 25 minutes

Say Turn to Test 3 on page 118.

Check to see that the students have found page 118.

Say Look at your answer sheet. Find the part called Test 3, Spelling. All your answers for this test should be marked on your answer sheet, not in your book.

Check to see that the students have found the correct part of the answer sheet.

Say This test will check how well you can find misspelled words. Remember to make sure that the circles for your answer choices are completely filled in. Press your pencil firmly so that your marks come out dark. Completely erase any marks for answers that you change.

Look at the words for Sample A. Find the word that has a spelling mistake. If none of the words has a mistake, choose the last answer, No mistakes. Mark the circle for your answer.

Allow time for the students to mark their answers.

Say Answer circle D, *c-a-c-t-i-s*, should have been marked because it is a misspelling of the word *c-a-c-t-u-s*. If you chose another answer, erase yours and fill in answer circle D now.

Check to see that the students have filled in the correct answer circle.

Say Look at Sample B. Find the word that has a spelling mistake. If none of the words has a mistake, choose the last answer, *No mistakes*. Mark the circle for your answer.

Allow time for the students to mark their answers.

Say Answer circle N should have been marked because all the words are spelled correctly. If you chose another answer, erase yours and fill in answer circle N now.

Check to see that the students have filled in the correct answer circle.

Unit 11 Test Practice
Test 3 Spelling

Directions: Fill in the space for any word that has a spelling mistake. If there is no mistake, fill in the last answer space.

Sample A		
	A	obscure
	B	revision
	C	solution
*	D	cactis
	E	(No mistakes)

Sample B		
	J	scrambling
	K	umpire
	L	rebellion
	M	tradition
*	N	(No mistakes)

1
- A level
- B planet
- *C takle
- D victory
- E (No mistakes)

2
- *J aquareum
- K skinny
- L business
- M fountain
- N (No mistakes)

3
- A shower
- *B forebid
- C college
- D narrow
- E (No mistakes)

4
- J risky
- K capture
- L graceful
- M vanish
- *N (No mistakes)

5
- *A strenth
- B pencil
- C observe
- D comparing
- E (No mistakes)

6
- J finger
- *K crumbel
- L multiply
- M shiver
- N (No mistakes)

7
- A sleeve
- B buckle
- C hallway
- *D phlat
- E (No mistakes)

8
- J celebrate
- K operate
- *L supplly
- M sample
- N (No mistakes)

9
- A unloaded
- B lightning
- C connection
- *D gient
- E (No mistakes)

10
- J clever
- *K gathred
- L weary
- M pebble
- N (No mistakes)

GO

118

Say Now you will do more spelling items. Look for a word that has a spelling mistake. If none of the words has a mistake, choose the last answer. Work by yourself. When you come to the GO sign at the bottom of the page, turn to the next page and continue working. Work until you come to the STOP sign at the bottom of page 119. When you have finished, you can check over your answers to this test. Then wait for the rest of the group to finish. Any questions?

Answer any questions that the students have.

Say Start working now. You will have 20 minutes.

Allow 20 minutes.

Say It's time to stop. You have completed Test 3. Check to see that you have completely filled in your answer circles with dark marks. Make sure that any marks for answers that you changed have been completely erased. Now you may close your books.

Review the items with the students. Have them indicate completion of the lesson by entering their score for this activity on the progress chart at the beginning of the book. Then collect the students' books and answer sheets if this is the end of the testing session.

Unit 11   Test 3 **Spelling**

11　A　uniform
　　　B　blaming
　　　C　ferry
　　　D　servant
　　＊E　(No mistakes)

12　J　container
　　　K　mining
　　＊L　handleing
　　　M　soften
　　　N　(No mistakes)

13　A　grammar
　　＊B　heatting
　　　C　remarkable
　　　D　manager
　　　E　(No mistakes)

14＊J　pertect
　　　K　fancy
　　　L　twinkle
　　　M　champion
　　　N　(No mistakes)

15　A　basement
　　　B　western
　　　C　cheaper
　　＊D　spiled
　　　E　(No mistakes)

16　J　marsh
　　　K　speech
　　＊L　decizhion
　　　M　memory
　　　N　(No mistakes)

17　A　travel
　　＊B　magicien
　　　C　included
　　　D　cheerful
　　　E　(No mistakes)

18　J　lampshade
　　　K　pocketbook
　　　L　scrapbook
　　　M　pancakes
　　＊N　(No mistakes)

19　A　tough
　　　B　balance
　　　C　stable
　　＊D　chokking
　　　E　(No mistakes)

20　J　scooter
　　　K　ceiling
　　＊L　emtied
　　　M　increase
　　　N　(No mistakes)

21＊A　stikking
　　　B　excellent
　　　C　cruel
　　　D　message
　　　E　(No mistakes)

22　J　tighten
　　＊K　hunderd
　　　L　wiggle
　　　M　partner
　　　N　(No mistakes)

STOP

119

Test 4
Capitalization

Administration Time: 20 minutes

Say Turn to Test 4 on page 120.

Check to see that the students have found page 120.

Say Look at your answer sheet. Find the part called Test 4, Capitalization. All your answers for this test should be marked on your answer sheet, not in your book.

Check to see that the students have found the correct part of the answer sheet.

Say This test will check how well you can find capitalization mistakes. Remember to make sure that the circles for your answer choices are completely filled in. Press your pencil firmly so that your marks come out dark. Completely erase any marks for answers that you change.

Look at Sample A. Read the answer choices. Find the answer that has a capitalization mistake. If there is no mistake, choose the last answer. Mark the circle for your answer on the answer sheet.

Allow time for the students to mark their answers.

Say Answer circle C should have been marked because *Liberia* should be capitalized. If you chose another answer, erase yours and fill in answer circle C now.

Check to see that the students have filled in the correct answer circle.

Say Look at Sample B. Find the answer that has a capitalization mistake. If there is no mistake, choose the last answer. Mark the circle for your answer.

Allow time for the students to mark their answers.

Say Answer circle J should have been marked because *Cold War* should be capitalized. If you chose another answer, erase yours and fill in answer circle J now.

Test Practice
Test 4 Capitalization

Directions: Fill in the space for the answer that has a mistake in capitalization. Fill in the last answer space if there is no mistake.

Sample A
- A   My best friend grew up in
- B   Africa. His father worked
- * C   in liberia for ten years.
- D   (No mistakes)

Sample B
- * J   The cold war was a term
- K   used to describe the rivalry
- L   between certain countries.
- M   (No mistakes)

1
- A   The narrator of S. E. Hinton's
- B   novel, *The Outsiders*, is a young
- * C   man named pony boy Curtis.
- D   (No mistakes)

2
- J   After the hairdresser listened
- * K   to my request, she asked, "are
- L   you sure you want it that short?"
- M   (No mistakes)

3
- A   The student government team
- B   from my school planted an oak tree
- * C   last year to celebrate arbor day.
- D   (No mistakes)

4
- J   Borah Peak, the tallest mountain
- K   in Idaho, rises over 12,000 feet and
- * L   is a part of the northern rockies.
- M   (No mistakes)

5
- A   The team gave Carly Childer the
- B   nickname "Lightning" Childer after
- C   her speedy feats at the World Cup.
- * D   (No mistakes)

6
- J   If you're looking for quilt fabric,
- * K   you should visit Anna Lena's quilts
- L   on the north side of the peninsula.
- M   (No mistakes)

7
- * A   The nine-banded Armadillo is
- B   a small American mammal found
- C   in the southeastern United States.
- D   (No mistakes)

8
- * J   Whenever I see uncle Filbert,
- K   he tells me I have the same
- L   mischievous nature as Dad.
- M   (No mistakes)

9
- A   Last fall we took a field trip
- * B   to the State Capital and got to
- C   meet some of our representatives.
- D   (No mistakes)

10
- J   The city zoo has a new program.
- * K   student workers are paid to help with
- L   the feeding and care of the animals.
- M   (No mistakes)

GO ➡

120

Check to see that the students have filled in the correct answer circle.

Say Now you will do more items. Look for an answer that has a capitalization mistake. If none of the answers has a mistake, choose the last answer. When you come to the GO sign at the bottom of the page, continue working. Work until you come to the STOP sign at the bottom of page 121. When you have finished, you can check over your answers to this test. Then wait for the rest of the group to finish. Any questions?

Answer any questions that the students have.

Say Start working now. You will have 15 minutes.

Allow 15 minutes.

Say It's time to stop. You have completed Test 4. Check to see that you have completely filled in your answer circles with dark marks. Make sure that any marks for answers that you changed have been completely erased. Now you may close your books.

Review the items with the students. Have them indicate completion of the lesson by entering their score for this activity on the progress chart at the beginning of the book. Then collect the students' books and answer sheets if this is the end of the testing session.

Unit 11 Test 4 **Capitalization**

11
A I bought an unusual reference book
B at a garage sale last Saturday. It's
✱ C called *Extremely weird Animals*.
D (No mistakes)

12
J Rich deposits of coal are found
✱ K in many parts of china. The areas
L with the greatest yield are in the north.
M (No mistakes)

13 ✱ A The substitute teacher said, "the
B principal tells me this class is one
C of the brightest he has ever met."
D (No mistakes)

14
J The next time you go to the coast,
✱ K take redwood highway and follow
L the signs for Goat Rock State Park.
M (No mistakes)

15
A Some musicians were invited to
B play music at the grand opening
✱ C of the museum of Modern Art.
D (No mistakes)

16
J In 1669, Sor Juana entered a
K convent in Mexico City and began
L writing poetry and religious dramas.
✱ M (No mistakes)

17 ✱ A 721 Covered bridge Court
B Bradford, VT 05033
C May 19, 2001
D (No mistakes)

18
J The Manager
K Music and More
✱ L Dear madam or sir:
M (No mistakes)

19
A My name is Patrice DeVoe, and
B I am writing about the summer job
✱ C you advertised in the Newspaper.
D (No mistakes)

20
J I am a responsible thirteen-year-
✱ K old with experience in retail. just
L check with any of my references.
M (No mistakes)

21
A I look forward to hearing from you.
✱ B respectfully yours,
C Patrice DeVoe
D (No mistakes)

121

Administration Time: 20 minutes

Say Turn to Test 5 on page 122.

Check to see that the students have found page 122.

Say Look at your answer sheet. Find the part called Test 5, Punctuation. All your answers for this test should be marked on your answer sheet, not in your book.

Check to see that the students have found the correct part of the answer sheet.

Say This test will check how well you can find punctuation mistakes. Remember to make sure that the circles for your answer choices are completely filled in. Press your pencil firmly so that your marks come out dark. Completely erase any marks for answers that you change.

Look at Sample A. Read the answer choices. Find the answer that has a punctuation mistake. If there is no mistake, choose the last answer. Mark the circle for your answer on the answer sheet.

Allow time for the students to mark their answers.

Say Answer circle B should have been marked. A comma is needed after *others* because it is a compound sentence. If you chose another answer, erase yours and fill in answer circle B now.

Check to see that the students have filled in the correct answer circle.

Say Look at Sample B. Find the answer that has a punctuation mistake. If there is no mistake, choose the last answer. Mark the circle for your answer.

Allow time for the students to mark their answers.

Say Answer circle L should have been marked because quotation marks are needed. If you chose another answer, erase yours and fill in answer circle L now.

 Test Practice
Test 5 **Punctuation**

Directions: Fill in the space for the answer that has a mistake in punctuation. Fill in the last answer space if there is no mistake.

Sample A		
	A	Audrey had a passion
*	B	for helping others so she
	C	aided hungry children.
	D	(No mistakes)

Sample B		
	J	She asked what I liked best
	K	about my trip. I told her
*	L	very honestly, The video arcade.
	M	(No mistakes)

1
A
* C   Rachel went for a long run
B   after dropping the mail at the
C   post office It was her routine.
D   (No mistakes)

2 * J   Uncle Sean lives in Cardiff Wales.
K   He moved there when he retired. All
L   he took with him was his dog, Nellie.
M   (No mistakes)

3
A   Hedrick wasn't nervous yet.
B   The piano recital was not until
* C   seven oclock, thank goodness.
D   (No mistakes)

4 * J   Where did this rain come from.
K   The weather forecast mentioned
L   only clear skies.
M   (No mistakes)

5
A   Mrs. Anundson, my teacher in
B   fifth grade, loved music but couldn't
C   sing no matter how hard she tried.
* D   (No mistakes)

6
J   "All you could see was meadow,"
* K   Grandfather recalled. I was just a
L   kid, but it took my breath away."
M   (No mistakes)

7 * A   A professor is a person, who
B   teaches a particular discipline
C   or subject in great depth.
D   (No mistakes)

8
J   "The weather is glorious, and
K   we're both sick of sitting indoors.
* L   How about a walk" Farah suggested.
M   (No mistakes)

9 * A   Dixie Trent a local reporter is
B   supposedly on assignment in Hawaii.
C   We suspect she's getting some rest.
D   (No mistakes)

10 * J   The fly's think of it as an invitation
K   whenever you go outside and
L   leave the front door wide open.
M   (No mistakes)

GO

122

Check to see that the students have filled in the correct answer circle.

Say Now you will do more items. Look for an answer that has a punctuation mistake. If none of the answers has a mistake, choose the last answer. When you come to the GO sign at the bottom of the page, continue working. Work until you come to the STOP sign at the bottom of page 123. When you have finished, you can check over your answers to this test. Then wait for the rest of the group to finish. Any questions?

Answer any questions that the students have.

Say Start working now. You will have 15 minutes.

Allow 15 minutes.

Say It's time to stop. You have completed Test 5. Check to see that you have completely filled in your answer circles with dark marks. Make sure that any marks for answers that you changed have been completely erased. Now you may close your books.

Review the items with the students. Have them indicate completion of the lesson by entering their score for this activity on the progress chart at the beginning of the book. Then collect the students' books and answer sheets if this is the end of the testing session.

 Unit 11 Test 5 **Punctuation**

11   A   The telephone repairperson
   *B   said "Your line is not dependable,
    C   so I'm going to have to replace it."
    D   (No mistakes)

12   J   Grandmother Gersich took great
   *K   pleasure in her family she gathered
    L   us around as a hen does her chicks.
    M   (No mistakes)

13 *A   I put on a cap, and some mittens
    B   before setting out into the snow to
    C   sled, skate, and throw snowballs.
    D   (No mistakes)

14   J   A newborn blue whale gains about
    K   200 pounds a day because its mother's
    L   milk is so rich and filled with protein.
   *M   (No mistakes)

15   A   Every Saturday morning at the deli,
    B   Jared helped his father prepare the
   *C   potato macaroni and tuna salads.
    D   (No mistakes)

16   J   Grandfather thinks the reason his
    K   mother sent him on errands was
    L   to help "keep him out of trouble."
   *M   (No mistakes)

17   A   239 Wisteria Lane
    B   Portland, OR 97213
   *C   November 12 2001
    D   (No mistakes)

18   J   Governor John A. Kitzhaber
    K   900 Court Street NE
    L   Salem, OR 97301-4047
   *M   (No mistakes)

19 *A   Dear Mr. Kitzhaber
    B   I'm writing on behalf of the Earth
    C   Club at Cedar Park Middle School.
    D   (No mistakes)

20   J   We'd like to know if you'd be able
    K   to speak to us about what you're
   *L   doing to protect our environment?
    M   (No mistakes)

21   A   We look forward to hearing from
       you.
   *B   Sincerely
    C   Stephen J. Weeks
    D   (No mistakes)

123

Administration Time: 15 minutes

Say Turn to Test 6, Part 1 on page 124.

Check to see that the students have found page 124.

Say Look at your answer sheet. Find the part called Test 6, Part 1, Usage. All your answers for this test should be marked on your answer sheet, not in your book.

Check to see that the students have found the correct part of the answer sheet.

Say This test will check how well you can find mistakes in English usage and expression. Remember to make sure that the circles for your answer choices are completely filled in. Press your pencil firmly so that your marks come out dark. Completely erase any marks for answers that you change.

Look at Sample A. Read the answer choices. Find the answer that has a mistake in usage. If there is no mistake, choose the last answer. Mark the circle for your answer on the answer sheet.

Allow time for the students to mark their answers.

Say Answer circle D should have been marked because none of the answers has a mistake in English usage. If you chose another answer, erase yours and fill in answer circle D now.

Check to see that the students have filled in the correct answer circle.

Say Look at Sample B. Find the answer that has a usage mistake. If there is no mistake, choose the last answer. Mark the circle for your answer.

Allow time for the students to mark their answers.

Say You should have marked answer circle L because the word *here* should be spelled *hear*. If you chose another answer, erase yours and fill in answer circle L now.

Unit 11 Test Practice
Test 6 Part 1 Usage

Directions: Fill in the space for the answer that has a mistake in usage or expression. Fill in the last answer space if there is no mistake.

Sample A	A	Lori pushed herself to be the
	B	fastest runner on the team. Being
	C	pretty fast wasn't good enough.
	∗D	(No mistakes)

Sample B	J	Kelly asked the teacher to
	K	repeat the question. She
	∗L	couldn't here well.
	M	(No mistakes)

1
A   Hound dogs are supposed to
B   have a good sense of smell, but
∗C ours can't seem to smell nothing.
D   (No mistakes)

2
J   If you enjoy singing, you
∗K might could look into joining a
L   vocal group or a community choir.
M   (No mistakes)

3
A   Jamal and Jesse are the
∗B bestest of buddies. Whatever one
C   does, the other must also do.
D   (No mistakes)

4
∗J I never been to Niagara Falls
K   before. I heard it is one of the most
L   popular tourist spots in the world.
M   (No mistakes)

5
A   Nico's face was so pale, it looked
B   like a sheet. He said he'd simply
C   decided to stay out of the sun.
∗D (No mistakes)

6
∗J The mouses in the story had
K   personalities that made them seem
L   more like humans than like animals.
M   (No mistakes)

7
A   At the beginning of the party, the
B   hostess told everyone to feel free
∗C to help theirselves to anything.
D   (No mistakes)

8
J   It will be strange when my brother
∗K goes away to college. Me and him
L   have shared a room for fifteen years.
M   (No mistakes)

9
∗A Apricots makes up a large
B   percentage of the produce grown
C   and sold on Mr. Caspar's farm.
D   (No mistakes)

10
∗J This here bike is worth more
K   than what I paid for it because of
L   all of the special features I added.
M   (No mistakes)

124

Check to see that the students have filled in the correct answer circle.

Say Now you will do more items. Look for an answer that has a mistake in usage. If none of the answers has a mistake, choose the last answer. Work until you come to the STOP sign at the bottom of the page. When you have finished, you can check over your answers to this test. Then wait for the rest of the group to finish. Do you have any questions?

Answer any questions that the students have.

Say Start working now. You will have 10 minutes.

Allow 10 minutes.

Say It's time to stop. You have completed Test 6, Part 1. Check to see that you have completely filled in your answer circles with dark marks. Make sure that any marks for answers that you changed have been completely erased. Now you may close your books.

Review the items with the students. Have them indicate completion of the lesson by entering their score for this activity on the progress chart at the beginning of the book. Then collect the students' books and answer sheets if this is the end of the testing session.

Test Practice

Test 6 Part 1 **Usage**

Directions: Fill in the space for the answer that has a mistake in usage or expression. Fill in the last answer space if there is no mistake.

Sample A	A	Lori pushed herself to be the
	B	fastest runner on the team. Being
	C	pretty fast wasn't good enough.
	*D	(No mistakes)

Sample B	J	Kelly asked the teacher to
	K	repeat the question. She
	*L	couldn't here well.
	M	(No mistakes)

1
A   Hound dogs are supposed to
B   have a good sense of smell, but
*C ours can't seem to smell nothing.
D   (No mistakes)

2
J   If you enjoy singing, you
*K might could look into joining a
L   vocal group or a community choir.
M   (No mistakes)

3
A   Jamal and Jesse are the
*B bestest of buddies. Whatever one
C   does, the other must also do.
D   (No mistakes)

4
*J I never been to Niagara Falls
K   before. I heard it is one of the most
L   popular tourist spots in the world.
M   (No mistakes)

5
A   Nico's face was so pale, it looked
B   like a sheet. He said he'd simply
C   decided to stay out of the sun.
*D (No mistakes)

6
*J The mouses in the story had
K   personalities that made them seem
L   more like humans than like animals.
M   (No mistakes)

7
A   At the beginning of the party, the
B   hostess told everyone to feel free
*C to help theirselves to anything.
D   (No mistakes)

8
J   It will be strange when my brother
*K goes away to college. Me and him
L   have shared a room for fifteen years.
M   (No mistakes)

9
*A Apricots makes up a large
B   percentage of the produce grown
C   and sold on Mr. Caspar's farm.
D   (No mistakes)

10
*J This here bike is worth more
K   than what I paid for it because of
L   all of the special features I added.
M   (No mistakes)

124

Test 6 Part 2
Expression

Administration Time: 25 minutes

Say Turn to Test 6, Part 2 on page 125.

Check to see that the students have found page 125.

Say Look at your answer sheet. Find the part called Test 6, Part 2, Expression. All your answers for this test should be marked on your answer sheet, not in your book.

Check to see that the students have found the correct part of the answer sheet.

Say This test will check how well you know English expression. Remember to make sure that the circles for your answer choices are completely filled in. Press your pencil firmly so that your marks come out dark. Completely erase any marks for answers that you change. Read the directions for each section. Mark the space for the answer you think is correct. Work by yourself. When you come to the GO sign at the bottom of a page, turn the page and continue working. Work until you come to the STOP sign at the bottom of page 127. When you have finished, you can check over your answers to this test. Then wait for the rest of the group to finish. Do you have any questions?

Answer any questions that the students have.

Say Start working now. You will have 20 minutes.

Allow 20 minutes.

Test Practice
Test 6 Part 2 **Expression**

Directions: For questions 11–14, choose the best way to write the underlined part of the sentence.

11 We shop less during the summer **because** our vegetable garden keeps us well stocked.
  A although   B until   C despite   **✱ D** (No change)

12 Because the defendant had not committed the crime, he was eager **proving** his innocence.
  ✱ J to prove   K when he proves   L about to prove   M (No change)

13 The ship's captain worried until he **has seen** that his crew would do a fine job.
  ✱ A saw   B sees   C will have seen   D (No change)

14 The lifeguard was friendly and **cautiously** when she approached the child.
  J a caution   K it was a caution   **✱ L** cautious   M (No change)

15 **Which of these would be most appropriate as a beginning for an essay?**

A   Wearing uniforms wouldn't be that bad if they were stylish and we could figure out a way to choose ones that everyone could agree upon. Many students from other countries wear school uniforms.

C   If you make students wear school uniforms, they will figure out ways to get around it. Making somebody do something is not a good way to earn their respect. Wearing uniforms isn't either.

B   When people don't have to worry about what they are wearing, they can really be themselves. Besides, clothes aren't all that important if you think about it. Uniforms would help everyone get along.

✱ D   Requiring school uniforms would be positive in the sense that a student could concentrate on learning rather than making a fashion statement, but it would be negative in the sense that it could limit creativity.

125

Directions: Use this paragraph to answer questions 16–21.

> [1] The early umbrellas of ancient Egypt and Babylonia were a symbol of wealth and sunshades mostly used as. [2] Umbrellas come in a wide variety of colors. [3] The umbrella was not really used for rain until the 1700s in Europe. [4] A more fashionable umbrella called a parasol was introduced in the 1800s. [5] These were usually quite decorative but made of silk and lace. [6] Rain umbrellas were made of wood and oilcloth to repel moisture.

16 Choose the best opening sentence to add to this paragraph.
  J Some people think that carrying an umbrella is a sign of weakness.
  K The umbrella is something that should not be taken for granted.
  L It is fascinating to learn about inventions.
*M Like many everyday things, the umbrella has an interesting history.

17 Which sentence should be left out of this paragraph?
  A 1
*B 2
  C 3
  D 4

18 Where is the best place for sentence 6?
  J Where it is now
  K Between 1 and 2
*L Between 3 and 4
  M Between 4 and 5

19 What is the best way to write the underlined part of sentence 1?
  A as sunshades mostly used.
  B used as mostly sunshades.
*C used mostly as sunshades.
  D (No change)

20 What is the best way to write the underlined part of sentence 5?
  J until
*K and
  L yet
  M (No change)

21 Choose the best concluding sentence to add to this paragraph.
  A Modern umbrellas come in all sizes, shapes, colors, and fabrics.
  B Some umbrellas are so small you can store them in a purse.
  C If people used umbrellas more often, they would get sick less often.
*D None of these umbrellas worked quite as well as those we have today.

Say It's time to stop. You have completed Test 6, Part 2. Check to see that you have completely filled in your answer circles with dark marks. Make sure that any marks for answers that you changed have been completely erased. Now you may close your books.

Review the items with the students. Have them indicate completion of the lesson by entering their score for this activity on the progress chart at the beginning of the book. Then collect the students' books and answer sheets if this is the end of the testing session.

 Unit 11 Test 6 Part 2 **Expression**

Directions: For questions 22–25, choose the best way of writing the idea.

22 *J On my bookshelves lay a thick blanket of dust.
　 K A thick blanket of dust, it lay on my bookshelves.
　 L On my bookshelves, a thick blanket of dust lay there.
　 M A thick blanket of dust, on my bookshelves it lay.

23 A After the snowman gave it a carrot, Jake took a picture of it.
　 *B Jake took a picture of the snowman after he gave it a carrot for a nose.
　 C Taking a picture of the snowman and giving it a carrot for a nose was Jake.
　 D Jake, he gave the snowman a carrot for a nose, and he took a picture of it.

24 J In the abandoned tower about the birds, the students studied them.
　 K The students studied in the abandoned tower for the birds that nested.
　 L The birds that nested in the abandoned tower the students studied.
　 *M The students studied about the birds that nested in the abandoned tower.

25 A Better pay the workers demanded before signing the contract.
　 B The workers before signing the contract, they demanded better pay.
　 C Better pay the workers demanded the contract they signed before.
　 *D Before signing the contract, the workers demanded better pay.

26 Which of these would be most appropriate in a letter requesting a chance to interview a zoo employee?
　 J Lots of people think zoos are really neat, but sometimes that's not true. One reason I wanted to do this assignment is because I think zoos are controversial. Can I talk to someone about this?
　 K Is there any way to hook me up with someone at the zoo? If not, could you send me a bunch of material I could use to get an idea about zookeepers and what they do? If so, how soon can you send it?
　 L If it wouldn't be too much trouble, I was wondering if there is anyone there at the zoo I can talk to for a while. Even though I don't care for zoos, I have always liked animals.
　 *M I am writing to inquire about the possibility of interviewing one of the zoo's employees. I'm doing a research project on zookeepers and would appreciate the chance to speak with someone firsthand.

Administration Time: 25 minutes

Distribute scratch paper to the students.

Say Turn to Test 7, Part 1 on page 128.

Check to see that the students have found page 128.

Say Look at your answer sheet. Find the part called Test 7, Part 1, Math Concepts. If you need to, you may work on scratch paper, but be sure to mark all your answers for this test on your answer sheet.

Check to see that the students have found the correct part of the answer sheet.

Say This test will check how well you understand and solve mathematics problems. Remember to make sure that the circles for your answer choices are completely filled in. Press your pencil firmly so that your marks come out dark. Completely erase any marks for answers that you change.

Look at Sample A. Read the problem and the four answer choices. Then solve the problem. On your answer sheet, find the answer circles for Sample A. Mark the circle for the answer to the problem.

Allow time for the students to mark their answers.

Say Answer circle D should have been filled in because *9* is the greatest common factor of 18 and 81. If you chose another answer, erase yours and fill in circle D now.

Check to see that the students have filled in the correct answer circle.

Say Now do Sample B. Solve the problem and mark the circle for the answer you find.

Allow time for the students to mark their answers.

Say Answer circle L should have been filled in. If you chose another answer, erase yours and fill in circle L now.

Test Practice
Test 7 Part 1 **Math Concepts**

Directions: Read each mathematics problem. Choose the best answer.

Sample A	Which is the greatest common factor of 18 and 81?
	A 3
	B 6
	C 8
	*D 9

Sample B	Which is greater in value than 0.5?
	J 0.471
	K 0.05
	*L 0.589
	M 0.0392

1 Which is the same as eight hundred twelve thousand, three hundred forty-four?
A 81,234
*B 812,344
C 80,012,344
D 80,012,000,344

2 A measurement of 2 meters probably describes the length of a/an
J city block.
*K couch.
L school bus.
M adult person's arm.

3 Which figure is missing in this pattern?

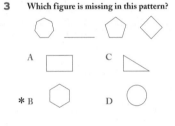

A
C
*B
D

4 The best unit for measuring the cost of a new CD is
*J tens of dollars.
K hundreds of dollars.
L thousands of dollars.
M millions of dollars.

5 What should replace the △ to make the number sentence true?
$(6 + 3) \times \triangle < 30$
*A 3
B 4
C 5
D 6

6 Which of the following statements is true?
J $\frac{1}{9} > \frac{1}{7}$
K $\frac{1}{8} < \frac{1}{9}$
*L $\frac{1}{7} < \frac{1}{4}$
M $\frac{1}{4} > \frac{1}{3}$

GO →

128

Check to see that the students have filled in the correct answer circle.

Say Now you will solve more mathematics problems. Work by yourself. Remember that you may use scratch paper to solve the problems. When you come to the GO sign at the bottom of a page, turn to the next page and continue working. Work until you come to the STOP sign at the bottom of page 130. When you have finished, you can check over your answers to this test. Then wait for the rest of the group to finish. Any questions?

Answer any questions that the students have.

Say Start working now. You will have 20 minutes.

Allow 20 minutes.

---

7 About what fraction of the circle is shaded?

  A   Less than $\frac{1}{4}$

  B   Between $\frac{1}{4}$ and $\frac{1}{2}$

＊C   Between $\frac{1}{2}$ and $\frac{3}{4}$

  D   More than $\frac{3}{4}$

8 How should the numeral 749.5132 be written if it is rounded to the nearest hundredth?

  J   700

  K   750

  L   749.5

＊M   749.51

9 The set of numbers {4, 8, 16, 24, 32, 36, 60} can best be described as a set of

  A   prime numbers.

  B   odd numbers.

  C   squares of numbers.

＊D   multiples of 4.

10 Which fraction is not equal to 0.75?

  J $\frac{3}{4}$

＊K $\frac{2}{3}$

  L $\frac{6}{8}$

  M $\frac{9}{12}$

11 If m is a positive number, what should replace the ☐ to make the equation true?

$$m \div \square = m$$

＊A   1

  B   0

  C m

  D n

12 Jeremy was flipping coins. He flipped the first coin twice. The first time it landed heads up. What is the chance that it also landed heads up the second time?

  J   1 in 4

  K   3 in 4

＊L   1 in 2

  M   1 in 3

13 Which is the correct solution to $0.6 \times \square = 0.48$?

  A   0.08

＊B   0.8

  C   8

  D   80

14 The numbers in the table below are related to each other by the same rule. What number is missing in the second row?

Row 1	3	6	12	24	48
Row 2	16	19	25	☐	61

＊J   37

  K   38

  L   48

  M   50

GO ➤

129

Say It's time to stop. You have completed Test 7, Part 1. Check to see that you have completely filled in your answer circles with dark marks. Make sure that any marks for answers that you changed have been completely erased. Now you may close your books.

Review the items with the students. Have them indicate completion of the lesson by entering their score for this activity on the progress chart at the beginning of the book. Then collect the students' books and answer sheets if this is the end of the testing session.

15 When $a = 5$ and $b = 7$, which of these is the value of $3a + 4b$?
- A 19
- B 35
- *C 43
- D 49

16 Which solid figure could be formed using all the pieces at the right?

- J A sphere
- *K A pyramid
- L A cone
- M A cylinder

17 If $55 \div a = 11$, what is the value of $11 \times a$?
- A a
- *B 5
- C 11
- D 55

18 Scores of 67, 71, 68, and 73 were recorded. The average (mean) of these 4 scores is about
- J 60.
- *K 70.
- L 75.
- M 280.

19 In what order should you place the numbers 4, 6, 8, and 10 into the boxes below so that the largest possible answer will be formed?

☐ − ☐ + ☐ − ☐
- A 4, 6, 8, 10
- B 6, 8, 10, 4
- *C 8, 4, 10, 6
- D 10, 8, 4, 6

20 Which is an obtuse angle?
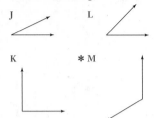

21 Which of the following is not the same as $\frac{4}{28}$?
- A $\frac{1}{7}$
- *B $4\frac{1}{28}$
- C $\frac{8}{56}$
- D $\frac{12}{84}$

Unit 11 · Test 7 Part 2
Math Estimation

Administration Time: 15 minutes

Distribute scratch paper to the students.

Say Turn to Test 7, Part 2 on page 131.

Check to see that the students have found page 131.

Say Look at your answer sheet. Find the part called Test 7, Part 2, Math Estimation. If you need to, you may work on scratch paper, but be sure to mark all your answers for this test on your answer sheet.

Check to see that the students have found the correct part of the answer sheet.

Say This test will check how well you understand and solve estimation problems. Remember to make sure that the circles for your answer choices are completely filled in. Press your pencil firmly so that your marks come out dark. Completely erase any marks for answers that you change.

Look at Sample A. Read the problem and the four answer choices. Then solve the problem. On your answer sheet, find the answer circles for Sample A. Mark the circle for the answer to the problem.

Allow time for the students to mark their answers.

Say Answer circle D should have been filled in because *100,000* is the closest estimate of the solution. If you chose another answer, erase yours and fill in circle D now.

Check to see that the students have filled in the correct answer circle.

Say Now do Sample B. Solve the problem and mark the circle for the answer you think is best.

Allow time for the students to mark their answers.

Unit 11 · Test Practice
Test 7 Part 2 **Math Estimation**

Directions: Read each mathematics problem. Choose the answer that is the best estimate of the exact answer.

Sample A	The closest estimate of 475 × 225 is ____.
	A 100
	B 1,000
	C 10,000
	* D 100,000

Sample B	The closest estimate of 71.3 ÷ 0.71 is ____.
	J 0.1
	K 1.0
	L 10
	* M 100

22 Dinah leaves home at 8:43 A.M. and arrives at her grandfather's house at 10:12 A.M. The closest estimate of how long it takes Dinah to get to her grandfather's house is ____.
 A 1 hour
 * B 1 hour 30 minutes
 C 2 hours
 D 2 hours 30 minutes

23 Which best shows how to get the closest estimate of $7\frac{4}{5} + 3\frac{1}{3} + 9\frac{3}{4}$?
 * J 8 + 3 + 10
 K 8 + 3 + 9
 L 8 + 4 + 10
 M 7 + 3 + 9

24 A piece of ribbon is 4 feet 3 inches long. The ribbon costs 28¢ per foot. The closest estimate of the cost of the piece of ribbon is ____.
 A $1.10
 * B $1.20
 C $1.30
 D $1.40

25 471 ÷ 98 is ____.
 J less than 2
 K between 2 and 4
 * L between 4 and 6
 M more than 6

26 A can of green paint costs $9.16, and a can of yellow paint costs $11.89. About how much more does the can of yellow paint cost than the can of green paint?
 * A $3
 B $4
 C $5
 D $6

STOP

131

Say Answer circle M should have been filled in because the closest estimate to the solution is 100. If you chose another answer, erase yours and fill in circle M now.

Check to see that the students have filled in the correct answer circle.

Say Now you will solve more estimation problems. Work by yourself. Remember that you may use scratch paper to solve the problems. Work until you come to the STOP sign at the bottom of the page. When you have finished, you can check over your answers to this test. Then wait for the rest of the group to finish. Any questions?

Answer any questions that the students have.

Say Start working now. You will have 10 minutes.

Allow 10 minutes.

Say It's time to stop. You have completed Test 7, Part 2. Check to see that you have completely filled in your answer circles with dark marks. Make sure that any marks for answers that you changed have been completely erased. Now you may close your books.

Review the items with the students. Have them indicate completion of the lesson by entering their score for this activity on the progress chart at the beginning of the book. Then collect the students' books and answer sheets if this is the end of the testing session.

Unit 11

Test Practice

Test 7 Part 2 **Math Estimation**

Directions: Read each mathematics problem. Choose the answer that is the best estimate of the exact answer.

Sample A	The closest estimate of 475 × 225 is _____.	**Sample B**	The closest estimate of 71.3 ÷ 0.71 is _____.
	A 100		J 0.1
	B 1,000		K 1.0
	C 10,000		L 10
	*D 100,000		*M 100

22 Dinah leaves home at 8:43 A.M. and arrives at her grandfather's house at 10:12 A.M. The closest estimate of how long it takes Dinah to get to her grandfather's house is _____.
A   1 hour
*B   1 hour 30 minutes
C   2 hours
D   2 hours 30 minutes

23 Which best shows how to get the closest estimate of $7\frac{4}{5} + 3\frac{1}{3} + 9\frac{3}{4}$?
*J   8 + 3 + 10
K   8 + 3 + 9
L   8 + 4 + 10
M   7 + 3 + 9

24 A piece of ribbon is 4 feet 3 inches long. The ribbon costs 28¢ per foot. The closest estimate of the cost of the piece of ribbon is _____.
A $1.10
*B $1.20
C $1.30
D $1.40

25 471 ÷ 98 is _____.
J   less than 2
K   between 2 and 4
*L   between 4 and 6
M   more than 6

26 A can of green paint costs $9.16, and a can of yellow paint costs $11.89. About how much more does the can of yellow paint cost than the can of green paint?
*A $3
B $4
C $5
D $6

STOP

131

Test 8 Part 1

Math Problem Solving

Administration Time: 20 minutes

Distribute scratch paper to the students.

Say Turn to Test 8, Part 1 on page 132.

Check to see that the students have found page 132.

Say Look at your answer sheet. Find the part called Test 8, Part 1, Math Problem Solving. If you need to, you may work on scratch paper, but be sure to mark all your answers for this test on your answer sheet.

Check to see that the students have found the correct part of the answer sheet.

Say This test will check how well you understand and solve word problems. Remember to make sure that the circles for your answer choices are completely filled in. Press your pencil firmly so that your marks come out dark. Completely erase any marks for answers that you change.

Look at Sample A. Read the problem and the four answer choices. Then solve the problem. On your answer sheet, find the answer circles for Sample A. Mark the circle for the answer to the problem. If the correct answer is not given, choose answer D.

Allow time for the students to mark their answers.

Say Answer circle C should have been filled in because the correct answer to the problem is 1,440. If you chose another answer, erase yours and fill in circle C now.

Check to see that the students have filled in the correct answer circle.

Say Now do Sample B. Read the problem and the four answer choices. Then solve the problem. On your answer sheet, find the answer circles for Sample B. Mark the circle for the answer

---

Test Practice
Test 8 Part 1 **Math Problem Solving**

Directions: Read each mathematics problem. Choose the best answer.

Sample A
There are 60 minutes in an hour and 24 hours in a day. How many minutes are in a day?
A   84
B   624
✱ C   1,440
D   Not given

Sample B
Karen is 15 years old. She is 3 times older than her brother. In 5 years, how many times older than her brother will Karen be?
J   3
K   4
L   5
✱ M   Not given

1 Brook wants to buy a new camera. She has saved $165, but her mom said that she could use only $120 of her savings. The new camera she wants costs $270. How much more money does Brook need to pay for the new camera?
A $5
B $45
✱ C $150
D   Not given

2 In one month, Brook earned $7 doing her chores. She earned three times as much cleaning her grandmother's house and twice as much walking the neighbor's dog. She also earned $12 washing cars. How much did she earn that month from those 4 jobs?
J $47
✱ K $54
L $61
M   Not given

3 When she had enough money for the camera, Brook bought the camera for $270. She decided to buy a camera bag for $20 and a package of film for half the cost of the camera bag. She also paid for a tripod, which was twice the cost of the package of film. What else does Brook need to know to figure out how much she spent?
A   The cost of the package of film
B   The cost of the tripod
C   The cost of the package of film and the tripod
✱ D   Brook needs to know nothing else.

4 Brook plans on taking her camera on vacation with her family. She brings a roll of film that can take 38 pictures. She takes an average of 6 pictures per day. A good estimate of how many days it will take Brook to finish the roll of film is given by
J   multiplying 40 times 6.
K   subtracting 6 from 40.
✱ L   dividing 40 by 6.
M   adding 40 and 6.

GO

132

---

to the problem. If the correct answer is not given, choose answer M.

Allow time for the students to mark their answers.

Say Answer circle M should have been filled in because the correct answer is not one of the choices. If you chose another answer, erase yours and fill in circle M now.

Check to see that the students have filled in the correct answer circle.

Say Now you will solve more mathematics problems. Remember that you may use scratch paper to solve the problems. When you come to the GO sign at the bottom of the page, continue working. Work until you come to the STOP sign at the bottom of page 133. When you have finished, you can check over your answers to this test. Then wait for the rest of the group to finish. Any questions?

Answer any questions that the students have.

Say Start working now. You will have 15 minutes.

Allow 15 minutes.

Say It's time to stop. You have completed Test 8, Part 1. Check to see that you have completely filled in your answer circles with dark marks. Make sure that any marks for answers that you changed have been completely erased. Now you may close your books.

Review the items with the students. Have them indicate completion of the lesson by entering their score for this activity on the progress chart at the beginning of the book. Then collect the students' books and answer sheets if this is the end of the testing session.

---

5 Ms. Basile is hosting a summer basketball camp that has 4 levels with 18 students in each level. The campers practiced a drill that requires groups of 6 players. How many groups of 6 can be formed using the players from all of the levels?
  A 11
* B 12
  C 13
  D Not given

6 Ms. Basile had the players scrimmage. Twelve of the players played a game that was 10 minutes long. Of these 12 players, 4 played on the green team and the rest played on the blue team. How can Ms. Basile find out the number of players on the blue team?
* J Subtract 4 from 12.
  K Subtract 4 from 10.
  L Subtract 4 from 12 and then divide the answer by 10.
  M Subtract 10 from 12 and then divide the answer by 2.

7 Sometimes Ms. Basile works with one-third of the 18 students in a group. The other players practice in groups of 3. How many groups of 3 players are practicing during this time?
* A 4
  B 6
  C 54
  D Not given

8 The campers need to practice some plays where the level 2 players and the level 3 players are partners, but there are more level 3 than level 2 players. Which of the following pieces of information is needed to allow Ms. Basile to figure out how many players in level 3 will not have partners?
  J The total number of players at camp that day
  K The total number of level 3 players at camp
  L The total number of level 1 players at camp
* M The total number of level 2 players at camp

9 Craig and Nicole helped their parents paint the house. They painted for 4 days. Each day Nicole used 3 quarts of paint and Craig used 5 quarts of paint. How many quarts did they use in all?
  A 8
  B 15
* C 32
  D Not given

10 One day Craig and Nicole's mom came home with a new kind of paintbrush and said that it worked three times faster than the old brushes. With her old brush, Nicole could use 3 quarts of paint in one day. If the brush works as her mom claims, how many quarts of paint could Nicole use with it in 2 days?
  J 2
  K 5
  L 6
* M 18

Administration Time: 20 minutes

Distribute scratch paper to the students.

Say Turn to Test 8, Part 2 on page 134.

Check to see that the students have found page 134.

Say Look at your answer sheet. Find the part called Test 8, Part 2, Data Interpretation. If you need to, you may work on scratch paper, but be sure to mark all your answers for this test on your answer sheet.

Check to see that the students have found the correct part of the answer sheet.

Say This test will check how well you understand and solve problems involving a graph or chart. Remember to make sure that the circles for your answer choices are completely filled in. Press your pencil firmly so that your marks come out dark. Completely erase any marks for answers that you change.

Look at the chart for Sample A. Read the problem and the four answer choices. Then solve the problem. On your answer sheet, find the answer circles for Sample A. Mark the circle for the answer to the problem. If the correct answer is not given, choose answer D.

Allow time for the students to mark their answers.

Say Answer circle B should have been filled in. If you chose another answer, erase yours and fill in circle B now.

Check to see that the students have filled in the correct answer circle.

Say Now you will solve more mathematics problems. Remember to make sure that the circles for your answer choices are completely filled in. Press your pencil firmly so that your marks come out dark. Completely erase any marks for answers that you change.

Unit 11 **Test Practice**
Test 8 Part 2 **Data Interpretation**

Sample A	State	Area (in Sq. Mi.)	Forested Areas (in Acres)
	Colorado	104,091	22,271,000
	Idaho	83,564	21,726,600
	Montana	145,388	22,559,300
	New Mexico	121,593	18,059,800
	Utah	84,899	15,557,400

About how much more forested area is in Colorado than in New Mexico?
A 1 million acres
∗ B 4 million acres
C 5 million acres
D Not given

Directions: Use the graph below to answer questions 11–14.

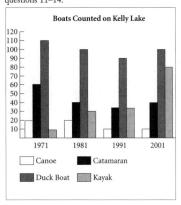

Boats Counted on Kelly Lake

☐ Canoe   ■ Catamaran
■ Duck Boat   ▨ Kayak

11 In which year was the smallest number of boats counted?
A 1971
B 1981
∗ C 1991
D 2001

12 If you were at Kelly Lake, which type of boat would you be most likely to see?
J Canoe
∗ K Duck boat
L Catamaran
M Kayak

13 Which type of boat has increasing counts for each of the years shown?
A Canoe
B Duck boat
C Catamaran
∗ D Kayak

14 What is the best estimate of the number of catamaran boats that will be counted in 2004?
∗ J Between 10 and 20 boats
K Between 40 and 50 boats
L Between 70 and 80 boats
M Between 90 and 100 boats

GO

134

Remember that you may use scratch paper to solve the problems. When you come to the GO sign at the bottom of the page, continue working. Work until you come to the STOP sign at the bottom of page 135. When you have finished, you can check over your answers to this test. Then wait for the rest of the group to finish. Any questions?

Answer any questions that the students have.

Say Start working now. You will have 15 minutes.

Allow 15 minutes.

Say It's time to stop. You have completed Test 8, Part 2. Check to see that you have completely filled in your answer circles with dark marks. Make sure that any marks for answers that you changed have been completely erased. Now you may close your books.

Review the items with the students. Have them indicate completion of the lesson by entering their score for this activity on the progress chart at the beginning of the book. Then collect the students' books and answer sheets if this is the end of the testing session.

 Test 8 Part 2 **Data Interpretation**

Directions: Use the graph below to answer questions 15–18.

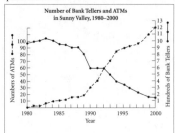

15 In 1992, how many bank tellers were there in Sunny Valley?
A 6,000
*B 600
C 60
D 6

16 During which of the following periods did the number of ATMs change the least?
*J 1980–1985
K 1985–1990
L 1990–1995
M 1995–2000

17 About how many years did it take for ATMs to triple in number after 1989?
A 1 year
B 2 years
*C 3 years
D 10 years

18 What relationship is shown in this graph?
J The number of ATMs increased faster than the number of bank tellers increased.
*K As the number of ATMs increased, the number of bank tellers decreased.
L The number of banks decreased, but the number of ATMs increased.
M As the number of bank tellers decreased, the size of banks decreased.

135

Test 9 Math Computation

Administration Time: 20 minutes

Distribute scratch paper to the students.

Say Turn to Test 9 on page 136.

Check to see that the students have found page 136.

Say Look at your answer sheet. Find the part called Test 9, Math Computation. If you need to, you may work on scratch paper, but be sure to mark all your answers for this test on your answer sheet.

Check to see that the students have found the correct part of the answer sheet.

Say This test will check how well you can solve computation problems. Remember to make sure that the circles for your answer choices are completely filled in. Press your pencil firmly so that your marks come out dark. Completely erase any marks for answers that you change.

Look at Sample A. Read the problem and the four answer choices. Then solve the problem. On your answer sheet, find the answer circles for Sample A. Mark the circle for the answer to the problem. If the correct answer is not given, choose answer D.

Allow time for the students to mark their answers.

Say Answer circle A should have been filled in. If you chose another answer, erase yours and fill in circle A now.

Check to see that the students have filled in the correct answer circle.

Say Now do Sample B. Solve the problem and mark the circle for the answer you find. Mark the circle for the answer you think is best.

Allow time for the students to mark their answers.

Test Practice
Test 9 Math Computation

Directions: Solve each problem. Choose the answer you think is correct. If the correct answer is not given, fill in the space for the last answer, *N*.

Sample A $\frac{5}{12} + \frac{1}{12} =$
- *A $\frac{6}{12}$
- B $\frac{6}{24}$
- C $\frac{5}{12}$
- D N

Sample B $6\overline{)258}$
- J 21
- K 41 r2
- *L 43
- M N

1. 6,276 + 208
- A 6,384
- *B 6,484
- C 7,474
- D N

2. $875 \div 25 =$
- J 20 r15
- *K 35
- L 350
- M N

3. 6.7 − 0.2
- A 4.5
- B 4.7
- C 65
- *D N

4. 7,625 − 1,481
- *J 6,144
- K 6,234
- L 9,106
- M N

5. $30 \times 900 =$
- A 270
- B 2,700
- *C 27,000
- D N

6. $0.13 \times 7 =$
- *J 0.91
- K 9.1
- L 91
- M N

7. $\frac{1}{6} \times \frac{5}{9} =$
- *A $\frac{5}{54}$
- B $\frac{1}{9}$
- C $\frac{1}{3}$
- D N

8. $27 \div 6 =$
- J 4.4
- *K 4.5
- L 40
- M N

9. 0.17 × 0.04
- *A 0.068
- B 0.68
- C 6.8
- D N

10. $\frac{1}{5} + \frac{3}{8} =$
- J $\frac{1}{8}$
- K $\frac{4}{13}$
- *L $\frac{23}{40}$
- M N

11. $\frac{4}{9} - \frac{1}{6} =$
- A $\frac{3}{18}$
- *B $\frac{5}{18}$
- C 3
- D N

STOP

136

Say Answer circle L should have been filled in because the solution to the problem is 43. If you chose another answer, erase yours and fill in circle L now.

Check to see that the students have filled in the correct answer circle.

Say Now you will solve more computation problems. Remember that you may use scratch paper to solve the problems. Work until you come to the STOP sign at the bottom of the page. When you have finished, you can check over your answers to this test. Then wait for the rest of the group to finish. Any questions?

Answer any questions that the students have.

Say Start working now. You will have 15 minutes.

Allow 15 minutes.

Say It's time to stop. You have completed Test 9. Check to see that you have completely filled in your answer circles with dark marks. Make sure that any marks for answers that you changed have been completely erased. Now you may close your books.

Review the items with the students. Have them indicate completion of the lesson by entering their score for this activity on the progress chart at the beginning of the book. Then collect the students' books and answer sheets if this is the end of the testing session.

Test Practice
Test 9 **Math Computation**

Unit 11

Directions: Solve each problem. Choose the answer you think is correct. If the correct answer is not given, fill in the space for the last answer, *N*.

| Sample A | $\frac{5}{12} + \frac{1}{12} =$ | * A $\frac{6}{12}$
B $\frac{6}{24}$
C $\frac{5}{12}$
D N | Sample B | $6\overline{)258}$ | J 21
K 41 r2
* L 43
M N |

1 6,276
+ 208

A 6,384
* B 6,484
C 7,474
D N

2 875 ÷ 25 =

J 20 r15
* K 35
L 350
M N

3 6.7
− 0.2

A 4.5
B 4.7
C 65
* D N

4 7,625
− 1,481

* J 6,144
K 6,234
L 9,106
M N

5 30 × 900 =

A 270
B 2,700
* C 27,000
D N

6 0.13 × 7 =

* J 0.91
K 9.1
L 91
M N

7 $\frac{1}{6} \times \frac{5}{9} =$

* A $\frac{5}{54}$
B $\frac{1}{9}$
C $\frac{1}{3}$
D N

8 27 ÷ 6 =

J 4.4
* K 4.5
L 40
M N

9 0.17
× 0.04

* A 0.068
B 0.68
C 6.8
D N

10 $\frac{1}{5} + \frac{3}{8} =$

J $\frac{1}{8}$
K $\frac{4}{13}$
* L $\frac{23}{40}$
M N

11 $\frac{4}{9} - \frac{1}{6} =$

A $\frac{3}{18}$
* B $\frac{5}{18}$
C 3
D N

STOP

136

Unit 11 Test 10
Maps and Diagrams

Administration Time: 25 minutes

Say Turn to Test 10 on page 137.

Check to see that the students have found page 137.

Say Look at your answer sheet. Find the part called Test 10, Maps and Diagrams. Mark all your answers for this test on your answer sheet.

Check to see that the students have found the correct part of the answer sheet.

Say This test will check how well you can use maps and diagrams. Remember to make sure that the circles for your answer choices are completely filled in. Press your pencil firmly so that your marks come out dark. Completely erase any marks for answers that you change.

Look at the map and read the question for Sample A. On your answer sheet, find the answer circles for Sample A. Mark the circle for the answer to the question.

Allow time for the students to mark their answers.

Say Answer circle C should have been filled in because Route 14 probably has a bridge. If you chose another answer, erase yours and fill in circle C now.

Check to see that the students have filled in the correct answer circle.

Say Now you will answer more questions. Mark your answers on the answer sheet. When you come to a GO sign, turn the page and continue working. Work until you come to the STOP sign at the bottom of page 139. When you have finished, you can check over your answers to this test. Then wait for the rest of the group to finish. Any questions?

Answer any questions that the students have.

Unit 11 Test Practice
Test 10 Maps and Diagrams

Directions: Read each question. Choose the best answer.

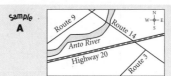

Sample A

Which highway probably has a bridge?
A Route 3
B Highway 20
*C Route 14
D Route 9

Directions: Harold used these diagrams to make two different paper helicopters for his five-year-old cousin to play with. The numbers shown are in inches.

Patterns

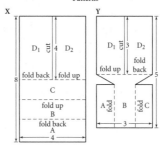

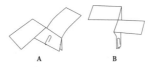

1 What do the dotted lines represent?
A Where to use a paper clip
*B Where to fold the paper
C Where to cut a straight line
D Where the wings are

2 What is the purpose of the cuts?
J To make the bottom of the helicopters
K To make two helicopters out of one
*L To make the helicopter wings
M To make the helicopter wings smaller

3 Which parts of the helicopters need to be clipped together?
A The wings
*B The bodies
C The tops
D The backs

4 Which of these is the smallest piece of paper from which helicopter Y could be made?
J 5" × 10"
K 6" × 4"
L 3" × 4"
*M 4" × 5"

5 When the helicopters are assembled, which section cannot be seen?
A A   C C
*B B   D D

6 Which of these could be the last step in assembling one of the helicopters?
J Fold C across B
K Fold A back from B
*L Attach a paper clip
M Cut D1 from D2

137

Say Start working now. You will have 20 minutes.

Allow 20 minutes.

Test 10 **Maps and Diagrams**

Directions: A rafting tour company's brochure has this map and table about its rafting trips. Use them to answer questions 7–11.

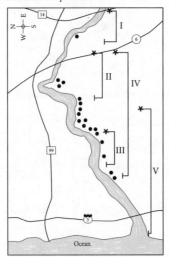

| | local road | ✳ | start and end of trip | trip #s in Roman numerals |
| 99 | local road | | ⊢——⊣ = 1 mile | ● rapids |

Trip	Miles	Time (hours)	Open
I	4	4	May–July
II	5	4	June–July
III	3	2	July–Aug
IV	13.5	7	June–Aug
V	12	8	July–Sept

7 Which raft trip is both the shortest and the least difficult?
* A I
  B II
  C III
  D IV

8 On which raft trip do the rafts travel about one-and-a-half miles per hour?
  J II
  K III
  L IV
* M V

9 How is raft trip IV different from raft trip V?
  A Raft trip IV covers fewer miles.
* B Raft trip IV has more rapids.
  C Raft trip IV ends in the ocean.
  D Raft trip IV is for less advanced rafters.

10 Which raft trips have the most miles of territory in common?
  J II and IV
  K IV and III
* L IV and V
  M III and V

11 Which raft trip would be the most challenging?
  A I
  B II
  C III
* D IV

GO

138

172 Unit 11 **Test Practice**

Say It's time to stop. You have completed Test 10. Check to see that you have completely filled in your answer circles with dark marks. Make sure that any marks for answers that you changed have been completely erased. Now you may close your books.

Review the items with the students. Have them indicate completion of the lesson by entering their score for this activity on the progress chart at the beginning of the book. Then collect the students' books and answer sheets if this is the end of the testing session.

 Unit 11 Test 10 **Maps and Diagrams**

Directions: The map below shows part of a planet with some land and water masses. The planet also rotates in the same way as earth. Use the map to answer questions 12–18.

12 For which two cities is there probably a difference in time?
* J Shreve and Tola
  K Shreve and Vint
  L Scio and Clespo
  M Scio and Vint

13 Where is the mouth of Moon Bay?
  A 20°N and 20°W
* B 12°N and 15°E
  C 5°S and 15°W
  D 10°S and 20°E

14 When it is midnight in Vest, about what time is it in Phila?
  J Noon
  K Five hours later
  L A few hours earlier
* M Midnight

15 Where is the point 45°S, 15°E located?
  A In the Green Sea
* B Near Scio
  C In Halo Bay
  D Near Clespo

16 Which city would be likely to have the most snow-related sports activities?
  J Clespo
  K Vint
  L Tola
* M Kaido

17 Which city is found approximately 40° west of the mountain range?
  A Tola
  B Shreve
* C Vest
  D Scio

18 How many degrees north is Phila from Scio?
  J About 5
  K About 10
* L About 30
  M About 60

 STOP

139

Test 11
Reference Materials

Administration Time: 25 minutes

Say Turn to Test 11 on page 140.

Check to see that the students have found page 140.

Say Look at your answer sheet. Find the part called Test 11, Reference Materials. Mark all your answers for this test on your answer sheet.

Check to see that the students have found the correct part of the answer sheet.

Say This test will check how well you understand reference materials. Remember to make sure that the circles for your answer choices are completely filled in. Press your pencil firmly so that your marks come out dark. Completely erase any marks for answers that you change.

Look at the guide words from a dictionary and read the question for Sample A. On your answer sheet, find the answer circles for Sample A. Mark the circle for the answer to the question.

Allow time for the students to mark their answers.

Say Answer circle C should have been filled in because homburg would be found on *page 633*. If you chose another answer, erase yours and fill in circle C now.

Check to see that the students have filled in the correct answer circle.

Say Now you will answer more questions. There are different kinds of questions in this test, so be sure to read the directions for each part carefully. Mark your answers on the answer sheet. When you come to a GO sign, continue working. Work until you come to the STOP sign at the bottom of page 142. When you

have finished, you can check over your answers to this test. Then wait for the rest of the group to finish. Any questions?

Answer any questions that the students have.

Say Start working now. You will have 20 minutes.

Allow 20 minutes.

Test Practice
Test 11 Reference Materials

Directions: Read each question. Choose the best answer.

Sample A

hold •	hollow	631
holly •	holy	632
homage •	homework	633
homey •	homonym	634

On which page would you find the word *homburg*?
A 631
B 632
*C 633
D 634

Directions: This is part of an index from a book called *How to Design and Build Fences and Gates*. Use the index to answer questions 1–4.

F
Fence, basket-weave, 29; gate on, 84; cleaning, 71; design of, 7, 47; extending an existing, 68–70; plywood, 29; repair, 75–77; styles of, 20–34
Finish, 51, 70; application, 71; preservative, 70–71; pressure-treated lumber, 51; restore old finish, 75
Footing, 36; concrete, 45, 54, 62; earth-and-gravel, 45, 54, 62; materials for, 54
Foundation (see Footing)
G
Gate, bamboo and wood, 80; to build, 91–92; in a chain-link fence, 74; frame, to measure, 91; perimeter, 4, 85; hardware, 89–91
H
Handles, gate, 90
Hardware, gate, 82, 89–91
Hinge, gate, 90, 91
L
Lumber, choosing, 51–53; dimensions of, 53; to handle, 51; to order, 54–55; pressure-treated, 51, 52; sources of, 94; storing, 55
M
Metal, for fencing, 6, 9, 18; for gates, 82; ornamental, 34; sources of, 94

1 Which page would explain how to fix an old fence?
A 7
B 47
C 71
*D 76

2 Which page would describe how to store your fence lumber?
J 44
K 51
*L 55
M 94

3 Which page would list places you could get ornamental metal for a fence?
A 6
B 18
C 34
*D 94

4 Which page would tell you how to build a sturdy foundation for a fence?
*J 45
K 55
L 85
M 91

GO

140

Directions: At the top of each page in a dictionary, there are two guide words. They are the first and last words on that page of the dictionary. Use the guide words and page numbers below to answer questions 5–8.

ebullient	• echolocation	320
ecology	• ectoblast	321
ectoderm	• edutainment	322
Edwardian	• egocentric	323
egotism	• eightpenny	324

5 On which page would you find the word *eider*?
A   321
B   322
C   323
∗ D   324

6 On which page would you find the word *economics*?
J   320
∗ K   321
L   322
M   323

7 On which page would you find the word *edifice*?
A   320
B   321
∗ C   322
D   323

8 On which page would you find the word *effectual*?
J   320
K   321
L   322
∗ M   323

Directions: Before you use certain reference materials, you need to decide exactly which word or phrase to use to find the information you want. We call this word or phrase the *key term*. In questions 9–12, select the best key term.

9 Which key term should you use to find information about Loretta Walsh, the first woman to enlist in the U.S. Navy?
∗ A   Walsh, Loretta
B   United States
C   Navy
D   Women enlistees

10 Which key term should you use to find out how a plasterlike material called *gesso* is made by dissolving white chalk and glue in water.
J   Glue
∗ K   Gesso
L   Chalk
M   Plaster

11 The name *daisy* has been given to many different flowers, some of which are in the scientific grouping *Chrysanthemum*. Which key term should you use to find pictures of different daisies?
A   Chrysanthemum
B   Flower
∗ C   Daisy
D   Plant

12 Which key term should you use to find out how modern churns made of stainless-steel drums and paddles transform cream into butter?
J   Modern
K   Stainless
L   Cream
∗ M   Butter

141

Say It's time to stop. You have completed Test 11. Check to see that you have completely filled in your answer circles with dark marks. Make sure that any marks for answers that you changed have been completely erased. Now you may close your books.

Review the items with the students. Have them indicate completion of the lesson by entering their score for this activity on the progress chart at the beginning of the book. Then collect the students' books and answer sheets if this is the end of the testing session.

Directions: Use this dictionary page and the guides below it to answer questions 13–17.

---

squinch (skwĭnch) *n.* a small arch built across the interior angle between two walls

sta•bler (stā′blər) *n.* a person who runs a horse stable

ste•nog•ra•pher (stə nŏg′ra fər) *n.* a person who specializes in taking dictation in shorthand

steph•a•no•tis (stĕf′ə nō′tĭs) *n.* a vine having fragrant, waxy, white flowers and leathery leaves

ste•ve•dore (stē′vĭ dôr, -dōr) *n.* a firm or individual engaged in the loading or unloading of a vessel

sti•fling (stī′f lĭng) *adj.* suffocating; oppressively close

sti•pend (stī′pĕnd′, -pənd) *n.* 1. periodic payment or scholarship 2. fixed or regular pay; salary

stip•ple (stĭp′əl) *tr.v.* to paint, engrave, or draw by means of dots or small markings

stir•ring (stûr′rĭng) *tr.v.* 1. rousing or thrilling, as in a stirring speech 2. active or bustling, as in a business office

stor•ied (stôr′ēd, stōr-) *adj.* having stories or floors; a two-storied home

---

1. Pronunciation Guide:

ă	sat	ŏ	lot	ə	represents
ā	day	ō	so	a	in alone
ä	calm	ŏŏ	look	e	in open
â	pare	ōō	root	i	in easily
č	let	ô	ball	o	in gallop
ē	me	ŭ	cut	u	in circus
ĭ	sit	û	purr		
ī	lie				

2. Abbreviations: *n.*, noun; *tr. v.*, transitive verb; *adj.*, adjective; *pl.*, plural

---

13 What is the plural of *stipend*?
* A stipends
  B stipendes
  C stipendies
  D stipendses

14 Which word fits best in the sentence "He found the crowded bus _____"?
  J stifled
* K stifling
  L stiflement
  M stifleness

15 Which word fits best in the sentence "The attorney needed a _____ to take notes while he spoke"?
  A stipend
  B stevedore
* C stenographer
  D stabler

16 In which sentence is the first form of the word *stirring* used correctly?
* J Kareem's speech was so stirring that the council applauded.
  K All of the animals in the zoo were stirring by nine o'clock.
  L Teresa found the constant stirring of the liquid tiresome.
  M The young women had started a stirring new business.

17 How do the two pronunciations of *storied* differ?
  A The accent is on different syllables.
  B The *e* is pronounced differently.
  C The *i* is pronounced differently.
* D The *o* is pronounced differently.

142

Unit 11 Test 12 Science

Administration Time: 45 minutes

Say Turn to Test 12 on page 143.

Check to see that the students have found page 143.

Say Look at your answer sheet. Find the part called Test 12, Science. Mark all your answers for this test on your answer sheet.

Check to see that the students have found the correct part of the answer sheet.

Say This test will check how well you understand science. Remember to make sure that the circles for your answer choices are completely filled in. Press your pencil firmly so that your marks come out dark. Completely erase any marks for answers that you change.

Read Sample A to yourself. Think about the question and look at the answer choices. On your answer sheet, find the answer circles for Sample A. Mark the circle for your answer.

Allow time for the students to mark their answers.

Say Answer circle B should have been filled in because *light* travels fastest. If you chose another answer, erase yours and fill in circle B now.

Check to see that the students have filled in the correct answer circle.

Say Now do Sample B. Read the question and decide which answer is correct. Mark the circle for the answer you think is best.

Allow time for the students to mark their answers.

Say Answer circle L should have been filled in because you would be most likely to find *decomposers* in a compost pile. If you chose another answer, erase yours and fill in circle M now.

Check to see that the students have filled in the correct answer circle.

Unit 11 Test Practice
Test 12 Science

Directions: Read each question. Choose the best answer.

Sample A Which of these travels fastest?
- A Sound
- *B Light
- C Satellites
- D Rockets

Sample B Which kind of organisms would you be most likely to find in a compost pile?
- J Producers
- K Scavengers
- *L Decomposers
- M Producers

1 Over thousands of years, giraffes' necks have become longer so that they can reach leaves from taller trees. This is an example of
- A elasticity.
- B elongation.
- *C adaptation.
- D reproduction.

2 Which of the following statements about recycling is true?
- J Peanut shells must be crushed before they are recycled.
- *K Recycling helps to preserve natural resources.
- L Mixing glass and paper is the most efficient way to recycle.
- M Recycling plastic pollutes more than making new plastic.

3 Which factor is most responsible for moving a sailboat through water?
- A The temperature of the water
- B The mass of the boat
- *C The force of the wind
- D Friction in the water

4 Which of these is true about Earth's crust?
- J It is made of frozen water near the poles.
- K It is solid all the way to the center of Earth.
- L It is made mostly of water.
- *M It is about 10 to 50 kilometers thick.

143

Say Now you will answer more questions. Mark your answers on the answer sheet. When you come to a GO sign, turn the page and continue working. Work until you come to the STOP sign at the bottom of page 152. When you have finished, you can check over your answers to this test. Then wait for the rest of the group to finish. Any questions?

Answer any questions that the students have.

Say Start working now. You will have 40 minutes.

Allow 40 minutes.

Directions: Use the information below to answer questions 5–8.

Some scientists trained lab rats to expect a hard pellet of food to fall into their dish when they heard a buzzer. Then they tried the experiment below.

A rat was placed in a cage that had an area of two feet square. After ten minutes, a buzzer was sounded. Food was dropped into the rat's dish. The scientists noted whether or not the rat moved toward the dish.

This procedure was followed using nine hard food pellets and again using nine grapes that were the same size as the food pellets. Different rats were used for each repetition. Rats moved toward the food dish seven times when a hard food pellet was dropped into it but only three times when they received a grape.

5 Which question is this experiment designed to answer?
  A Do rats like grapes better than they like hard food pellets?
 ∗ B Will rats respond in the same way to hard pellets and grapes?
  C Does the size of a piece of food matter to a rat?
  D Is a rat more likely to approach food with which it is unfamiliar?

6 Why do the scientists use a different rat for each trial?
  J To make sure the rats weren't too tired to respond
  K To make sure the rats could hear the buzzer
  L To make sure the rats were the same size
 ∗ M To make sure the rats were hungry

7 Why did the scientists wait 10 minutes before sounding the buzzer and giving the food?
 ∗ A To give the rat time to become familiar with the cage
  B To give the rat time to find its food dish
  C To give the rat more time to digest its previous meal
  D To give the rat time to fall asleep

8 Which change to this experiment would make the results difficult to interpret?
  J Using a rectangular cage instead of a square one
 ∗ K Waiting longer after the buzzer to give a rat a grape than a hard food pellet
  L Using seventeen grapes and seventeen hard food pellets
  M Waiting twenty minutes before sounding the buzzer to give the rat its food

GO

9 Which of these is <u>not</u> a chemical reaction?

*A Water freezing into ice

B Silver becoming tarnished

C Cider turning to vinegar

D An iron nail becoming rusty

10 Why do some plants have brightly colored flowers?

J So that they will have a more pleasant scent

*K So that they can attract insects

L So that they can live longer

M So that they can absorb more sunlight

11 On a dry day, Fred's hair stood up straight after he put on a sweater. Why did this happen?

A The sweater's mass attracted Fred's hair.

*B Fred's hair became electrically charged when he put on the sweater.

C Heat makes air molecules rise, and the hair was pulled along with it.

D The dryness made the molecules in his hair stiffer.

12 One important way in which birds are different from mammals is

*J a bird's bones are lighter.

K a mammal generates its own warmth.

L a bird eats only plant matter.

M a mammal eats only other animals.

13 A cross-country skier may put wax on the bottom of skis before using them in the snow. Why would the wax help the skier?

A The wax melts the snow under the skies.

*B The wax lessens the friction between the skis and the snow.

C The wax makes more snow stick to the skies.

D The wax lessens the gravitational pull of the ground.

 GO

Directions: Use the information below to answer questions 14–17.

Julia had several miniature rose bushes. She wanted to see if there was something she could do to have them produce more blooms. She did the following study.

The rose bushes were all in pots and were all on the same shelf in her greenhouse. She chose four bushes at random for her study. After weighing each pot to make sure they were all of equal weight, she gave each plant water mixed with rose food. Each plant received exactly the same amount of water, but some received more rose food than others. She watered each plant twice a week at the same time. Julia kept track of the amount of rose food each plant was to get at each watering and did not change that amount during her study. She counted the blossoms on each bush once a week for a total of three weeks. Her results are shown in the table below

Week	Plant	Amount of Food	Number of Blossoms
1	1	0 grams	1
	2	1 gram	3
	3	2 grams	4
	4	3 grams	4
2	1	0 grams	2
	2	1 gram	4
	3	2 grams	8
	4	3 grams	9
3	1	0 grams	3
	2	1 gram	7
	3	2 grams	12
	4	3 grams	14

14 **Which of these best states the question Julia is trying to answer?**
J How long should you wait for rose bushes to get blossoms?
∗K What is the best amount of food to give a rose bush?
L How many blossoms can a rose bush have?
M What makes a rose bush bloom?

15 **What was changed on purpose so that its effects could be studied?**
∗A The amount of food each bush got
B The amount of water each bush got
C The number of blossoms on each bush
D The length of time for blossoms to appear

16 **Based on the results of her study, which of these is the best conclusion Julia can reach?**
J It takes three weeks for a rose bush to produce blossoms.
K A rose bush needs more food than other kinds of plants.
L Rose food has no effect on the number of blossoms a rose bush produces.
∗M Rose food can help a rose bush produce more blossoms.

17 **Suppose Julia observed no rose blossoms on any of her bushes after three weeks. What should she try?**
A Look for blossoms twice a week
B Double the amount of water for each plant
C Try a different kind of rose bush
∗D Double the amount of food for each plant

GO

146

18 **Which of these would increase the pressure inside a volcano?**
* J An increase of the temperature inside the volcano
K Lava flowing down the sides of the volcano
L Smoke coming out of the top of the volcano
M Ash forming around the area of the volcano

19 **Why are areas around the North and South Poles the coldest parts of Earth?**
A The ice and snow around the poles keep them colder.
B Magnetic forces within the Earth draw ice to the poles.
* C The poles receive less of the sun's energy.
D Constant winds blow cold air toward the poles.

20 **How is a canyon usually formed?**
J Lava from a volcano carves out the canyon.
K Magnetic forces within the Earth pull the ground down.
* L The flow of a river erodes the ground.
M Rocks roll down a mountain.

21 **Why does the moon shine?**
A Its atmosphere is electrically charged.
B It is made of glowing rocks.
C It reflects light from Earth.
* D It reflects light from the sun.

22 **Which of these forces has the greatest effect on a ball rolling down a hill?**
J Light
K Magnetism
* L Gravity
M Friction

Directions: Use the information below to answer questions 23–27.

Two scientists thought they had discovered a cure for the common cold. They designed the following experiment to test the substance.

The scientists used twenty-seven subjects who had a cold. They measured the volume of mucus each subject produced in half an hour and took the temperature of each subject. The scientists then administered the substance dissolved in water to nine of the subjects. To a second group of nine they gave water without the substance dissolved in it. The third group of nine received no treatment.

A day later, the scientists measured the mucus production and took the temperature of each subject. They found that seven of the nine subjects in the group that received the substance dissolved in water showed decreased mucus production and a lower temperature. Only one person in the group that received water without the substance showed decreased mucus volume and a lower temperature. No one in the third group had an improvement of either symptom.

23 **Why was one of the groups given water without the substance?**
   A To show that water alone could improve the symptoms of a cold
 * B To show that the substance and not the water improved the symptoms
   C To show that colds improve over time
   D To show that temperature and mucus production are caused by a cold

24 **Why did the scientists measure mucus volume and take each subject's temperature before giving them their treatments?**
   J To make sure the sickest people got the substance
   K To make sure each subject's temperature was the same
 * L To find a beginning point from which to measure change
   M To determine how long the subjects had been sick

GO

Unit 11 Test 12 **Science**

25 **What was changed on purpose to observe its effects?**
∗ A The substance that the subjects received
B The volume of mucus a subject produced
C The length of time a subject had been ill
D The temperature of each subject

26 **What should the scientists do about the two people who received the substance but did not show improvement of their symptoms?**
J Check to see if there was something in the water they drank
K Conduct the study again, but doubling the amount of water given to subjects
L Conduct the study again using only these subjects
∗ M Examine other things that may explain these results

27 **What can the scientists conclude about their results?**
A This substance can cure the common cold.
B Water can help cure colds.
∗ C This substance can relieve a cold's symptoms.
D A cold is caused by germs that are hard to kill.

28 **Some foods are processed more than others. Which of the foods below is processed the <u>most</u> before it is eaten?**
J A raisin
K A carrot
∗ L A donut
M An apple

29 **Plants grow well in soil that has many nutrients. What is the main component of this type of soil?**
∗ A Decaying plant parts
B Dust that has been blown by the wind
C Rocks that have been worn by wind and water
D Sand that has been exposed to sunlight

topsoil

149

Directions: Use the information below to answer questions 30–33.

A hungry cat will patiently observe a mouse and try to pounce on the smaller animal when it comes closer to the cat. Mice are often fast enough to get away from the cat. Marilyn thought that the long hairs at the end of a mouse's ears helped the mouse feel the air that the cat disturbed as it pounced. She designed an experiment to test her idea.

A cat was placed in an outdoor pen that was fifteen feet in diameter. After twenty minutes, a mouse was placed into the pen. Marilyn observed whether the mouse was able to escape from the cat. Seven of the mice had ear hair of normal length. Seven others had the hair at the ends of their ears trimmed short. A different cat was used each time. Of the mice with untrimmed ear hair, five escaped the cat. Only two of the mice whose ear hairs had been trimmed escaped the cat.

30 **What question is Marilyn's study designed to answer?**
  J Can mice escape from cats?
  K Do cats prefer to chase mice with hairier ears?
  L Can short ear hair help mice move faster?
  * M Does feeling moving air help a mouse escape from a cat?

31 **What is the reason for a different cat being used for each trial?**
  A Some cats do not like to eat mice.
  * B Using different cats makes the results more valid.
  C A different colored cat will be easier for a mouse to see.
  D Cats get sleepier if they have eaten a mouse.

32 **What is changed on purpose for its effects to be studied?**
  J The speed of the air a cat disturbs when it pounces
  * K The length of the ear hairs of the mice
  L The length of time it takes the cat to pounce
  M The breed of the cat

33 **What change to Marilyn's experiment would make her results more difficult to interpret?**
  * A Using just one cat
  B Using twenty mice in each group instead of just seven
  C Using a pen that is ten feet in diameter
  D Using a black cat for each trial

GO

150

34 In cold weather, a liquid is sprayed on planes to remove ice from their wings. Which of these statements is true about the de-icing liquid?

   J It generates static electricity that repels water.

   K It creates more friction than water.

   L It is made of a substance that burns like gasoline.

  * M It has a lower freezing point than water.

35 Which of these is most responsible for Earth's seasons?

   A The melting of the polar icecaps

  * B The tilt of Earth

   C The shifting of tectonic plates

   D The moon's gravity

36 Which of the planets below is closest to Earth?

   J Jupiter

  * K Venus

   L Uranus

   M Pluto

37 Which of these is an example of friction?

   A A stick floats in water even if the water is rough.

  * B It is harder to push a chair across a rug than a smooth floor.

   C A ball thrown into the air speeds up as it returns to Earth.

   D Two objects with different masses fall at the same rate in a vacuum.

38 All of these are characteristics of an insect except one. Which is <u>not</u> a characteristic of an insect?

   J Six legs

   K Three body parts

  * L Fur or hair

   M An external shell

Say It's time to stop. You have completed Test 12. Check to see that you have completely filled in your answer circles with dark marks. Make sure that any marks for answers that you changed have been completely erased. Now you may close your books.

Review the items with the students. Have them indicate completion of the lesson by entering their score for this activity on the progress chart at the beginning of the book.

Discuss the tests with the students. Ask if they felt comfortable during the tests, or if they were nervous. Were they able to finish all the questions in each test? Which tips that they learned were most helpful? Did they have any other problems that kept them from doing their best?

Go over any questions that caused difficulty. If necessary, review the skills that will help the students score their highest.

 Unit 11 Test 12 **Science**

39 Fossils can help scientists discover all of these about dinosaurs except
  A whether they ate plants or other animals.
 ✳B what kind of sounds they made.
  C how big they were.
  D how many legs they used for walking.

40 Which of these was probably invented first?
  J The radio
  K The camera
  L The electric motor
 ✳M The sailboat

41 Which of these proves that air has weight?
  A The moon is smaller than Earth and has almost no air.
  B A pilot needs oxygen in order to fly a plane high into the atmosphere.
 ✳C A balloon full of air weighs more than the same balloon without air.
  D Fish can breathe under water.

42 An example of weather changing the surface of Earth is
 ✳J wind creating sand dunes.
  K rain falling on a parking lot.
  L snow causing cars to slow down on a highway.
  M sun evaporating water from the surface of a lake.

43 Which of these animals can control its own body temperature?
  A A fish
  B A grasshopper
 ✳C A mouse
  D A frog
